EXCHANGE IDEOLOGIES

EXCHANGE IDEOLOGIES

Commerce, Language, and Patriarchy
in Preconflict Aleppo

Paul Anderson

CORNELL UNIVERSITY PRESS   ITHACA AND LONDON

Copyright © 2023 by Cornell University

All rights reserved. Except for brief quotations in a review, this book, or parts thereof, must not be reproduced in any form without permission in writing from the publisher. For information, address Cornell University Press, Sage House, 512 East State Street, Ithaca, New York 14850. Visit our website at cornellpress.cornell.edu.

First published 2023 by Cornell University Press

Librarians: A CIP catalog record for this book is available from the Library of Congress.

ISBN 978-1-5017-6827-9 (hardcover)
ISBN 978-1-5017-6830-9 (paperback)
ISBN 978-1-5017-6828-6 (pdf)
ISBN 978-1-5017-6829-3 (epub)

Contents

Acknowledgments	vii
Note on Transliteration	ix
Introduction: Exchange Ideologies, Patriarchy, and Economic Liberalization in Syria	1
1. Aleppo in Space and Time	23
2. Exchange Ideologies of Urban-Rural Difference	40
3. Merchant Patriarchy and the State	58
4. Economic Patriarchy and Contested Modernities	76
5. The Hospitality Economy	95
6. Civic Patronage	119
7. Affective Economies of Sincerity and Economic Liberalization in Aleppo	140
Conclusion: Exchange Ideologies and the Futures of the Syrian Nation	160
Notes	175
References	181
Index	197

Acknowledgments

Many debts have been accrued in the writing of this book. The research on which it is based would not have been possible without the friendship, patience, and critical insights of many brilliant and warm people in Syria who welcomed and supported me throughout the process. Many have to remain anonymous, but using the names I have given them in this book, I am particularly grateful to Fuad Umar, Abu Zaki, Hamdi Umar, Muhammad Sanub, Saad Ibrahim, Salam Umar, Nasir Tabkhi, Muhammad Tabhki, Adil Barakat, Abdurrahman and Ahmad Umar, Nur Tabbakh, Alaa al-Din Tufayl, and Muhyi Umari, for giving so generously of their time and for teaching me so much.[1] Particular thanks goes to Mohammad Berro, Abu Taha, Abu Anas, Abu Mahmoud, Abdellatif, Abdurrahman, Ra'd, Nur, Rima Umari, Georges Jabbour, Sylvia Zalloum, Fouad Mohammad Fouad, Zuhair, Ghassan, and MK for their generous hospitality and for making my stay such an enjoyable one. Students and fellow researchers at the Departments of Geography and Philosophy at the University of Aleppo provided invaluable support and intellectual advice in the study of Aleppo's yarn market, which features in chapter 4. I am grateful to Annika Rabo and John Borneman for their generous introductions to colleagues and friends in Syria. I am also grateful to the Institut Francais du Proche Orient in Aleppo for hosting me and providing a congenial and intellectually supportive environment during my fieldwork, especially to the Director Thierry Boissiere, and to Jamal Barout and Louma Samaan for advice and support. Irene Mendoza offered encouragement and friendship throughout the research.

I did the research for and writing of this book in the School of Social and Political Science at the University of Edinburgh and then as a lecturer in the Faculty of Asian and Middle Eastern Studies at the University of Cambridge. I have been fortunate to have truly remarkable mentors and colleagues at both institutions. Particular thanks goes to the brilliant Tobias Kelly and Francesca Bray, and to Magnus Marsden and Sandy Robertson, who gave guidance, inspiration, and critical appraisal throughout. At Edinburgh I also benefited from discussions and seminars with Jonathan Spencer, Janet Carsten, Iris Jean-Klein, Charles Jedrej, Dmitri Tsintjilonis, Stefan Ecks, and Rebecca Marsland. Since I left Edinburgh, Yasir Suleiman and Magnus Marsden have provided numerous opportunities for me to develop as a researcher. Financial support for this research was provided in the form of a research studentship from the Centre for the Advanced Study of the

Arab World. The work on Yiwu was supported by the European Research Council under the European Union's Horizon 2020 research and innovation programme 669 132—TRODITIES, "Yiwu Trust, Global Traders and Commodities in a Chinese International City."

I am particularly grateful to Magnus Marsden, who invited me to participate in this research project on the city of Yiwu, which features in chapter 2 and the conclusion, and to colleagues on the TRODITIES project. Magnus has shaped my thinking about commerce, merchants, and anthropology in general. I am also grateful to colleagues and friends at Cambridge and beyond who provided invaluable companionship, intellectual nourishment, and support, in particular Timothy Tang, Alice Wilson, Yasir Suleiman, Amira Bennison, Andrew Marsham, Christine Van Ruymbeke, Khaled Fahmy, Assef Ashraf, James Montgomery, Geoffrey Khan, Charis Olszok, Michael Rand, Yaron Peleg, Farida El-Keiy, Mahbod Ghaffari and Saussan Khalil. Andreas Bandak has helped me develop my thinking about Syria and anthropology in general. Audiences at the Universities of Sussex, Copenhagen, Cambridge, the London School of Economics, Brunel, and Al-Akhawayn provided valuable feedback. I am grateful to Magnus Marsden, Amani Maihoub, Alice Wilson, and two anonymous reviewers for Cornell University Press for commenting with such insight on the manuscript. Jim Lance, Clare Jones, and Susan Specter at Cornell University Press, and Mary Gendron and Irina Burns at Westchester Publishing Services, helped guide the book into production with skill, warmth, and professionalism, and I am grateful to Susan Storch for preparing the index. I thank my parents for their love and support. Above all, Amani has been my bedrock of support and joy. Without her constant love, wisdom, intelligence, and understanding, the book could never have been written, and I dedicate the book to her. I take sole responsibility for any errors and shortcomings contained in the text.

Portions of chapter 6 were previously published in "L'argent et les affaires a Alep: Succes et faillite d'un 'ramasseur d'argent' dans les annees 1980–2009" (Money and commerce in Aleppo: The rise and fall of a "money gatherer," 1980–2009), in *Alep et ses territoires: Fabrique et politique d'une ville 1868–2011*, ed. J.-C. David and T. Boissière (2013).

Note on Transliteration

Arabic words have been transliterated using an amended version of the *International Journal of Middle East Studies* system. No diacritical marks are used, but 'ayn is rendered as ' and hamza as '. Colloquial words are rendered phonetically. Arabic words common in English follow English spellings.

EXCHANGE IDEOLOGIES

Introduction

EXCHANGE IDEOLOGIES, PATRIARCHY, AND ECONOMIC LIBERALIZATION IN SYRIA

"We don't have two prices here, as God is my witness, our first price is our last price!" Despite frequent attempts by his mainly female clientele to negotiate a price discount on the household items he sold from his shop near Aleppo's bazaar, Fuad Umar invariably refused to bargain. As a regular guest of the shop before the Syrian uprising, I was used to hearing his polite but firm refusals, however insistent his customers' demands became. In moments between dealing with customers, he sometimes asserted his personal integrity with rhetorical flourishes and in a tone of masculine decisiveness, exclaiming, "In Islam, you cannot cheat even a Pharaoh!" His adult son Hamdi, who worked alongside him, adopted the same stance, telling customers, "Our price is not two prices," and telling me that, "in Islam you are held to account for every word that you say." In other words, even a white lie spoken in the course of a sale would render haram or unlawful any profit gained from it. It was no surprise that Hamdi's position was identical to his father's; he deferred unquestioningly to his father and often seemed to be a model of filial obedience and devotion, opening the shop early each day before his father arrived, greeting him respectfully, and executing his instructions without delay. For his part, Fuad acted as a pedagogue to his sons in the shop, offering moral instruction and guidance, reminding them to pray and to keep precise accounts. He prided himself on this, telling me, "This is one of the few markets in Aleppo where you still see fathers sitting alongside their sons, instructing them."

The two positions Fuad adopted in the shop—refusing to bargain on price and commanding the labor and obedience of his sons—may appear to be separate issues, but they were connected. In both, Fuad approximated the ideal of a man whose "word is not two words" (kalimatuh mu kalimatayn)—who was not unstable or inconsistent in his speech but whose words were definitive and decisive, worthy at once of trust and obedience. This was an idiom of masculine maturity. In Aleppo's markets, merchants and shopkeepers tended not to recognize an arbitrary age of majority; a person was no longer a boy (walad), no longer young or small (sghir), simply when it could be said of him that "his word is not two words." The unchanging speech was also an idiom of patriarchal authority; a father whose instructions were challenged or questioned by his children could say, "don't try and discuss it, my first word is my last" (literally: "my word will not become two words" [la tnaqishni, kalimati ma btsir itnayn]). A patriarch was a man of whom it could be said that "his word is heard" (kalimatuh tusma'); in other words, trusted and obeyed.

On one level, Fuad's refusal to bargain could be read as an instance of religious morality. He and his family were adherents of a Sufi piety movement, which censured bargaining in the name of sincerity (al-sidq). In the words of one adept, "when you tell the client a price higher than what you would take, this means you have an evil intention in your heart and are also forcing him to do the same by offering a price lower than the one he would pay" (Pinto 2006, 169). But there is more to Fuad and Hamdi's refusal to bargain than a religiously sanctioned moral precept of honesty. There is also a language ideology—a culturally specific notion of language, of what language is and does, and of what is signified by different ways of speaking. Language ideologies are "shared bodies of commonsense notions about the nature of language in the world" (Rumsey 1990, 346) or "cultural representations of the nature of language" (Robbins 2001, 592). Hamdi's maxim that "in Islam you are held to account for every word that you say" conveyed an understanding of language as accountable, irrevocable, and having an irreducible moral weight. Once spoken, words cannot be taken back, and they are always in the balance on the Day of Judgement. The patriarchal ideal of having trusted and socially consequential speech—a word that "would not become two words," and a word that was "heard"—conveyed an understanding that what language does is to bind the self and move others. Crucially, as the sociolinguist Kathryn Woolard observed, "ideologies of language are not about language alone" but rather "enact ties of language to identity" (1998, 3).[1] Aleppine traders, for example, constituted social categories through their language ideologies: a real merchant (tajir) was someone whose first word was his last, while a trader whose speech was insubstantial and unreliable chatter (haki) was closer to a child (walad) than a merchant.

It is hard to speak of language ideologies in this context without also speaking of what we might call commerce ideologies: culturally specific notions of what commerce is, and of what is signified by different ways of trading. By commerce ideologies I mean sets of ideas about the moral and social characteristics associated with particular forms of trade: including, for example, what constitutes civilized or uncivilized, authentic or inauthentic, respectable or unworthy ways of trading. Language ideologies and commerce ideologies were closely interwoven in Aleppo's bazaar; ideas about speech were drawn into culturally specific construals of what it meant to trade and to be a real merchant. For Fuad, to trade was to put one's honor at stake through speech; to be a reputable merchant in a retail setting was to have unwavering speech and to refrain from bargaining. Within this ideological construal of respectable commerce, ways of trading could also constitute social categories, much as sociolinguists have argued about modes of speaking. Fuad sometimes made caustic remarks about shopkeepers who "say a hundred lire for something worth ten," referring to them not as merchants (tjjar) but as deceivers or the rip-off crowd (ghashashin). Here the social categories of real merchants and deceivers were constituted through a culturally specific notion of what trade was and what was signified by different modes of transacting and speaking.

Similar cultural construals of commerce could also be seen in wholesale markets in Aleppo's bazaar. Wholesale merchants often emphasized the importance of reputation and trust, priding themselves on an image of commerce in Aleppo in which reputation still counted for something, and trade was still made by verbal promises, rather than on collateral, by bank guarantees, or simply in cash. This was a commerce ideology—a culturally specific representation of what it meant to trade; namely, to transact by verbal commitment or by word (bi'l-kalimeh), on reputation, by trust ('a-l-thiqa). In an Islamic formulation, referencing virtues associated with the Prophet Muhammad, trade could be described simply as sincerity and trustworthiness (al-sidq wa'l-amaneh). In another formulation, trade was synonymous with keeping one's word, illustrated by the ethical precept that "whoever has sold has sold, and whoever has bought has bought" (illi baʿ baʿ wa illi shtara shtara). In other words, trade meant keeping promises to buy or sell at a certain price even if the price in the wider market changed before the goods were handed over.

Rather than seeing these concepts of commerce simply as expressions of Islamic tradition or culture, I ask about their intertwining with language ideologies, their role in constituting social identities, statuses, and hierarchies, and the historical conditions under which they gained traction in society. This book is a study not of the morality of exchange, but of exchange ideologies—commerce ideologies and their intertwining language ideologies—among Aleppo's merchants during the first decade of Bashar al-Asad's rule in Syria (2000–2009). It approaches exchange ideologies as the structured and socially situated ways in which processes of commerce and exchange were construed and represented, assigned morally and politically charged characteristics, and linked to categories of social identity and difference. The book documents commerce/language ideologies in everyday interactions, inquiries into their historical conditions of possibility, and identifies their social effects; for example, in drawing boundaries of inclusion and exclusion, and buttressing or challenging social hierarchies.

Patriarchal Structures of Market Membership

An important reason to pay attention to commerce and language ideologies in this period is because they played a role in the reproduction and legitimation of social hierarchies, and in particular hierarchies of patriarchy. By patriarchy I do not mean only domination of women by men, but a structure of father-authority, "a system of government in which men rule societies through their position as heads of households" (Walby 1989, 214, referring to Weber [1947] 2009), requiring the subordination of junior men as well as of women. Among Aleppo's merchants, patriarchal social structures organized access to credit, credit guarantees, information, and—through patriarchally structured informal arbitration mechanisms—commercial rights in the market. The book focuses on two patriarchal forms that organized access to these goods: the extended patrilineal merchant family or house (bait) and the gathering (jamaʿa), a leader-centered network of loyal peers and dependents that revolves around a fraternal patriarch. These structures enabled merchants to become legible and locatable to others, and also organized access to political support.

The book analyzes these as structures of social membership in the market, following feminist scholarship on citizenship in the Middle East, which argues patriarchal families often mediate membership of the polity, as the state recognizes and interacts with citizens as members of families, through their fathers, rather than directly as rights-bearing individuals. Suad Joseph (2005, 149) describes state-citizen relations as governed by a kin contract in which persons belong to families before they belong to the state; thus, citizenship depends on family membership (Joseph 1996a, 7). This kin contract of citizenship is connected to a system of family relations which she calls "patriarchal connectivity," which fosters "selves with fluid boundaries who defer to males and elders" (Joseph 2005, 154; see also Joseph 1993, 1994). Although much scholarship in this vein focuses on the ways in which women are brought into the nation-state as second-class citizens, this book brings patriarchy into the discussion of markets.[2] It analyzes the ways in which patriarchal authority operated within markets, arguing that membership of markets often depended on membership of families or networks that subscribed to ideals of kin-like connectivity.

The book's empirical focus is mainly on relations among men rather than relations between women and men. Women were often excluded from or marginal to the commercial sociality of the merchant strata described here. They did not participate in merchants' spaces of sociability beyond the family.[3] From the perspective of the milieu of mercantile sociability, women's main role was to ensure family respectability through embodying modesty.[4] In market spaces, women were visible as tourists, tour guides, and customers—predominantly as retail customers, with some small wholesalers visiting from provincial towns within Syria, and some female importers visiting from abroad, especially from Turkey, Russia, and Central Asia. Women played other less publicly visible roles in the market, supplying tailoring and machine labor for textile businesses. In some cases, they provided capital, but as a rule they did not manage it.[5] I encountered one rare case of a female industrialist (see chapter 3), but even she had to negotiate patriarchal norms to participate in the market. The book addresses this gendered exclusion indirectly by analyzing structures of social membership of the market and the exchange ideologies coproduced with them.

Patriarchal structures and their associated ideologies of commerce and language were not an ingrained cultural form, but a function of the ways in which the state simultaneously intervened in and kept its distance from the market and managed relations with merchant elites. In addition to access to commercial goods, patriarchal hierarchies structured access to political elites, as the regime recruited merchant patriarchs as relays of state-society relations, allowing them to channel petitions on behalf of their constituencies. This structure of state-merchant interaction reinforced the authority of patriarchal leaders vis-à-vis their constituencies. Patriarchal norms also became salient in the market because of the absence of a reliable juridical state and a robust framework of individual rights, which might have challenged vested interests among regime elites. Without access to dependable formal legal institutions, Aleppo's merchants instead relied on their own constructs of reputation and creditworthiness to regulate commerce. Reputation was typically conceived of as a patrilineally transmissible good—as an asset a father could pass on to sons. This conception justified senior men's interventions in the lives of junior males on behalf of the family name; it had the effect of buttressing patriarchal hierarchies in the family and the market. Patriarchal structures and ideologies of commerce had room to flourish because the regime lacked either the capacity or the willingness to institute reliable formal legal institutions, instead leaving the function of market regulation to families and kinship-like forms such as the mercantile gathering.

If patriarchal structures were elicited and reinforced by the regime's modes of managing merchant constituencies in Aleppo, exchange ideologies of language and commerce were an important means by which these structures were reproduced in everyday life as meaningful and legitimate social forms. To the extent that traders such as Fuad associated unwavering speech both with real merchants and with patriarchs, this commercial virtue was construed in a way that buttressed a gendered social hierarchy. In this commerce/language ideology, a respected merchant was imagined as one whose word was heard, both in the market—where he could do deals through uncollateralized verbal commitments, and where he refused to enter into bargaining conversations with retail customers—and in the family, where he demonstrated his authority over family members. In this cultural construal of the respected merchant as a patriarch, a trader commanded credit from peers and trust from retail customers as he commanded obedience from sons. This is not to say that all merchants who could command uncollateralized credit in the market had sons or presided over their family labor in their shops. Rather, patriarchal social hierarchies, which were pervasive in the market, were made to appear natural by language/commerce ideologies, which figured trusted and unwavering speech both as an essential component of real and virtuous commerce and as a patriarchal characteristic. One social effect of commerce and language ideologies, then, was to legitimize and naturalize gendered social hierarchies entailed by the regime's mode of interacting with Aleppo's merchant bourgeoisie.

Patriarchal ideals were also coproduced with cultural conceptions of Aleppine commerce as a domain of autonomy from the state. In the 1960s and 1970s, the Baathist state had rooted itself in Damascus and marginalized the northern hub of Aleppo, which became a center of opposition to the state; in the 1980s, the regime put down an Islamist revolt in the northern cities of Aleppo and Hama. Even in the 2000s, merchants in Aleppo still understood their counterparts in Damascus to be more closely associated with and more reliant on the Baathist state for their access to commercial opportunity and financing. Several prominent merchant families prided themselves on a pre-Baathist commercial heritage, articulating this in terms of the city's authenticity (al-asala) and its autonomy through the sentiment that "the state is far from here." They placed cultural value on the provision of credit and dispute resolution informally, from within merchant networks, in a way that was independent of and illegible to the state. Among the city's leading merchants, cultural conceptions of Aleppine identity developed, in which commerce was construed as a domain of autonomy from the state and its juridical and financial institutions. Consequently, it was construed as properly depending on uncollateralized verbal commitments, and on trust and reputation among merchants, rather than on bank guarantees.

Commerce, conceived of as a domain of autonomy from the state, was premised on the ideal of a merchant universally recognized among his peers as creditworthy, and on the ideal of an independent arbiter who possessed a social authority autonomous of the state. In Aleppo, both these forms of standing were construed on a patriarchal basis, as leading merchants and commercial arbiters were recognized as those whose words are heard, and as each performed their status by demonstrating authority over sons and male juniors and subordinates. This commerce ideology—in which proper trade meant Aleppine autonomy, distinction from Damascus, and distance from the Baathist state—was coproduced with patriarchal hierarchies and norms.

Ideology as a Methodological Lens

To study notions of commerce and language as ideological means to see them as socially situated and contestable. As Friedrich (1989) and Woolard (1998) both note, to call a cultural notion or representation ideological is to emphasize that it reflects the concerns of a particular social and historical position; that it is inevitably "partial, interest-laden, contestable and contested" (Woolard 1998, 10, referring to Hill and Mannheim 1992, 382). While I have been talking in the abstract of "Aleppo's leading merchants," the ideologies of language and commerce discussed above expressed the interests and perspectives of merchant houses of pedigree (asl wa fasl) who enjoyed an established reputation, wealth, and a social position of notability. They belonged to a merchant stratum that was well-capitalized, male-dominated, and committed to an idea of Aleppine distinctiveness vis-à-vis the city's rural hinterland and to some extent vis-à-vis Damascus. Yet within this stratum, alongside old merchant houses of pedigree, and in a somewhat competitive relationship with them, were new entrants to the market. These enterprising individuals had not inherited merchant capital and reputation but had flourished with Aleppo's industrial renaissance (al-nahda al-sinaʿiyya) and Syria's partial economic liberalization during the 1990s and 2000s, including the signing of free trade agreements with Turkey and the wider Arab world under Bashar al-Asad. Some of the most successful and ambitious entrepreneurs who benefited from these changes sought election to the city's merchant chambers. The book contrasts the social structures and exchange ideologies of these two groups of merchant elites: old merchant houses of pedigree and ambitious, new merchant-industrialists. Some in the latter group, lacking membership of established merchant houses, construed notability not in terms of pedigree but in terms of charisma—a God-given ability to gather supporters and resources around them. This idea of notability was reflected in their construals of commerce and speech;

within their circles, to be a merchant was to know how to gather (bya'rif yajma'); to be a notable (akabir) or a personality (shakhsiyya) was to speak, host, and extend credit in ways that were characterized by graciousness (adab) and generosity (karam).

Chapters 2–4 focus on merchant houses of pedigree, whereas chapters 5 and 6 consider new entrants to the market among whom access to commercial goods—credit, information, opportunity, and arbitration—was organized not through patriarchal families but through a different social formation: the gathering. This was a leader-centered network of customers and associates coalescing around a principal merchant who acted as creditor and host. The central figure constituted himself as a leader not by exercising authority over sons but by acting as creditor and host to his constituency of followers. Commerce/language ideologies in this setting emphasized not the authority of the father but the charisma and grace of the creditor-host. The gathering was a fraternal patriarchy, built not around the authority of a father, but around the central figure's status as a first among equals. He demonstrated his excellence in the generosity with which he hosted customers and forgave debts, and the measured speech with which he chased late debts and presided as a host. The extension of hospitality and credit through which he maintained this position were construed as relations of mutual identification with his closest followers. By offering a permanent line of credit, the central figure was said to be mutually identified with the buyers, entering into a kind of partnership (mitl sharakeh) with them. Guests at his gathering also construed their relations with him in terms of mutuality, characterizing their speech as not restrained or formal, as in the expression "we are not shy of each other." By characterizing their modes of commerce and speech as expressions of mutuality, merchants construed the gathering as a kin-like formation, in which members were mutually identified with each other and bound by expectations of loyalty. This cemented the authority of the central figure, who was then able to presume on members of his gathering for commercial and political support. As in the case of established merchant houses, the effect of these commerce/language ideologies of mutuality was to naturalize patriarchal hierarchies and structures of market membership.

To study notions of commerce and language as ideological also means to see them as embedded in other social and political processes. Since traders' commerce/language ideologies were often coproduced with patriarchal authority structures in the market, they were ultimately grounded in the mechanisms by which the Syrian regime interacted with Aleppo's merchant bourgeoisie under Bashar al-Asad. Chapter 2 considers another way in which everyday construals of commerce and language intertwined with state-market relations. It describes contests for influence in Aleppo's markets and merchant chambers between two rival groups of social and economic elites. On the one hand, was a long-established commercial bourgeoisie of merchant families who intermarried, who prided themselves on their Aleppineness and their independence of the state, and whose leaders could often trace their trading lineages back to a period before the advent of Baathist rule in 1963. On the other hand, was a state-dependent bourgeoisie, who had prospered since the 1980s through state contracts, and who identified with villages and clan solidarities rooted in Aleppo's hinterland. The Alawite-dominated regime pursued a divide-and-rule policy, maintaining these Sunni trading bourgeoisies as competing elites in the city's markets and merchant chambers.

These contests were reflected in everyday life through stereotypes among the first group—Aleppo's established merchant houses—about the rural and clannish traders who had become their competitors in the city. The incumbent merchant lineages who self-identified as urban, construed their competitors in the city as culturally different—as rural and clannish—in part by characterizing their modes of commerce and speech. On the one hand, their competitors dealt only in cash; unlike them, they said, "rural" clans "do not entrust" or sell goods on credit and "have no [notion of the] accountable person." On the other hand, since their competitors remained outside the incumbents' networks of commercial arbitration, they deemed their speech as lacking urban Islamic civility: in a dispute they would "shout" and "make problems" rather than say "God will hold to account." Stereotypes of urban-rural difference emerged through characterizations of exchange, commerce, and language. Modes of commerce and exchange were construed as signs of social and moral character (cf. Woolard 1998, 19). To entrust in marriage and commerce, to trade on credit, to speak with civility, and to submit to established networks of accountability, were all construed as signs of authentic urbanity. To refuse to entrust or sell on credit, and to shout, was to be clannish and beyond the pale of urban civility. The effect of these characterizations of exchange, commerce, and language was to naturalize a distinction between urban and rural, and to reinforce assumptions of radical cultural difference between Sunnis from the countryside and Sunnis from the city. Commerce/language ideologies mediated contests for urban leadership and brought the Alawite-led regime's divide-and-rule strategies vis-à-vis Sunni elites into everyday life.

Urban merchants' claims about the uncouthness of rural modes of commerce and speech raise another methodological issue: where exchange ideologies are to be located. One approach locates ideology in explicit discourse as ideational forms: ideas in conscious thought that are capable of being said. Another approach sees ideology as prereflective, and immanent in socially organized material practices (Woolard 1998, 5–6). This book analyzes exchange ideologies across both these sites. Chapter 2 argues that the same commerce ideology—whereby trading on credit and by reputation was seen as the foundation of an authentically urban order and identity—could be both articulated in explicit discourse and lie immanent in practices of precise accounting. Accounting absorbed much time and collective labor in parts of Aleppo's bazaar and could be performed semipublicly in front of visiting customers and suppliers. Through their accounting practices, merchants maintained their family reputation in the market and disciplined their sons to do the same; but also enacted their urbanity and commitment to credit-based commerce as the foundation of an urban order. When they disparaged clannish modes of exchange, they explicitly articulated a commerce ideology of credit-and-civility as the foundation of urban order. But this exchange ideology was also immanent in practices of accounting and in the verbal etiquette of dealing with customers.[6]

Dialogue between Anthropology and Sociolinguistics

Sociolinguists have studied how language ideologies—cultural representations of language—enable social actors to project as natural and common-sensical what are, in reality, arbitrary ideas about different social types and their distinct characteristics. Describing how this works in the case of language ideologies, Woolard (2008) observes that people commonly connect particular ways of speaking with particular types of speakers, connections which Peirce (1960) terms indexical. Michael Silverstein (2003) distinguished between different orders of indexicality. In the first order, people notice particular ways of speaking, and connect them to a particular class, gender, ethnicity, or group membership (Woolard 2008). In the second order, people think or talk about connections in politically or morally loaded ways, treating ways of speaking as signs of a particular "social, political, intellectual or moral character" (Woolard 1998, 19). These second-order connections are ideological in that they posit as natural an arbitrary relation between linguistic forms and a particular "type" of person. As Judith Irvine and Susan Gal (2000) argued, ideology works as people ignore or erase any information that does not fit the picture, and as they further map particular ways of speaking onto other signs of social difference.

Representations of commerce, and of the meaning and value of particular commercial forms, could work in similar ways and intertwine with language ideologies. The book borrows and draws from sociolinguistic approaches to language ideologies. Chapter 2 shows how an exchange ideology and language ideology intertwined to constitute urban merchant identity and distinction vis-à-vis rural incomers. Chapter 4 describes how well-capitalized merchants in Aleppo's wholesale yarn market denigrated poorer and socially marginal day traders who engaged in highly leveraged speculative bets on yarn futures. The men of capital and substance described the speculators as children engaged in un-Islamic betting that was little more than chatter (haki). By contrast, they emphasized their generational position, Islamic propriety, and ability to command obedience and credit through their "words." Here, ideologies of speech and exchange—what it meant to chatter vis- à-vis trading on one's word—intertwined to constitute them as merchants with Islamically endorsed patriarchal authority.

Such intertwinings of representations of language and of commerce constitute a challenge to sociolinguistics not to treat language as a bounded field of social practice, but to think about language as one form among others of exchanges that mediate social structures. As Woolard notes, "The point of the comparative study of language ideology is to examine the cultural and historical specificity of construals of language, not to distinguish ideology of language from ideology in other domains of human activity. Exclusion of some cultural conceptualizations because language is not sufficiently focal in them would be an ironic outcome to this attempt to denaturalize our own intellectual tradition's compartmentalization and reification of communicative social practices" (1998, 4).[7] In a further challenge to the reification of language, the book shows that ideologies of language and of other cultural forms could overlap and intertwine. Rather than treating language as a de facto bounded field of human practice, or privileging language ideologies as a uniquely powerful medium for creating social identities, we should broaden the field of inquiry beyond language to see how different ideologies of exchange interact and are coproduced with one another, intertwining to constitute social types and statuses.

The proposal to subsume the study of both commerce and language ideologies within a broader study of "ideologies of exchange" takes up a suggestion by the anthropologist Joel Robbins. Robbins (2001) argues that in any culture, there are correlations between a culture's language ideologies and ritual ideologies—that is, its understanding of what ritual is and does. He develops his argument in a discussion of Roy Rappaport's theory of ritual. Robbins argues that Rappaport's own implicit language ideology, which viewed language as a suspect medium unable to guarantee truthful communication, inspired his view of ritual—as the place that people turn to for trustworthy—indexical—communication. But, Robbins argues, where people have a different linguistic ideology—for example, if they do not worry about language as a flawed vehicle for conveying inner truth—they will see ritual differently. Understandings of the function of rituals and of the function of language in any given culture will be connected because both are part of the same "well-structured ideological domain." He concludes that "one should situate the study of ritual as communication within a framework that takes account of ideologies of language. Indeed, it would perhaps be profitable to adopt some term of art such as "ideologies of communication" to refer to a culture's whole set of ideas about how information flows between people and between people and the natural and supernatural worlds" (Robbins 2001, 599). I approach commerce in much the same way as Robbins does ritual: placing "commerce ideologies" alongside language ideologies and situating them both within a broader field of inquiry in order to track the connections and relations between them. I do not make a diachronic argument about the effects of historical shifts in language ideologies on understandings of commerce, which is the direction that Robbins takes his argument about ritual. Rather, I offer synchronic observations that concepts of language and of commerce were articulated together as part of the same process of formulating social identities and differences and justifying hierarchies.

Economic Liberalization in Syria

Through its analysis of Aleppine merchants' exchange ideologies, the book also addresses the broader political, social, and cultural dynamics of economic liberalization in Syria under Bashar al-Asad. In the 1990s, facing a shortage of foreign exchange and unable to sustain the costs of popular subsidies and mass public sector employment, the Syrian regime had started to dilute its commitment to Baathist socialism. Sectors of the economy run by the state were privatized; and in 1991 a law was passed to entice private investment. Economic reform was given renewed emphasis when the current president Bashar al-Asad took office in 2000 (Perthes 2004). The regime licensed private banks (2003) and signed free trade agreements with neighboring Arab countries (2005) and with Turkey (2007). Bashar al-Asad vaunted the model of "public private partnerships" and declared a "social market economy" in 2005 at the 10th Baath Party Congress. Many have argued that underneath the language of reform, the economic changes mainly benefited narrow networks of elites.[8] Indeed, much scholarly literature on economic liberalization or infitah in Syria has emphasized the dimension of crony capitalism in which economic networks of privilege comprising regime officials, their business partners and proxies, secured monopolies, free credit, and the bulk of private contracts.[9] Scholars have argued that economic liberalization took that shape because the overriding logic was a political rather than an economic one: to enable the Asad regime to retain its grip on power by cultivating powerful elites whose position and prosperity were dependent on the survival of the regime. In this perspective, infitah is part of a process of authoritarian "upgrading" (Heydemann and Leenders 2013), enabling political elites to appear modern and provide a measure of economic liberalization while retaining political control and capturing the lion's share of economic benefits for themselves (Donati 2020).

While the capture of the state and economy by narrow networks posed problems for the regime's legitimacy in wider society, it has also been argued that the regime's approach to economic liberalization managed to win over sections of the wider urban bourgeoisie. In these accounts, the policies and language of neoliberalism or post-populism—championing the capacities and values of the private sector, opening sectors of the economy previously controlled by the state, and reducing popular subsidies—appealed to urban merchants and landowners. Cities benefited from free trade agreements that stimulated commerce and consumption of imported goods, while the countryside suffered from the reduction of subsidies on agricultural inputs, fuel, and food, impoverishing the regime's previous constituencies of workers and peasants (Hinnebusch and Zintl 2015b; Pierret 2015).

Amid this analysis of economic interests, less attention has been given to what politically managed economic liberalization and authoritarian upgrading actually looked like among urban bourgeoisies, beyond the networks of privilege. What forms of economic, social, and cultural life emerged beneath the stratum of regime cronies, among the much larger swathes of the more autonomous commercial bourgeoisie, which had traditionally operated in and around urban bazaars, and in sectors such as light manufacturing and the import and distribution of consumer goods? How did economic, social, and cultural forms among this stratum work to maintain or unsettle the political status quo, to perpetuate or undermine the regime's power?

In Aleppo, these more autonomous commercial strata had been a source of political opposition to the regime in the 1970s and early 1980s. But by the 1990s and through the 2000s, many had reached an accommodation with the regime. To some extent, economic liberalization in the 1990s and privatization under Bashar al-Asad had enlarged their space of operation and profit. But the political logic of authoritarian resilience still required the regime to prevent the emergence of a politically powerful, cohesive, independent merchant bourgeoisie. It did so in part through a strategy of divide-and-rule, which separated wealthy Sunni strata into a state-dependent contractors' bourgeoisie, and a relatively autonomous traditional merchant bourgeoisie. The regime also prevented the emergence of a merchant bourgeoisie as an independent, cohesive political force that could articulate shared class interests by co-opting leaders of the merchant bourgeoisie into its patron-client networks. For the most part, it did not accord them monopolies, free credit, or state contracts as it did its cronies and networks of privilege. Instead, it enabled them to access permits, protection from prosecution, and petitioning rights for redress in cases of grievous predation by state agents or proxies through informal relations with regime patrons, known as relations ('alaqat) or friendship (suhba) with officers and officials.

These policies shaped the economic, social, and cultural forms that mediated infitah among Aleppo's merchant bourgeoisie. The recruitment of leading merchants into the regime's patron-client networks had the effect of empowering merchant patriarchs.[10] It also reinforced patriarchal structures of social membership in the market. By social membership I mean the terms under which a person was known, recognized, invited, listened to, accorded weight, and given access to goods of various kinds, such as opportunities, information, credit, and arbitration. The book considers how persons accessed these goods as members of a merchant house (bait) or gathering, which were patriarchal social formations in which male elders, or male leaders who exemplified masculine ideals—of generosity (karam), civility (adab), and charisma (hudur)—had authority and expected to be deferred to. Although these may not have been the only structures that afforded merchants market access, they could be influential, and became salient in the absence of a reliable juridical-bureaucratic state and a legal framework of individual rights. I analyze their dynamics and how they contributed to the regime's resilience in chapters 3–5. These membership structures brought larger swathes of the merchant bourgeoisie (those beneath merchant patriarchs who accessed goods through these structures) into a political economy subordinated to regime patronage. Scholars have used the lens of business networks to analyze crony capitalism and state capture in Syria by narrow bands of economic and political elites (see, e.g., Haddad 2020). I argue that an ethnography of social membership structures in the market helps us understand how the much larger swathes of Aleppo's merchant bourgeoisie were brought into the regime's political economy and became invested in the status quo under Bashar al-Asad.

The favoring of urban over rural economies, and the regime's divide-and-rule policy toward merchant elites, also led to contests of urban notability. The Baathist regime had come to power in the 1960s by removing the previously dominant class of urban notables. But with successive waves of economic liberalization in the 1970s, 1990s, and 2000s, the regime increasingly recognized and cultivated merchants as prominent social figures (Abboud 2018). It allowed leading merchants to stand for election to the conformist national parliament and used elections to Aleppo's merchant chambers to gauge the size and influence of support bases and determine who was worth co-opting into its patron-client networks, as Lisa Blaydes (2010) argued of Egypt. The regime allowed those successful in these elections a measure of influence, allowing them to present informal petitions to political elites. In this sense, it recruited them as relays of state-society relations and accorded them a kind of notability, albeit a politically subordinated one. At the same time, as I noted above, the regime fostered rivalries between different elite social groups: a state-dependent bourgeoisie and an autonomous commercial bourgeoisie. One way in which it did so was by allowing rival commercial elites to stand as candidates in politically managed elections to the city's merchant chambers, and to compete for influence and civic status by acting as public sponsors of urban clubs and infrastructure. I analyze these dynamics, and their relation to authoritarian rule, in chapters 2, 3, and 6. These forms of state-merchant interactions created the conditions for claims of social distinction and contestations of authentic urbanity, which expressed the regime's strategy of divide-and-rule vis- à-vis Sunni elites. At the same time, the discourse of notability was not totally controlled by the regime. While the regime sought to construct an arena of urban notability that was purely civic and politically neutered, some merchants sustained an ideal of notability as having a religious basis and being politically independent.

Post-Baathist Modernities

Much attention has been paid to the shifting class configurations and political loyalties entailed by processes of economic liberalization in Syria. This book considers a less-studied topic: the cultural dimensions of infitah—the shifting idioms and moralities of the public sphere, the contestations of modernity, and the shifts in social imaginaries that unfolded as part of this multifaceted process.[11] An early encounter in my fieldwork illustrated the ways that ideas of modernity were shifting. Two years before the outbreak of the 2011 Arab revolts, I was sitting in a drawing-room in a genteel suburb of Damascus, on a comfortable armchair almost knee to knee with a former political adviser to President Hafez al-Asad, whom I had been advised by a previous fieldworker to approach as a gatekeeper for my research into Aleppo's traders. The sharp-eyed septuagenarian paused briefly as his wife intervened with a tray of homemade ice cream. She hovered at the door briefly, and then her husband continued: "you are looking for the traditional trader, the one sitting in the bazaar. But *you* are the traditional one! You should be looking for the young businessman in his office faxing Shanghai. I will introduce you to one such businessman, a man who is young like you. Already he has launched the magazine, *Syria Forward*. Maybe he will make you famous."

It is striking that a former adviser to Hafez al-Asad should celebrate as a symbol of Syrian modernity and as an exemplar of the nation's future a young private-sector entrepreneur. The Baathist regime through which the adviser had risen had espoused an ideology of socialist modernity, promising national transformation, with the state and the worker as the agents of modernization. Yet, with his celebration of a dynamic young media entrepreneur, the owner of *Forward Magazine*, the former presidential adviser was perfectly in tune with the times. While Hafez al-Asad had maintained a public ideology of austere socialism, his son Bashar al-Asad had overseen a shift in official discourse, championing entrepreneurial initiative. Under Bashar al-Asad, Syria's urban bourgeoisies were no longer the historical enemies of the nation (Sottimano and Selvik 2008). These new imaginings of commerce and merchants were tied to shifts in the political economy: the decline of Baathism as a model of state-led development and the emergence of the project of infitah. What was at stake in these shifts was not just official positions on the proper limits of the market or the extent of redistribution, but an idea about how to be modern: who should be the agents of social transformation and the exemplars of national modernity.

Under Bashar al-Asad, the regime moved away from Baathist ideology and socialist modernity and sought to articulate instead what I call an "entrepreneurial modernity" in which citizens would aspire to create jobs rather than become employees. Syria was also entering into free trade agreements with regional and transregional partners, and this outward-looking modernity was a central part of the regime's self-promotion and its ideological interpellation of Syrian citizens (Wedeen 2019). Merchants were drawn into this new state project of modernity as they were cast by political elites as agents and embodiments of social change—as "figures of modernity" (Barker, Harms, and Lindquist 2013).[12] One feature of economic liberalization in Syria, then, was that commerce and merchants emerged as significant sites for marking and contesting modernity. Yet others, especially bazaar-based merchants and owners of family businesses, were cast as traditionalists, even overbearing patriarchs, and thus figured as symbols of unmodernity and barriers in the path of national progress.

Those vulnerable to this categorization made counterclaims. Some weeks after leaving the Adviser's drawing-room, I met Fuad Umar, the trader who ran a simple shop retailing household items close to the center of the old markets in Aleppo. He belonged to an extended merchant family of pedigree, and at first sight appeared to conform to the image of traditionalism described by the Adviser: in his office was a phone but no fax; in front of him was an accounting ledger which he filled in by hand; and throughout the day he commanded the labor of his sons who deferred to him without question. Yet Fuad contested representations of economic patriarchy as unmodern, telling me of a team of Japanese scientists who had visited his market to discover how a family business run by one man could be so efficient and competitive; he also insisted on the social value of "fathers working alongside their sons, instructing them," seeing it as a bulwark against the specter of corruption (al-fasad) encroaching on society. He construed his modes of commerce in relation to ideals of modernity—as efficient and as the basis of national moral renewal, an authentic Islamic modernity. Such construals could unsettle regime discourses of modernity. At the same time as they chafed against the state project of modernity, economic patriarchs were empowered by the regime's approach to the market and merchant elites.

With the ideological turn away from Baathist socialism, then, trade was becoming central to the ways in which political, economic, and cultural elites imagined and contested what it meant to be modern. Bazaar-based merchants were drawn into the state's project of modernity in ways that were contested and sometimes contradictory. Chapter 4 explores these contestations of post-Baathist modernity: the interactions between a state project of entrepreneurial modernity and a bazaar-based imaginary of patriarchal modernity. The latter was in some respects a counterproject to state modernity, but in other ways buttressed by it. The book thus approaches Syrian merchants not only as figures of modernity, but also as cultural producers of the modern—as agents who shaped and reshaped imaginations of Syria's place in the world and of collective Syrian futures. Studies of the constitution and contestation of Middle Eastern modernities have tended to focus on actors who self-consciously seek to engage in cultural production: religious actors, musicians, artists, popular media, and intellectuals.[13] But imaginings and contestations of modernity are not limited to sites of self-consciously cultural production and consumption. Aleppine merchants were also culturally and politically engaged actors, who fashioned ideas of the relationship between commerce, urban heritage, modernity, and national identity. The book draws here on Magnus Marsden's (2016) approach to merchants as cultural and political actors. It argues that their agency lies not only in their sponsorship of cultural productions, but in the everyday ways in which they construed the business of commerce as a culturally and politically meaningful practice.

Through the analysis of exchange ideologies, the book explores the diverse social, cultural, and economic forms that actually took shape under the banner of economic liberalization. It relates these to the ways in which the regime managed relations with merchant elites so as to prevent the emergence of a cohesive and powerful merchant class and ensure the resilience of authoritarian rule. For the most part, these economic, social, and cultural forms buttressed authoritarian rule: patriarchal membership structures incorporated middle merchant strata, and contestations of urban notability kept social elites divided. But to some extent they also partially unsettled authoritarian rule, as merchants contested the regime's project of modernity and expressed lukewarm sentiments toward its constructs of urban notability.

Fieldwork among Merchants

I first visited Syria for Arabic study for nine months in 1997–98, returned for another period of study in 2006, and then conducted the bulk of the fieldwork on which this book is based over fifteen months in 2008–9; I supplemented this with fieldwork among Syrian merchants in China conducted between 2016 and 2019.[14] I had been introduced to various merchants in Aleppo's bazaar by two anthropologists who had previously worked there. The interlocutors in Aleppo with whom I developed long-term relations and held repeated in-depth conversations were roughly evenly split between manufacturers, wholesalers, retailers, and professional roles (such as brokers, accountants, managers, and lawyers), although many were active in more than one of these domains. Most owned or ran small partnerships or family businesses with between zero and eight employees (although five of my key interlocutors employed more than fifty), and some of my long-term interlocutors were employees.

In Aleppo, I was attached to the Institut Francais d'Etudes du Proche Orient in Aleppo, a French research institute under the umbrella of the French Foreign Ministry, which arranged my research visa. As the former colonial power, France retained some sway in the country, and in the aftermath of the Hariri affair—in which the Syrian state was suspected of involvement in the assassination of the former Lebanese prime minister Rafic Hariri in 2005—the Syrian regime was for a time looking to President Nicolas Sarkozy for its diplomatic rehabilitation. Although I did not shape my research questions to fit any agenda of the French Foreign Ministry, I benefited from their patronage for research access. This probably shaped how I was seen by my Syrian interlocutors and, in some cases, increased or confirmed the suspicion of me. Some inquired about the funding and ultimate purposes of my research; many others were acutely conscious of the colonial historical contexts which had led British and French researchers to conduct research in the region.

The post–9/11 securitization of the Middle East as an object of policy interest both facilitated and obstructed my research. I was not studying security-related matters or Islamist movements, but I benefited from post–9/11 public funding made available through the UK research councils for the "advanced study of the Arab world." The securitization of Islam led to a measure of cooperation between the British and Syrian states at the time of my research and probably also discouraged those active in mosque study circles from talking to me. Early in my fieldwork, I socialized with a young trader who was active in a Sufi piety movement, who introduced me to his study circle, but then abruptly cut off the contact. My British nationality also shaped perceptions of my research and how it might be used. Another former colonial power in the region, Britain continued to assert itself militarily and diplomatically in the Middle East. During my fieldwork in Syria, Britain was an occupying military power in neighboring Iraq, having participated in the war in 2003 to dislodge the Iraqi regime. It also maintained diplomatic and economic pressure on the Syrian regime because of its support for Hezbollah. Merchants, in particular, were often conscious that their country was subject to economic sanctions and internationally isolated; several were sensitive to the rhetoric of the "axis of evil" that was circulating globally at the time, and Syria's position within it as a "rogue state". Israel's bombing of Gaza in December 2008 and January 2009 was particularly prominent in people's minds, and most saw the United Kingdom, the United States, France, and Israel as part of the same diplomatic and military front, arrayed against the interests of Palestinians in particular and Arabs in general. Many generously exempted me from any criticism, saying "governments and people are not the same."

In urban settings and among social elites such as merchants, it was hard to reach the anthropological textbook ideal of participant observation. I was more of an observer than a participant in most commercial exchanges in the market, and my attempts to participate in the labor of shopkeeping by folding textiles and moving and storing goods, were generally short-lived. Conducting fieldwork among traders exemplifies Bourdieu's observation that the position of the ethnographer is a distorting one: "The anthropologist's particular relation to the object of his study contains the makings of a theoretical distortion inasmuch as his situation as an observer" is "excluded from the real play of social activities by the fact he has no place (except by choice or by way of a game) in the system observed and has no need to make a place for himself there" (Bourdieu 1977, 1). What I did participate in, and necessarily sought to make a place for myself in, albeit a temporary one, was merchants' patterns of sociability and visiting. I was positioned within these in particular ways. One example is the writing of fieldnotes, which positioned me firmly but sometimes awkwardly within local forms of sociality. Fuad, who was seeking to discipline one of his sons for what he saw as his errant behavior—skiving off work and visiting nightclubs—told me to "write about him in your books—you have notebooks? Do it, I don't mind!" He went on to say how shameful ('ayb) it was that a person who carried the name of his lineage would behave as his son did. In another shop, one of the staff noted down his sales in the same kind of pad that I used for my scratch notes. Fuad's rhetoric of co-opting ethnographic inscription drew my attention to the parallels between ethnographic, commercial, and moral accounting and led me to focus on these processes, which I explore in chapter 2.

Because anthropological research is immersive and therefore necessarily limited in scope, it may be asked whether it is valid to draw conclusions about the dynamics of merchant society on the basis of interactions, however detailed and sustained, with a relatively limited number of interlocutors. The book does not claim to provide an account of Aleppine mercantile society writ large, or to present case studies that are representative of a larger whole. Rather, it seeks to think through the terms and stakes of the particular social worlds it describes. The chapters describe individuals, families, and networks drawn from differently positioned business strata: established merchant families; emerging industrialists; smaller entrepreneurs operating in the interstices of the networks of emerging industrialists; and a businessman from a state-dependent clan. The chapters also explore different historical periods, from the 1980s to 2019, although most of the ethnographic descriptions are drawn from the late 2000s.

Argument and Organization of the Book

The book argues that economic liberalization in Aleppo under Bashar al-Asad was a cultural process, because it involved shifting notions of the merchant in relation to society and polity and shifting notions of commerce. The book documents how certain modes of commerce were assigned socially and morally charged characteristics—being construed, variously, as expressions of authentic urbanity, patriarchal authority, Islamic modernity, a kinship-like mutual identification, and Aleppineness. These shifting notions or commerce ideologies can be studied much like language ideologies—as cultural representations that mediate social structures. Studying both language and commerce ideologies as subsets of an overarching category of exchange ideologies reveals how the two often overlapped and interacted to reinforce merchant hierarchies and notions of social identity and difference. A critical context in which traders' exchange ideologies were articulated in Aleppo were patriarchal structures of social membership of the market—the patrilineal merchant family and the leader-centered gathering. Merchants' exchange ideologies were co-produced with these structures and constituted them as meaningful and legitimate social forms. Patriarchal structures of social membership were, in turn, fostered by the regime's approach to merchant elites and had the effect of tying parts of Aleppo's commercial bourgeoisie to the political status quo, although they could also generate a degree of background noise of dissatisfaction.

Chapter 1 offers an introduction to the city of Aleppo, tracing its shifting location in the nation-state and regional and transregional economies under Baathist rule. This chapter introduces the main merchant strata considered in the book and locates them within a wider history of state-market relations in Syria. Chapter 2 then elaborates on the concept of exchange ideologies, showing how for some elite merchants, representations about commerce were a way of asserting what it meant to be authentically Aleppine. Established merchant lineages in Aleppo represented honor-based trade as a form of urbanity and themselves as authentically Aleppine.[15] The chapter situates these exchange ideologies as part of a rivalry between state and commercial bourgeoisies in Syria, itself a product of a divide-and-rule strategy by the regime.[16]

Chapters 3 and 4 analyze exchange ideologies in which "respectable" merchants were construed as patriarchs, their respectability in the market being premised on their authority over sons. These notions served to naturalize structures of aged and gendered domination or economic patriarchy in the market. Chapter 3 considers how exchange ideologies of economic patriarchy were supported by the regime's mechanisms of state-merchant interaction. Chapter 4 looks at domains in which economic patriarchy was either evaded or contested and traces a nascent movement of social and political reform that cast economic patriarchy as out of step with Syrian modernity. Representations of commerce were a mode of imagining and contesting national modernity at a time of economic and social change.

Chapter 5 analyzes a mercantile gathering or leader-centered peer network as a form of social membership of the market and an associated exchange ideology, which construed certain commercial transactions and the exchange of hospitality within this network as a form of kinship-like mutuality. It connects this exchange ideology to the social position of an ambitious new entrant to the market, who needed to gather supporters and resources around him without relying mainly on familial networks. Hospitality enabled the principal merchant to engage and manage the tensions inherent in credit relations, and to construe credit-debt relations with his customers as a form of mutuality and mutual obligation. By fostering ideals of mutuality, he subordinated guests and debtors to himself, and secured their political loyalty when he stood for election to the board of Aleppo's Chamber of Industry. This hospitality economy incorporated his customers into a domain of political economy that was ultimately overseen by patrons in the regime.

Chapter 6 traces how merchants, once deemed social parasites in Baathist discourse, emerged as public figures and celebrities in Aleppo under Bashar al-Asad. As part of the economic liberalization permitted by the regime, political elites invited leading merchants to act as civic sponsors of urban associations and infrastructure, enabling them to achieve a kind of public renown. The most prominent were said to have cultivated a public (jumhur). This new status and understanding of the figure of the merchant emerged as part of an attempt by political elites to recruit politically compliant entrepreneurs and industrialists as rival relays of state-society relations.

Chapter 7 analyzes discourses about the place of sincerity, emotion, and affective connection in trade. It was common for merchants to claim sincerity in their interactions with customers, and this could be framed as an Islamic virtue. Others emphasized that they were sensitive to other merchants' orientations of good or bad will (or cinnamon) toward them. Some also emphasized their emotional sensitivity (al-'atifiyyeh) as a capacity for affective connection with others, including distant trading partners. Many understood the transaction of affects and intentions as a distinctively Aleppine and Eastern mode of commerce—one that connected them to Aleppines in the diaspora, and that could even transcend divides between Muslims and Jews from the city. This exchange ideology of Aleppine commerce enabled merchants to consolidate transnational networks and fashion new diasporic geographies as new possibilities for mobility emerged through the 1990s and 2000s.

The conclusion summarizes the main contributions of the book and discusses their relevance to the Syrian crisis. It also asks what happened to Aleppo's merchants and exchange ideologies after 2011. Aleppine and Arab merchants in the diaspora in China recalled a cosmopolitan ethos of commercial interaction, labeling this mode of commerce as authentically Syrian and Arab and indigenous to the region. This exchange ideology was a means of engaging in debates about the polity and contesting an increasingly dominant sectarian dynamic in the region. In this setting, commerce was emerging as a form of national heritage. This speaks to scholarship on the ways in which conflicts produce new forms of heritage.[17] Through this exchange ideology, merchants engaged in a diasporic debate about the future of the Syrian nation.

1
ALEPPO IN SPACE AND TIME

Aleppo has been perhaps the most heavily contested and brutalized city in Syria's civil war. Just mentioning the city's name brings to mind images and stories of human, material, and social devastation wreaked during the Battle of Aleppo (2012–16) that will take decades to mend. But in the years before the uprising, during the first decade of Bashar al-Asad's rule (2000–2010), this industrial city was finding its place in an expansive regional economy, exporting textiles to Turkey, Iraq, and across the Arab world and beyond, and acting as a regional forwarding point for consumer goods imported from China. These modern-day commercial connections recalled a glorious trading history. Aleppo was once the third largest city in the Ottoman Empire, an entrepot on the Silk Route connecting trading posts across Eurasia. The historian Arnold Toynbee commented, "plant yourself, not in Europe, but in 'Iraq. . . . It will become evident that half the roads of the Old World lead to Aleppo, and half to Begrám" (1961, 1). Merchants from across Eurasia came to seek their fortunes in the city, which boasted the largest souks in the empire, trading Venetian silk, spices, Persian silk, soap from Baalbek, cotton from Amman, and much else besides (Tracy 2009). This trade earned the city a mention in Shakespeare's *The Merchant of Venice*. Some of the first consulates in the world were opened in the city: the Republic of Venice (1548), France (1560), England (1583), and the Netherlands (1609). Commerce gave the city a cosmopolitan feel; by the eighteenth and nineteenth centuries, alongside Muslim traders from the Ottoman Empire, the city's elite merchants included Armenians, Greeks, Christian Arabs, Europeans, and Jews from Venice and Livorno (Momdjian 2017). In the late nineteenth century, Aleppo was one of the intellectual hubs of the nahda, the great cultural and scientific flourishing in the Arab world, and one of the centers of modern Arab journalism, alongside Beirut and Cairo.

The imposition of artificial national borders by European powers carving up the Ottoman Empire after World War I cut Aleppo off from its hinterland. The high point of Eurasian trade had already passed, and the city's importance as a commercial crossroads had also declined with the opening of the Suez Canal in 1869. But its confinement within the boundaries of the new nation-state presaged Aleppo's declining fortunes. Economically, Aleppo continued to thrive under the French mandate (1920–46) and early independence period (1946–63) through the agricultural exploitation of cotton in the Jazira, the city's hinterland to the East. But as political power was centralized in Damascus, particularly with the advent of the Baathist state in 1963, Aleppo increasingly fell behind Damascus in economic development.

Despite its relative economic stagnation under much of Baathist rule, Aleppo retained a strong sense of its identity, character, and excellence. This could be expressed in an attachment to heritage and pride in "authentic" cultural forms—from religious learning and folk music, to traditions of cuisine and commercial savviness, to folkish notions of joviality, good humor, and sincere heartedness (Shannon 2006). In 2008, a poet of the city, Fouad Mohamed Fouad, observed that Aleppines are proud of their Aleppineness (al-halabiyya), even to the extent of becoming inward-looking and socially conservative. In part this pride in Aleppineness was a legacy of the Ottoman era when loyalties had been defined largely in local (as well as imperial) terms; through much of the twentieth and early twenty-first century, urban identities in Syria arguably remained stronger than the national one (Salamandra 2004). In part, the attachment to Aleppineness was an expression of this merchant city's understanding of itself as distanced from the state and distinct from Damascus, whose business networks were more closely aligned with the Baathist regime.

The city of Aleppo lies almost entirely in a shallow bowl-like depression in the ground. Within this vast bowl, there was before the uprising typically a sense of bustle, with traffic and pedestrians and shops on most thoroughfares. Almost everywhere inside the periphery, there was a sense of dense urban fabric. The city retained some green spots but over the past century, most had been encroached upon by building, whether formal or informal; the main river now runs largely underground. Seen from the air, the city is dominated by the citadel, an imposing Crusader fortress built on a large rampart. The citadel, long an icon of the city, is said to be where Abraham stopped to water his sheep and goats. Around the citadel, old city gates and parts of the historical city wall stood remarkably intact, marking out the old city (li-mdineh) with its mostly covered bazaar complex dating back centuries. Like the bazaar, the Umayyad Mosque at the edge of the markets drew a mix of international tourists, local shoppers, and visiting merchants. The edges of the bazaar had been expanding since the early 2000s, transforming residential areas into commercial ones. An equally commercially vibrant downtown lay just to the north, and beyond them, Christian areas, including the historic Jdayde quarter. A nineteenth-century Jewish area, Jamiliyyeh, lies to the West, abutting onto up-market suburbs, boutiques, villas, and luxury flat developments that extend past the university district. Areas of densely packed informal housing circle the north of the city—largely Kurdish to the north, housing permanent residents and workers who migrated seasonally from Kurdish villages to the north and east. Areas of informal housing to the east and southeast had long served as an interface between the city and rural incomers from the Jazira (Hivernel 2000). For some of the sophisticated merchants who could afford residences in posher districts in the west, they gave onto the tribal or clannish hinterland and conjured up images of unmodernity. Several talked of the social problems caused by the migration of whole villages to the city's periphery, particularly after the drought that devastated the agricultural economy in 2006–7. Yet the hinterland also fed the city, supplied laborers for its factories, and shaped its rhythms. Countryside demand for the goods in the market remained significant, so a good harvest was good for business in the city.

Aleppo's urban periphery was clearly marked. Whereas Damascus is surrounded by a densely populated oasis, the Ghouta, Aleppo's surroundings are sparsely populated, creating a greater sense of urban edges and—despite the interlinkages between them—a perceived contrast between the urban and the nonurban. Aleppo's relationship to the Jazira was, between the mid-nineteenth and mid-twentieth century, one of political and economic domination, based on the exploitation by Ottoman (and then French) authorities of the Jazira's agricultural potential—especially cotton—and associated projects to sedentarize local populations. These had been implemented through a series of outposts—the towns of Raqqa and Deir al-Zur to the east—subordinated to Aleppo. With the advent of the Baathist state, transport and administrative infrastructures were reconfigured to connect and subordinate these areas to Damascus and to cut them off from Aleppo (Balanche 2014). Nevertheless, in 2008, members of Aleppo's merchant bourgeoisie could still evoke a sense of the city's superiority vis-à-vis its hinterlands, expressed in notions of urban sophistication and civility in relation to rural incomers and the backwardness of towns in the Jazira. At the same time, established urban merchants were also investing beyond the periphery: an era of industrial expansion since the 1990s had seen factories built in villages just beyond the beltway including on formerly agricultural land; a large state-run industrial zone was also opening up outside the city to the northeast.

Beyond the Kurdish and Turkmen areas to the north lies the Turkish border some thirty miles away. The Ottoman past is recent history for some, whose families are still spread on either side of the border. The Euphrates valley is fifty miles to the east, with trade routes extending to Mosul in Iraq. Over the centuries, the city had absorbed aspects of these diverse hinterlands and was culturally mixed; its location as a crossroads between different regions and routes afforded it a multiethnic and multicultural character. A history of dense interactions with the northern and Anatolian hinterland had made Turkmen and Kurds part of the urban fabric alongside the Arab Sunni population; connections with the Euphrates hinterland brought villagers with rural and Bedouin traditions, some of which remained important even as they embarked on urbanizing strategies; other Aleppines hailed from a Circassian background, one legacy of the Ottoman period and the waves of migration that had connected the empire to the Caucasus. After World War II, Syriacs and Armenians had swelled the Christian population. Aleppo historically had been an important Jewish center. Jewish economic migrations to Egypt and the United States in the early twentieth century, and further Jewish migrations after the establishment of the state of Israel in 1948, had depleted the population, with the remaining few hundred leaving Aleppo after Hafez al-Asad relaxed travel restrictions in 1992.[1] One indication of the continuing importance of the city to Jewish identities worldwide is the fact that a distinctive Aleppine rite and liturgy is still practiced in the diaspora, notably in New York. But in the central bazaar of Aleppo, markets were increasing homogenous in religious terms; the last Jews had left twenty years earlier, and most bazaar merchants were of Sunni Muslim background. Christian merchants tended to cluster outside the bazaar in specific quarters or sectors.

This book focuses on merchants of this dominant Sunni Muslim affiliation—those who lived and worked in or near the bazaar, those who operated factories supplying the city's central markets as well as markets and merchants further afield, and brokers who moved between them. For all their diversity and rivalries, most recognized a social order premised on ideals of respectability (akabiriyyeh) and governed by the accounting of reputation (suma'); and most recognized that these ideals were best embodied by those acknowledged as a noble or notable (akabir),[2] or a preeminent personality (shakhsiyya) possessing notability (wajaha). Merchants might disagree on which particular individuals merited these statuses, and even to some extent on what the basis of such preeminence was. But notables exemplified the sense in which all merchants could understand themselves as different from ordinary persons, and as participating in a social order that was distinct from wider society. The book analyzes these hierarchies of urban notability—their diverse forms, internal contestations, and the ways in which they interacted with state power. Some cultivated standing within these hierarchies through family and religious networks, and others through ostentatious hospitality and football sponsorship. This chapter plots out some of the histories from which this contested status of notability emerged. It does so by locating Aleppo's merchant networks in an ongoing and ever-shifting interaction between fields of commercial, religious, and political power. While it touches on urban history, political economy, and state-merchant relations, the chapter does not offer a continuous or exhaustive account of any of these. Instead, it follows the memories of the merchants I spoke to and sketches out the background to key events and periods that they themselves recalled.

Merchant-State Relations in Historical Perspective

In 2008, in some parts of Aleppo's bazaar, it was common to hear merchants nostalgically invoke a bygone era when morals were higher, trade was made on trust, and solidarity was strong between merchants. Some connected this to a time when religious knowledge was stronger and more authentic. This was remembered as a golden age before successive postcolonial governments had begun to encroach on the religious field, appropriating the waqfs or pious endowments through which merchants had funded independent religious scholars. Some merchant families that could trace their roots back beyond this period were conscious that their lineage had funded and affiliated themselves with Aleppo's prestigious religious scholars over a century earlier. This affiliation had been a source of prestige and a way of negotiating entry into the ranks of urban notability in the late Ottoman period. A class of notables had emerged as a politically dominant stratum of Syrian society in the second half of the nineteenth century.[3] In 1858, legal reforms had created a landowning class, and legislation passed in 1864 empowered landowners politically by placing them on administrative councils (Abboud 2018). Together, these measures created a new kind of political elite based on landownership (Khoury 1983) and consisting of property-owning families of religious scholars, merchants, and bureaucrats. The stratum of notables retained its power after the collapse of the Ottoman Empire as political intermediaries with local populations under the French mandate (1920–46). The French distributed collective land to the notables in return for their loyalty; smaller merchants were also invested in the system of notability as small landowners. Although a small group of notables was based in the countryside, power over rural affairs was largely concentrated among urban elites, which created resentment in the countryside.

The rule of the notables was increasingly challenged by popular social forces—peasants, workers, and middle classes—who were empowered by an expanding state (Abboud 2018). These challenges culminated in the Baathist coup of 1963, in which rural minorities took control of the state, leading to a "revolution from above" (Hinnebusch 2004) that dispossessed landed notables and an urban merchant class. The Baathist state came into being through a far-reaching program of land redistribution and nationalization of industries, which redistributed wealth to rural areas and popular constituencies. Led by military officers hailing from the countryside, it reversed the dynamic of urban-rural domination, creating urban resentment of the newly empowered rural strata. The Baathist state was also dominated by the Alawite minority, who were resented by elements of the Sunni majority, especially the notables who had previously been their overlords. If the notables had been drawn from landowning families often associated with prestigious Sunni religious learning, the Baathist state was run by a rurally rooted, heterodox minority that was avowedly secular. Resentment among leading merchants was particularly acute as the Baathist state introduced socialist policies, reducing space for private trade, and heralding the worker and the state as agents of social transformation, while traders came to be dubbed bourgeois reactionaries. In 2008, some merchants still scorned the nationalizations, recalling a successful company known for having five investors, which soon went bankrupt after the state took it over and installed five hundred workers.

When Hafez al-Asad became president in 1970, he consolidated power through a system of authoritarian control and patronage. He incorporated popular social forces through a large public sector, agricultural cooperatives, state-controlled unions of workers, peasants, and professionals, and the Baath Party. Enjoying oil rent and patronage from both the USSR and the Gulf states, he oversaw a large expansion of the public sector. This enabled him to build a political support base among the mass of public sector workers to add to the rural peasants who had benefited from Baathist land reforms and agricultural subsidies. Another facet of the state was a large military and security/domestic intelligence sector; these consisted of multiple competing agencies whose proliferating networks enriched themselves through control of industry and cross-border trade. The presidency sat atop the whole system. It consisted of mainly Alawite networks that controlled the army and competing intelligence services, which gave them autonomy from the party (Hinnebusch 2008). This regime (al-sulta) balanced above society. The pillars on which it rested—unions, the public sector, party, military, and security—constituted systems of patronage which incorporated many ordinary people into the Baathist political economy, and can be seen as a patrimonial system in which all resources flowed, ultimately, from the leader. The Baathist regime also sought to control society through security state informers. Asad's expansion of the public sector in this period also led to the creation of a new class of state contractors who grew visibly wealthy in a short period of time by depending on their proximity to the managers of public sector industries. They were referred to as a new class (tabaqa jadidah) because of their emergence as a new stratum with a distinct source of wealth. Asad had created a new rival bourgeoisie dependent on state contracts. This crony economy favored Damascenes and Alawites. Aleppo's mainly Sunni merchants felt resentment at their dispossession and relative exclusion from benefits enjoyed by Damascene and state-dependent bourgeoisies. They expressed resentment against those whom they saw as lacking authenticity (asala)—a genuine commercial enterprise and skills—and as lacking pedigree (asl wa fasl), hailing from a humble social background, often with rural roots.

When Hafez al-Asad took power in 1970, he announced a corrective movement in 1970, to moderate the effects of Baathism. He gave some permission to trade to a (mainly Sunni) merchant bourgeoisie, especially in Damascus, to secure their loyalty. Aleppo's merchants, however, enjoyed less access to the state elites who were needed to facilitate commerce in the state-dominated economy. In frustration at their political and economic decline and loss of status at the hands of a rurally rooted regime, some of Aleppo's merchant notables supported the armed Islamist rebellion against Hafez al-Asad in 1979–82, which was centered on the northern cities of Aleppo and Hama. The regime crushed the uprising. A massacre in the city of Hama left perhaps 20,000 dead. In Aleppo, merchants remember soldiers forcing open the shops that had been closed in solidarity, raiding homes, and burning religious books. After the uprising, Aleppo's merchants faced years of exclusion from the regime's "networks of privilege" (Haddad 2020). By contrast, Damascene merchant leaders, who had supported the regime, reaped the rewards, with the head of the merchant chamber in Damascus allegedly told by Hafez al-Asad: "Syria is yours." Public investments and the development of a public industrial sector were focused on the coast, in rural areas, and in Damascus. Aleppo was starved of investment, its industrial tradition neglected by the state. Road networks also tended to isolate the city, connecting towns formerly in the city's orbit instead to Damascus (Balanche 2014). The city suffered from the closing of the Iraq-Syria border (1978–98) and from political problems between Syria and Turkey (until the late 1990s), which blocked Aleppo's regional connectivity. At the end of the 1980s, Aleppo's market was comparable in size to Homs rather than Damascus (Balanche 2014), and it mainly comprised small enterprises while Damascus comprised medium and large businesses.

The 1980s also saw the beginnings of a reorientation of Syria's political economy. Asad's public sector-based patrimonial economy arguably prioritized the stability of the state over economic productivity (Hinnebusch 2008), although the proliferating networks of self-enriching officers, officials, and contractors also put the notion of the state in question. Although aid from the oil-rich Gulf and the USSR kept the system afloat during the 1970s, by the mid-1980s, tensions were more obvious, culminating in 1986 in an acute shortage of foreign exchange. With inflation accelerating, the standards of living of salaried workers and civil servants declined. In 2008, even merchants recalled the period prior to the 1980s as one where "the lira could speak" and hold its own against other currencies. In the late 1980s, some in the regime wanted to reduce popular subsidies and privatize public industries; others worried about the effect such moves would have on the support base of the regime and about the likely demands of an empowered bourgeoisie for political liberalization (Hinnebusch and Zintl 2015a). The economic and political tensions of this period can be seen in Aleppo in the rapid rise and subsequent fall of financial entrepreneurs, dubbed money collectors. These individuals pioneered popular investment schemes that initially promised to meet the demand of salaried workers and small business owners for a regular income that kept pace with inflation. Chapter 6 follows the story of one of the largest entrepreneurs who used the funds he gathered to found a series of private industrial enterprises in Aleppo. He was subsequently prosecuted and imprisoned in the early 1990s. With his tens of thousands of investors he may have appeared as a possible independent support base, or his patron in the regime may simply have lost out in an internal power struggle. In any case, this was a period when there was internal tension in the regime about how to manage economic liberalization without seeing the emergence of a politically autonomous commercial bourgeoisie.

The solution that emerged was to liberalize selectively; that is, to ensure that the benefits of economic liberalization were captured by narrow, politically compliant networks of privilege. By 1990, the regime had decided that private investment was necessary to generate growth. But being unwilling to allow a politically independent bourgeoisie, it allowed only limited privatization, liberalization of trade and investment, and external investment, and ensured that the lion's share of benefits was distributed to compliant business networks (Kienle 1994). Those with powerful patrons and no political ambitions could become wealthy and even gain a public profile through sponsorship and elections. From the mid-1990s, leading merchants and industrialists were co-opted into parliament, but subjected to harassment and imprisonment if they became politically independent (Seif 1998). In 2008, some spoke of Aleppo's largest private yarn and textile industrialist, active in a domain traditionally dominated by the independent commercial bourgeoisie, as part of the regime. The fortunes of the city's private industrialists had revived in the second half of the 1990s because the regime had introduced tariffs on imports which encouraged investment in manufacturing. Political connections brokered through access to parliament and the boards of the chambers of commerce and industry provided new elites with the confidence to form industrial capital and invest in textile and yarn manufacturing in this period. These connections saw the emergence of a stratum of Sunni industrialists from outside the established families of pedigree.

New and old merchant families alike found opportunities in textile manufacturing through the 1990s, stimulated by demand from post-Soviet markets. These transnational connections were rooted in an earlier history of Soviet patronage of Syria. In the 1970s, the USSR had accepted payment in textiles and other consumables for its military hardware sold to the Syrian regime. This agreement, enabling the settlement of Syrian government debt through private exports, benefited Aleppo's textile manufacturers, who exported much of their output to the USSR through the 1980s. Russia was the most significant market, estimated at a third or more of all Syria's private exports; when the rest of the socialist bloc is included, the figure rises to 80 percent in 1989 (Perthes 1992). In 1991, the formal patronage ended, but the commercial networks endured, as Russian importers initially lacked commercial relations beyond the formerly socialist bloc, so they continued to depend on Syrian factories for the first few years. Syrian merchants talked of making profits of up to 300 percent in Russia in the 1990s. Aleppo's textile exporters also found demand for their relatively low-quality goods in post-Soviet Central Asia, in newly independent resource-rich countries that were developing middle classes and markets for imported consumer goods. A former manager of one of Aleppo's largest fabric factories claimed that he had been the first to sell into the market in Uzbekistan in 1993, and that a week after his first sale, the airplane from Tashkent was full of merchants seeking Aleppo's fabrics, from clothes and carpets to sofa furnishings and curtain fabrics. These connections also drew Syrian entrepreneurs to sojourn in Russia and post-Soviet Central Asia to organize the importation of Syrian goods.

Aleppo under Bashar al-Asad

In 2008, some merchants in Aleppo talked of the city having undergone an industrial renaissance (al-nahda al-sinaʿiyya) since the late 1990s. Aleppine industry had been catching up with Damascus since the 1990s. By 2004, Aleppo had more private industrial enterprises (10+ employees) than Damascus (974 to 633) and had 50 percent of all such enterprises in Syria (Balanche 2014). Damascus had more large enterprises (50+ employees) than Aleppo: 55 to 38. But between 1994 and 2004 (the last available data), the overall number of industrial enterprises remained steady in Aleppo, while declining in Damascus and nationally (Balanche 2014). After Bashar al-Asad inherited the presidency from his father in 2000, the regime accelerated market reforms, opened the banking sector, and liberalized import and export rules. It described the new approach in vague terms as a social market economy in an attempt to reassure those in the regime uncomfortable with the speed of change and the reduction of popular subsidies on food, fuel, and agricultural inputs that would harm the regime's traditional support base (Sottimano and Selvik 2008). In reality, the regime was retreating from its Baathist commitments to popular subsidies, mass public sector employment, and agricultural development. These reforms shifted the base of the regime away from traditional constituencies of workers and peasants toward economic elites and urban bourgeoisies in particular.

Under Bashar, the city also regained some of its former regional and transregional connectivity. In part this was due to the gathering pace of economic liberalization, and in part due to a political decision to reorient Syria's international relations. In 2005, at the height of Syria's isolation by the West after the assassination of Lebanese prime minister Hariri, Bashar reoriented Syria's foreign relations eastward toward China, Turkey, and the Gulf (Hinnebusch and Zintl 2015b). Syria joined the Greater Arab Free Trade Area on January 1, 2005. Relations improved with Turkey, leading to the signing of a Free Trade Agreement in 2007. The opening of the border with Iraq was particularly important, bringing Iraqi merchants and capital to the city, seeking alternative markets for provision and investment after the decimation of their country's industrial base after 2003. The 2003 US-led invasion and subsequent turmoil had weakened Iraq's industrial capacities and displaced Iraqi capital into Syria, making Aleppo a critical industrial and commercial node for supplying Iraqi markets (Arslanian 2009; Daher 2019).[4] Textile and clothing exports tripled from 2005 to 2006, according to official figures (Said 2010, 40). Alongside this growth in manufacturing, Aleppo became a commercial forwarding hub for the region, especially for Far Eastern imports, earning the city the nickname "the little China" (al-sin al-sghireh). Thus Aleppo benefited from an emerging regional economy connecting it both to Turkey and the Arab region. International connectivity improved (although it still lagged behind Damascus): regular direct flights started connecting Aleppo to Istanbul, the Gulf, Asia, and Africa (Balanche 2014). Foreign investment into Aleppo reached 36 percent of the national total, and the economy grew annually as a result in 2006–8 between 4 percent and 5 percent (Hinnebusch and Zintl 2015a).

The significance of these connections needs to be understood against a backdrop of barriers to other possible spaces of economic integration. In 1995, a Euro-Mediterranean Partnership was proclaimed between the fifteen member states of the European Union and twelve southern Mediterranean countries, with a vision of security and economic cooperation. But Syria did not ratify its participation until December 2008. This was partly because of concerns that the partnership would be unequal, imposing neoliberal economic governance on the

Syrian economy, while failing to remove trade barriers associated with the European Common Agricultural Policy.[5] But just as important, joining the Euro-Mediterranean partnership meant that Syrian exporters, the vast majority of whom were small and medium businesses, would need to accept costly industrial standards, which was feasible only for the largest enterprises. Some of the Aleppine textile entrepreneurs that exported to EU countries reported in 2009 that they regarded it as hazardous, because their manufacturing processes were often not able to guarantee the quality standards required by European markets.

Aleppo's better capitalized textile industrialists increasingly looked elsewhere for their export markets. Iraq and countries participating in the Greater Arab Free Trade Area provided important markets, but exporters like those described in chapters 4 and 5 also looked north and east to post-Soviet spaces, and south and west to the Horn of Africa, for their commercial fortunes. The factory described in these chapters employed around ninety staff and exemplified Aleppo's industrial renaissance. Production expanded rapidly from 2006, and the business integrated into regional and transregional markets. As well as supplying Syrian cities, it also exported to Arab countries, from Morocco to Iraq. Through a Syrian business partner in Dubai and other Syrian businessmen in the diaspora, the owners also exported fabric to the Horn of Africa and post-Soviet spaces of Russia and Central Asia, reaching markets in Addis Ababa, Somalia, Moscow, and Tashkent. Diasporic Syrian networks helped the owners to expand into these markets in the 2000s. They belonged to a stratum of well-capitalized textile industrialists who entered into transregional networks and circulations in the 2000s.

This industrial renaissance was undoubtedly uneven. Economic liberalization did not benefit all entrepreneurs in the city but had differentiated effects. Imports of cheap consumer goods from China put many small local manufacturers out of business or forced them to become importers and traders themselves, creating competition and cutting margins for longer established merchants who complained of the "crowd" of incomers and the decline of morals. As Samer Abboud (2018, 41) notes, "many in the business community did reap peripheral benefits of marketisation; but the overwhelming majority (more than 96 percent) of Syrian business enterprises were small (fewer than ten employees) and were on the peripheries" of these gains. In Aleppo, manufacturing enterprises employed, on average, five staff, and many lacked the scale to compete (Daher 2019).[6] Moreover, the industrial renaissance concentrated the surplus wealth that was derived from the exploitation of rural labor in the city rather than returning it to the countryside, exacerbating urban-rural divides (Balanche 2014). Industrial development increased land prices at certain edges of the city as the urban periphery expanded, and industrial zoning generated a real estate market. As those who sold up invested in commerce, more players entered urban trade, increasing competition for existing merchants. But in general, most rural strata lost out: economic liberalization saw cheap labor of the rural hinterland exploited again as it had been before the Baathist revolution.

Yet urban manufacturers with access to capital and the necessary facilitations took advantage of the regional integration and low labor costs. Larger operators who found an economic niche and who benefited from political support were able to flourish. There was a plentiful supply of land for industrial development at the urban periphery; rural migration into the city provided cheap low-skilled labor, and a low proportion of public sector workers (whose salaries were tripled in the first decade of Bashar's rule) also kept labor costs low—an important consideration for low-value-added industries such as textiles, which dominated the city (Balanche 2014). The opening of the banking sector created opportunities for the wealthiest industrialists to invest in the new financial enterprises and in the booming real estate market. At all stages, well-placed contacts in the state were essential in navigating economic liberalization; in many cases they made the difference between winners and losers. In a rapidly changing commercial environment, state officials were often involved in some way in the development and facilitation of private commerce. If anything, liberalization increased the role of state officials in mediating the opportunities for cross-border trade and the channeling of foreign investment. Scholars (e.g., Donati 2020) studied the ways that the regime captured the benefits of economic liberalization by turning over formerly public industries to compliant businesspeople who entered into partnerships with them. This has led scholars to propose a distinction between the "state-dependent bourgeoisie" and a "genuine commercial bourgeoisie" (Perthes 1997; Haddad 2020). But the distinction is blurred to some extent, as state-brokered advantage came not just come in the form of former state monopolies, but also in the form of access to information, quotas, licenses, and favor with customs officials. Autonomous commercial operators—competing for contracts "far from the state"—were also dependent on state contacts at critical junctures.

If Aleppo was, through much of the twentieth century, forced to submit to the hegemony of Damascus, the city was at the beginning of the twenty-first century finding its place once again in expansive regional and transregional geographies (see Balanche 2014, 64). As well as Turkey and Iraq, it was increasingly orienting itself to Asia and Africa; merchants were sending textiles to Central Asia and the Horn of Africa and fashioning the city as a regional forwarding point for Chinese imports. These processes benefited most of all those industrialists who enjoyed proximity to political power and who were able to reach the scale necessary to export. These larger industrialists appeared to inhabit a different world to most of Aleppo's commercial sector; they were embodiments of a new modernity, engaging in international travel, elite consumption, and acting as agents for the latest industrial machinery from China and Taiwan. Yet they were also connected to wider society as suppliers to the market, creditors, arbiters of disputes for less influential merchants, and visible civic sponsors of public goods. Thus, some textile industrialists made a rapid rise not only to wealth but also to public prominence. Their public profile reflected a shift in official ideology. With the waning of Baathism, official discourse cast entrepreneurs as agents of modernization (Sottimano and Selvik 2008). No longer the enemies of the nation as in Baathist ideology, leading merchants and industrialists were cast during Bashar al-Asad's first decade in power as visible social actors responsible for developing society—a position formerly assigned to workers and the state (Abboud 2015, 2018).[7] This shift did not solve the development problem; while the private sector expanded between 1990 and 2010, unemployment, precarity, and wage disparities all increased (Abboud 2018), with most suffering concentrated in rural areas and informal districts at urban peripheries.

Economic Liberalization as Cultural Process: Merchants as Public Figures

If under Hafez al-Asad the Baathist regime had sought to build both a nation and a modern centralized state which dissolved local oligarchies (Balanche 2014), under Bashar it also recognized and cultivated a sense of notability among leading merchants and industrialists, some of whom became public figures during the 2000s (Abboud 2018). This shift occurred as Bashar al-Asad sought to consolidate his power as president over the Baath Party by hollowing it out as a set of patronage networks and state-society relays. This left communal leaders and notables as the main channels through which ordinary people could seek redress. Thus notability was given renewed significance in the context of economic liberalization and post-Baathist reconfigurations of state-society relations. In the postpopulist era, the urban bourgeoisies were critical sources of revenue and support for the regime; one way to co-opt them was to offer leaders facilitations in exchange for revenue and fame as public sponsors of urban institutions and civic goods. This conferred status as notables from above. To decide who was worth co-opting, the regime relied on elections to merchant chambers, which demonstrated the status conferred on notables from below (see Blaydes 2010).

Leading figures achieved prominence through a variety of avenues: the city's merchant chambers, civic sponsorship, and informal commercial arbitration. Some cultivated standing through family and religious networks, and others through hospitality and football sponsorship. Some asserted their preeminence in terms that harked back nostalgically to an era of pre-Baathist notability. Others visibly embodied traits of youth and cosmopolitanism associated with Bashar's post-Baathist modernization of authoritarian power.

Pre-Baathist Notables

Merchant families with roots in the pre-Baathist period have been described as an "authentic" commercial bourgeoisie (Perthes 1997); that is, one that is independent of the state. This stratum was distinguished by its long-established commercial capital, experience, and networks. Because their extensive merchant family networks provided them with a relatively independent support base, an economically liberalizing regime could not afford to ignore them. Instead, through the 1990s and 2000s, the regime made moves to cultivate this stratum, acknowledging its leaders as notables by inviting them to act as civic sponsors, as well as by keeping open channels of petition and allowing independent merchants a quota of seats in Aleppo's merchant chambers. Among merchants, leaders of this stratum were recognized as notables for their pedigree; for the size and cohesiveness of their families; for their wealth and standing in hierarchies of respect, which enabled them to act as arbitrators in commercial disputes; and for their political influence, which enabled them to petition political or security elites.

This is the stratum I explore in chapters 2–4, which document the Souk Jarba notables and related leading merchant families with businesses across the city, including in and around the bazaar. They can be seen as a challenged notability, which the regime balanced against rival kinds of notables and rival power bases. Some were known for their piety, as they funded and courted the support of Islamic scholars. Those claiming pre-Baathist pedigree could also express indignation about bureaucratic encroachments on an older social-moral order, which they saw themselves as embodying; many also saw it as shameful to enter the employ of the state or intermarry with families of state officials. Yet this stratum was not wholly antagonistic to the regime. Some old merchant families entered into cautious business partnerships with the regime and profited as suppliers, for example as manufacturers of the fabrics used in school and military uniforms. Alongside these notable families were other less prestigious merchant strata—individuals and smaller families without pedigree as such, and with less ability to petition political or security elites, but who had internalized the norms of mercantile respectability and creditworthiness best embodied by the notables, such as submission to the disciplines of reputational accounting and to the authority of recognized arbitrators. When they had achieved a sufficient level of wealth and reputation, these lesser figures could also exercise a degree of notability in acting as arbitrators in smaller commercial disputes. They, too, could express resentment at state proxies whom they saw as outside the norms of urban merchant society.

Established merchants responded to the competition of powerful state proxies in part by decrying their lack of pedigree and hinting at the decline of morality they embodied. Reflecting on the changing dynamics of commerce, one merchant from a pre-Baathist family complained that the market and city as a whole had seen the influx of a crowd (zahmeh) of newcomers who had brought with them rurally based clannish ('asha'iri) ways of doing business. He was not expressing disdain for the rural poor but for more influential social and economic rivals. Aleppo's Chamber of Commerce—where his own family was influential—was dominated at the time by regime proteges whom urban merchants referred to as clans (al-'asha'ir). These were minor subgroups of tribes (al-qaba'il) who had been coopted by the regime as local extensions of the security state in and around Aleppo.

State-Affiliated Clans

The clans' rise to prominence had begun some thirty years earlier, when Hafez al-Asad had responded to the Islamist-led challenge of 1979–82 by recruiting loyalist militias to repress dissent in the steppe around Aleppo. They were rewarded economically, allowed to enrich themselves through forms of cross-border trade unavailable to other commercial strata, and offered state contracts in areas such as litter collection, road building, and phosphate mining. Economically empowered, they were able to enter into the city markets—traditionally the territory of urban merchants—as traders, at first in agricultural products, but later in industrial products such as yarn and real estate. Some gained considerable political power, rising to positions of prominence in the city's chambers of commerce and industry, where they came to dominate.

Although they became cash rich, they remained outside the networks of credit and social prestige that defined Aleppo's urban merchant hierarchies. Established urban merchants continued to regard them as outsiders. These politically influential clans were seen by incumbent urban merchants as rural incomers epitomizing the crony economy and its corruption. Their proximity to Asad's security state, and the relative autonomy from the law this conferred on them, contributed to an image of them as fearsome and uncouth—beyond the jurisdiction of the hierarchies of mercantile respect that governed much informal dispute resolution in the city. When they did marry into these hierarchies, it was the occasion for raised eyebrows and critical comments. The clans were Sunni rather than Alawite, but for the most part the commercial and familial networks of the city's Sunni-majority merchants remained closed to them.

The closure of urban networks to rural incomers reflected the regime's policy of fostering rival business elites and served to divide wealthy Sunni strata into competing groups. The social divide was reflected in residence patterns; the clans were head-quartered in the southeast district of Aleppo, at the gates to the city, in areas marked as unmodern by urban merchants inhabiting sophisticated (raqi) areas (see Meier 2014). Although some had invested in residences across the city, including in Aleppo's up-market western districts, they could speak of this as a strategy of infiltrating urban areas. The social divide was also perpetuated by discourses of authentic urbanity—in claims to be truly Aleppine (Halabi asli) or to have pedigree (asl wa fasl). When the clans emerged as powerful figures in Aleppo's merchant chambers, urban merchants identified them with the state, cast them as rural, and invoked notions of Aleppo's urban authenticity. In doing so, they perpetuated social divides that arguably played into a regime strategy of divide and rule vis-à-vis Aleppo's business elites.

Post-Baathist Notables

Another stratum considered in the book are leading Sunni industrialists without family pedigree who rose to prominence in the liberalizing era of the late 1990s and 2000s. As I noted above, the regime chose in this period to liberalize selectively, seeking to ensure that the benefits of economic liberalization were captured by narrow, politically compliant networks of privilege. In some cases, this happened through turning over formerly public industries wholesale (Donati 2020). But beneath this top tier, other elites benefited from less substantial but still significant forms of privilege: distribution of state-controlled assets, in the form of cheaper rent on industrial premises, commercially sensitive information, and larger quotas for imports or for the purchase of state-produced cotton. The most successful thrived from economic liberalization and industrial development in particular as Aleppo found its place in a regional network as a manufacturing hub. These constituted a new post-Baathist notability known for their wealth, as well as their connections among merchants and political elites. Because they were connected to a greater or less degree to networks of privilege, many were cautious about open criticism of the regime. But they saw themselves as part of urban merchant society and entered into business partnerships with the state only cautiously. Alongside this stratum was a group of managers, brokers, professionals (accountants), ad hoc importers, and businesspeople who found opportunities within these networks of more influential industrialists and merchants.

Mohannad, the central figure in chapters 5 and 6, is an example of the new industrialist stratum. He benefited from proximity to networks of privilege, but he was not part of the top tier. He did not assume control of a formerly public sector industry, nor was he part of the state-dependent contractors' bourgeoisie or the clans who were empowered through their incorporation into the security apparatuses and the control of cross-border trade. He operated in the textile sector, traditionally associated with the independent bourgeoisie in Aleppo, and was funded through a partnership with a minor merchant family from the bazaar. He was part of an elite stratum of Sunni industrialists without family pedigree who profited through access to independent capital and through varying degrees of access to networks of privilege. These new Sunni industrialists were a small but influential stratum. Many first accumulated capital by trading with Russia under the payments agreement through which the Syrian regime settled its weapons debts with the USSR by exporting domestically produced goods. Textile exporters in Aleppo were among those private entrepreneurs who benefited from this state-backed export, later developing profitable commercial relations with markets in post-Soviet republics. Some converted their profits into productive capital, establishing textile and then yarn factories in Aleppo in the 1990s. It was from this stratum that the regime invited leading merchants to act as sports and civic sponsors in return for facilitation (tashil) of their business interests. Some went further and were elected to parliament; by the 2000s, some referred to them as part of the regime.

These three groups were engaged in a contest for urban notability and precedence within the regime's patron-client networks. Notability was in part a matter of political influence and favor conferred on merchants through their connections with political elites. But notability was also a matter of status. Established merchant families and leading individuals performed their status as patrons and conservators of Aleppo's architecture, buildings, markets, and urban landscapes, as well as its traditions of commercial conviviality. The prestige of merchant lineages was connected to the city, and this connection needed to be continually reenacted to sustain a family's preeminence. Newer merchants—the post-Baathist notability—asserted their civic preeminence in other ways, funding urban sports clubs, either at the invitation of political elites in Damascus or in a bid to be noticed by them. Discourses about trade, about what it meant to be a merchant, and the relation between these and society and polity, figured prominently in this process and the rivalries between these groups. I call these representations of commerce and society "exchange ideologies." These are the focus of analysis in the following chapters.

2

EXCHANGE IDEOLOGIES OF URBAN-RURAL DIFFERENCE

Among Damascene merchants in the wholesale markets of Yiwu, a commercial city in the southeast of China where they sourced supplies, a person could hear it said of Aleppo's House of Umar that "they have a well-known name, immediately you will give them credit. They have been merchants for eighty years, from grandfather to father (abban 'an jidd)." But in Souk Jarba in Aleppo, where the Umar merchant family was based, you might have heard the opposite sentiment. Fuad Umar, a sixty-one-year-old wholesaler and retailer of household items, observed in 2008 that "once, Aleppo was a small city, and we were a big family; everyone knew our name. Now, no-one knows us! And Aleppo has become very large—it is bad for the health of the city . . . Good morals used to be enough for business—people would give you credit. Now, people don't do business with morals, only cash. Aleppo's society is clannish now, it is not so nice." He added that both the market and the city as a whole had seen the influx of a crowd (zahmeh) of newcomers who had brought with them rurally based clannish ('asha'iri) ways of doing business, resulting in the loss of calm (hudu') and a decline in moral interaction (al-ta'amul) in trade.

This chapter asks how and why differences between urban and rural people came to appear self-evident among merchants in Aleppo under Baathist rule. Rather than only being present in discourses about origin, it argues that they were also reproduced through everyday practices and understandings of trade, what I call exchange ideologies of differentiation. Ideas of urban-rural difference had become pertinent to the self-understanding of merchants such as Fuad because of the ways in which the Asad state had fostered rival merchant bourgeoisies; on the one hand, an autonomous commercial bourgeoisie, to which Fuad's House of Umar belonged and, on the other, a dependent state bourgeoisie that rivaled the influence of the autonomous merchant class. The regime's divide-and-rule policy maintained these bourgeoisies as competing elites in the city's markets and commercial chambers.

Exchange Ideologies of Differentiation

One puzzling feature of Fuad's complaints about rural incomers is how to make sense of such opposing evaluations of the Umar name. On the one hand, it is so widely known that it would immediately attract credit; on the other, it has declined to the extent that "no-one knows us!" Other merchants from established families agreed with Fuad's assessment of the changing modes of commerce in the city, observing that while urban merchants entrust goods on credit, the clans only do business in cash—they have no concept of credit or the accountable person. More widely shared still among Aleppo's urban bourgeoisie was the sentiment that the city had seen an influx of unruly forces from the countryside, who had brought about not just a challenge to dominant modes of commerce in the market but also a broader decline in honor-based forms of interaction and civility, in market and city alike.[1] What we see is a widely shared anxiety—prevalent among circles of established merchant elites and the wider urban bourgeoisie— that their preeminent position in the market and the city was being eroded by the rise of state-affiliated elites, whom they referred to as clans.

These anxieties crystallized in laments about the decline of credit-based commerce. I argue that one way to make sense of them is as an exchange ideology. By this I mean the structured and socially situated ways in which processes of commerce and exchange were construed, represented, and linked to categories of social identity and difference, as well as moral and aesthetic values. This approach draws heavily on the notion of language ideology from the field of sociolinguistics. Language ideologies have been defined as "shared bodies of common-sense notions about the nature of language in the world" (Rumsey 1990, 346) and as "cultural representations of the nature of language" (Robbins 2001, 592). Most scholars agree that "ideologies of language are not about language alone" but rather "enact ties of language to identity" (Woolard 1998, 3). Much like a language ideology, an exchange ideology specifies categories of identity and difference and markers of prestige. Borrowing Atiqa Hachimi's (2012, 322) description of language ideologies, an exchange ideology can be seen as a set of "ideas about what constitutes good or bad, vulgar or nice, civilized or uncivilized" ways of trading, rather than ways of speaking, which differentiate those said to trade in one way, from those said to trade in another.

In proposing the notion of exchange ideology by analogy with language ideology, this chapter seeks a cross-pollination between economic anthropology and sociolinguistics. Economic anthropologists have long studied the capacities of various kinds of material and immaterial exchange to create and define groups and relationships between groups (see, e.g., Malinowski 2013; Mauss 2002).[2] But they have paid comparatively little attention to metapragmatic discourse and orders of indexicality—the ways in which individuals reflect and comment on their exchange practices and use them to construct group boundaries and identities. Sociolinguists, by contrast, have developed sophisticated tools for understanding the links between language, identity, and social differentiation. But they have tended to view language and linguistic exchange in isolation from other kinds of exchange. Yet for Aleppo's merchants, trade and speech were not separate fields of practice, but part of a spectrum of modes of exchange that could be used interchangeably to index social identities. Fuad attributed the decline of honor-based forms of commerce to the increasing power of rural clans in the market, whereas other urban merchants claimed that the clans did not settle disputes in a civil way, by submitting to the authority of well-recognized arbitrators, but by shouting ('ayyat) and making problems. Fuad posited changing forms of commerce, and the decline of credit-based exchanges in particular, as evidence that the city was being ruralized and subjected to moral decline. In this case, both commerce and language provided the material for "semiotic processes of differentiation through which particular social identities [became] recognisable" (Rosa and Burdick 2017, 110).

As an example of the usefulness of sociolinguistic tools to make sense of ideologies of exchange, consider the way that Fuad and other Aleppine merchants construed clans as harbingers of cash-only commerce and the declining levels of trust that this implied. The sociolinguists Irvine and Gal (2000, 37) propose the term iconization to refer to the ways in which actors "treat linguistic signs as natural depictions or images of the inherent nature of speakers" (Woolard 2008, 438). This captures well the ways in which incumbent merchants in Aleppo rendered clans constitutionally unable to entrust, to trade on credit, because they lacked a conception of the accountable person. Irvine and Gal (2000, 38) also propose the term "fractal recursivity" to refer to the process whereby an "opposition salient at one level is projected onto other levels of a linguistic and social relationship" (Woolard 1998, 19). This, too, illuminates the way urban merchants could scale up the opposition between credit and cash to another level of opposition between civility and shouting. In doing so, they construed new entrants to the market as threats to an urban social order, which they saw themselves as embodying.

In this chapter I unpick the politics behind this ideology of exchange, describing how modes of commerce had come to code notions of urban-rural difference in Aleppo, and how these notions of difference had come to be politically and morally charged. To focus on the ideological construction of commercial interactions is to ask about the collective histories, social positions, and political struggles that account for these particular understandings of trade. What was at stake for urban merchants in assigning value to certain commercial forms—of entrustment and civility—and casting others out as beyond the scope of the city proper? An exchange ideology through which Aleppo's merchants and rural clans were figured as icons of incompatible forms of commerce and society reflected a commercial field (Bourdieu 1977) that was contested by two kinds of elites, whose leaders enjoyed distinct sources of power, capital, and prestige. On the one hand, merchants such as the House of Umar, who described themselves as authentically Aleppine (Halabi asli), pursued commercial and social credit within largely closed networks of commercial and marital entrustment, and sought prestige by associating themselves with self-consciously urban forms of heritage, such as Sufi religiosity, historic architecture, and family genealogies of urban pedigree. On the other hand, those who described themselves as clans were largely excluded from such networks. Instead, their leaders enjoyed access to state-brokered monopolies and licenses through their affiliation with the security apparatuses of the Syrian regime. Under Bashar al-Asad's first decade in power (2000–2010), these rival elites vied with each other within the same social field for control of Aleppo's merchant chambers and influence in the markets.

Urban and Rural Identities in Aleppo

Town-country tensions had long existed in Syria. In Aleppo, under the French mandate (1920–46), such divisions had been exacerbated by the French policy of empowering urban capitalists to exploit the cotton economy in the Euphrates valley (Weulersse 1946, quoted in Salamandra 2004, 12). The advent of the Baathist state in 1963 gave new force to urban-rural tensions, as rurally rooted officers of a humble social background dislodged urban notables from economic and political power and empowered previously dominated rural strata. There was also a sectarian dimension to the Baathist state: its leaders were drawn mainly from the Alawite confessional minority, regarded as heterodox by the Sunni majority. When Hafez al-Asad became president in 1970, he launched a corrective movement that courted the support of the Damascene merchant class. But tensions remained among urban elites, resentful at their fall from notability. The military was one of the pillars of the Baathist state, and its rise to power brought many Alawite peasants to the outskirts of Damascus (Salamandra 2004, 10). The Baathist state also empowered humbler rural strata. Some former peasants who had made money in the Gulf moved to Damascus, where they enjoyed strong links with the regime (Salamandra 2004, 8).

Christa Salamandra has analyzed the sectarian tensions that underpinned the rivalry between urban and rural elites in Damascus in the 1990s. Sunni elites in Damascus in the 1990s claimed that the city was becoming ruralized and corrupted by the influx of socially mobile state-dependent rural strata. Older Damascene families sought to distinguish themselves from these nouveaux riches rivals, and reassert their sectarian Sunni Damascene identity, by renovating the old city of Damascus and engaging in practices of consumption in styles they identified as authentically urban. Among this old Damascus movement, the category rural (rifi) could be code for Alawite. At the same time, as Salamandra argues, sect was not simply a marker of confessional identity, but an idiom of social difference that could be constituted by a variable mix of regional, linguistic, class, and cultural backgrounds (Salamandra 2004, 11). Laments about the ruralization of the city, and the valorization of urban modes of exchange, among Aleppo's Sunni merchants a decade later echo several features of the old Damascus movement analyzed by Salamandra (2004). Like their Damascene counterparts, some among Aleppo's bourgeoisie who "identified with the old social order" expressed a similar sense of "alienation" and a sentiment that the city "is becoming ruralised" and country people are inappropriate in the city (Salamandra 2004, 12).

Rival Bourgeoisies, the Shabiha, and Social Mistrust

In Aleppo, the rural rivals challenging incumbent merchant elites were not Alawite conscripts but the heads of minor clans from the steppe. Hafez al-Asad, confronting an Islamist-led challenge to his rule in the early 1980s focused on the north of the country, had co-opted the heads of rural clans to monitor movements around the northern cities of Aleppo and Hama, stem the supply of weapons from Iraq, and prevent members of the Muslim Brotherhood from taking refuge in the steppe (Rae 1999; Chatty 2010). They had been rewarded with money, but also contracts and positions in Aleppo's Chamber of Industry and in the Syrian parliament. They came to form a state-dependent bourgeoisie, composed of largely rural incomers, and were generally regarded as parvenus by the city's established merchant bourgeoisie, whose sources of wealth and opportunity were largely independent of the state.

These developments reflected shifts in political economy happening elsewhere in Syria. Across the country, in the 1980s and 1990s, new economic elites emerged who hailed from comparatively humble social backgrounds. Scholars have described these new elites as a "state bourgeoisie" of powerful officials and compliant businessmen who grew wealthy from public sector contracts, distinguishing them from an authentic "commercial bourgeoisie," which constituted an entrepreneurial and "traditionally resilient urban/Sunni" merchant class (Perthes 1997; Haddad 2012). These business networks emerged as economic liberalization was skewed toward the interests of regime cronies; as well as enjoying preferential access to state contracts, those close to the regime profited from politically engineered monopolies in newly liberalized sectors of the economy.

In Aleppo, rurally rooted clans loyal to the regime formed an important component of this state-dependent bourgeoisie. When Bashar al-Asad took over as president in 2000, the regime continued to outsource parts of the security field in Aleppo to local clans (Duhkhan 2014), rewarding their leaders with public sector contracts and trading concessions. Over time, they came to rival families such as Fuad's, from the city's established merchant bourgeoisie, for influence in the Aleppo's markets and commercial chambers. One of the clans whose dominant families were affiliated with the regime in 2009 was the Asasneh clan. They claimed membership of the Dulaim tribal confederation that stretched into Iraq. The clan had settled in Assan, a small town some twenty kilometers to the southeast of Aleppo, "over a hundred years ago," according to one of its leaders, and then spread to the city. In 2009, after waves of migration to the city, the population of Assan was estimated at some 10,000 people, while some 80,000 members were resident in Aleppo, according to the clan's notables.[3] In the city, the Asasneh sought to establish themselves in the city's markets. Their Facebook page reported in 2018 that the clan was "one of the oldest that settled the land of Aleppo from the south and is one of the first clans that entered the world of trade through the old markets of Aleppo."[4]

The families of the clan would be divided after 2011, with many of the educated and poorer families joining the revolution, while some of the wealthier and dominant families sided with the regime.[5] Some of the latter had been empowered politically and economically through their informal association with the security state since the 1980s. Abd belonged to one of these branches. The son of a senior member of a regime-affiliated family in the clan, he had lived in the southeast of the city, in a district called Nayrab Gate, until 2007. Then, at the age of twenty-four, he traveled to the market city of Yiwu in China, where he placed an order for car parts and began a career as an importer. When I met him in Yiwu in 2017, he was clearly proud of what he saw as the rise of his clan through its association with the state. As we sat in a café he favored because it was unfrequented by other Syrian merchants in the city, he told me, "We entered the state—the army, police, intelligence, judges, lawyers—and went into trade, and took concessions (munaqasat) to build roads and do construction projects for the state." These included maintaining water systems and managing litter collection. He added, "we went into all parts of the state; we are like a mafia, we have people in each domain. Like a mafia—but not a criminal mafia. There are parts who do illegal things, but a minority. The state cannot do anything against us, it is afraid. If an officer stops me for doing something wrong when I am driving, and asks to see my ID card, when he sees the name of the clan, he will just give it back and tell me not to do it again." His clan, he emphasized, was beyond other structures of accountability: "We settle accounts among ourselves" (nahsib lhsab bayn ba'd). Since 2011, his branch of the clan was—alongside the B. clan—one of those said to supply the regime with loyalist militias (shabiha). Abd was quite open about this. He said that some of the leaders of his clan became involved in mobilizing groups to repress protests and anti-regime activism, and they were rewarded with reconstruction and phosphate extraction contracts. He added that a government minister had recently intervened in an attempt to appoint him as the president of the Contractors' Union in Aleppo, which he saw as a gesture of thanks for his branch of the clan's mobilization against opponents of the regime, and an attempt to maintain their support.

For Abd in 2017, identifying as an Asasneh and as a shabiha was a way of claiming a certain prestige of military prowess, state-backed privilege, immunity from prosecution, and fearsomeness. The name "Asasneh" had long been known for its power and influence in the city of Aleppo.[6] This reflects the fact that the leaders of the clan enjoyed markedly different sources of power from the House of Umar—not social capital within expansive merchant networks of the established bourgeoisie, but positions and affiliations with the judicial and coercive arms of the state. Though the battle for Aleppo had accentuated the regime's reliance on loyalist clan families, they had long occupied a different position in Aleppo's commercial-cum-political field compared to longer-established merchant elites in the city. This left incumbent merchants vulnerable in the case of disputes, leading to mistrust and the closure of commercial and marital networks.

Figuring Otherness through Speech, Commerce, and Marriage

Before 2011, among Aleppo's established commercial bourgeoisie, this closure was policed through a combination of language and exchange ideologies, which cast clannish modes of speech and commerce, and sources of capital, as outside the scope of the city proper. In 2009, Fadi, a second-generation yarn broker based in Aleppo's bazaar, said, "When you work with someone, you are working with that House, that family of such-and-such, their family. We won't work with someone who has problems (mashakil), who has cheated others (nassab 'ala'l-'alem). Have you heard of the House of B.? These guys from the countryside, they are like the mafia, the new families. If someone says, I am from the House of B., we won't work with them. It is the same issue with marriage." Nur Tabbakh, a member of an established trading family, and a thirty-eight-year-old widow of a merchant from Hama who had settled in Aleppo said in the same year that

> old merchant families are refined (raqiyya). It means they are polite (muhadhdhaba), there is no shouting or cursing where there are disagreements... They have no problems with the state, no hint of criminality, no prison, no guns. If there is a disagreement, they won't shout, they won't say ugly words, they won't insult... Rich common families appeared in Aleppo in the last thirty years. We don't know their origins (usul), where they got their money from. They are... clans ('asha'ir): the owners of agricultural lands (mallakin aradiy), villagers (ahl al-daya'). They are from small villages, east of Aleppo... Forty years ago, they were unheard of. Now their names start to be heard all over the city... Some have a big influence in politics (markaz kabir bi ssiyasa).

Representations of modes of commerce, which constituted Aleppine merchants and nonurban clans as incommensurable social figures, could also focus on the question of credit. Ahmad Dabbagh was a yarn broker who hailed from a large merchant family established in Aleppo's bazaar since the Ottoman era. Again, in 2009, he drew a distinction between urban merchant networks and clans from Aleppo's hinterland. While he was complimentary of clans as having inherent goodness (tiba) and claimed to have friends among them, he argued that unlike urban merchants, clans did not trade on credit or practice notions of creditworthy personhood: "the clans, in Nayrab Gate and so on, have no practice of giving credit (dayn) and no [notion of the] creditworthy person (al-dhimma). If I buy 700,000 lire of goods on credit: I will pay 200,000 lire up front, then 50,000 a week. The clans do not do this. They have no concept of entrustment (amaneh)." He, too, located such clans outside the domain of urban civility: "If they lend money and someone refuses to pay it back, they resort to fighting and shouting (qatl wa 'ayyat), whereas we just say, 'God will hold to account (Allah yhasib)!'"

Ahmad deployed a mix of language and exchange ideologies to construe urban merchants and clans as different kinds of social beings; the former speak in tones of Islamic civility; the latter holler and shout; the former are persons of credit; the latter do not entrust and have no notion of the accountable self. The exchange ideology is akin to the language ideology with which it is closely entwined. As Kathryn Woolard notes, language ideologies are cultural representations that mediate between social structures and forms of speech, and underpin not only linguistic practice, but also fundamental notions of "person and social group" (Woolard

1998, 3). Exchange ideologies similarly mediate between social forms—the category of urban merchants—and exchange practices—credit-based trade and entrustment. Like language ideologies, they enact a social order, formulating and expressing basic notions of identity, group membership, and personhood.

Contesting Urban Leadership and Legitimacy

Such notions of identity and difference were expressed in the wider context of a struggle that pitted the city's established merchant bourgeoisie against a state-dependent bourgeoisie composed of largely rural incomers. One forum in which the contest between the state bourgeoisie and the commercial bourgeoisie came to a head was Aleppo's Chambers of Commerce and Industry. Leading families from the city's commercial bourgeoisie routinely stood for election to the board and expected to be represented. Fuad's House of Umar was among these: his cousin had recently stepped down as a vice president of one of the chambers. But members of the state-dependent bourgeoisie were also represented on the board. Salwa Ismail (2018, 83) reports that proregime clans and clients in the Chamber of Commerce ran underground import networks. Established merchants could resent their influence and complained about corruption. A senior Umar merchant claimed to have recently engineered the removal of a former president of the chamber by sending proof of his wrongdoing to an influential figure in the regime.

Alaa, a member of another leading merchant family, related to the House of Umar, anticipated a future in which urban merchants would run the Chamber of Industry differently. In the way he spoke, the terms of a discursive campaign against the state-dependent bourgeoisie were already present, in a kind of "hidden transcript" (Scott 1990) which had not yet declared itself in openly defiant terms. He said, "I don't want to talk about this, I don't want to name names. Who would you think should be in the Chamber of Commerce? The big merchants, the honest ones, with a good reputation, right? Not here, they are not the people who support trade, they just travel with the Ministers, to get the contracts, and keep them to themselves." Commenting on the Chamber of Industry, he said that "there are twelve of us and seven of the government on the board. The president is one of us. We cannot be part of the government because we are not part of the party or the army, and I am from the city. They are from the countryside. They come to the city, and after five years they look like us but on the inside they are very different. They are put in charge of things in commerce and industry that they know nothing about." Here an exchange ideology of differentiation came to the fore as a way of contesting the legitimacy of the power of clans and rural incomers in the city. It said that the state-dependent bourgeoisie are not persons of reputation; they know nothing about real commerce, they just get contracts from the state; they are totally different on the inside.

He spoke that way in 2009. Now let us skip forward to 2019. The intervening decade witnessed the Arab Spring, protests against the regime reaching Aleppo in 2012, the militarization of the conflict, and a brutal battle for Aleppo waged between multiple actors, but broadly between the regime and an opposition front, each with their various militias. The regime eventually won, but the conflict also saw the proliferation of opposition-aligned news outlets that have continued to broadcast and publish. Here is a piece of reporting from one of them, published online in 2019:

> The Asad regime surrounded Aleppo with a belt of slums inhabited by the people of the countryside and the clans coming from outside the city . . . While Aleppo is . . . the city that is supposed to be one of the most prominent strongholds of "civilization" in Syria . . . many neighborhoods of the old city of Aleppo are considered areas of tribal housing . . . Over the forty years that the Asad regime ruled . . . it deliberately strengthened a family from each clan and co-opted it by facilitating illegal business, providing investment facilities for it, and . . . expanding its influence and authority over the population of the city. There are many examples, such as the "Al Barri" family . . . [which] has had absolute power and power for decades . . . In addition, there are families from the "Al-Asasneh" clan whose leaders collect investments and funds with the regime, and have a brigade fighting alongside the regime.[7]

There are echoes here of mercantile exchange ideologies from the previous decade. The clans are construed as standing in contrast to the civilization of the city, as a rural threat to the established urban order, with leading families marked out by their engagement in illegal business and illegitimate forms of accumulation. Because of their role in the fighting, loyalist clans had become even more powerful economic and political actors in the intervening decade; the journalist's notion of a threatened urban order is one way of contesting the legitimacy of their position in the city. Anti-clan discourses that had been relatively hidden exchange ideologies in 2009 were by 2019 openly expressed as a form of political contestation.

Locating Exchange Ideologies

In the examples given above, ideas of urban and rural identity and difference are explicit in discourses about "people from the countryside," "clans from outside the city," and in claims about commerce, credit, refinement, civility, and civilization. Moreover, such claims were made in the context of overt struggles over power, wealth, and legitimacy. I argue below, however, that exchange ideologies through which merchants construed urban and rural identities did not always take the form of explicit discourses, nor were they always connected to overt political struggles. Exchange ideologies could also subsist in the everyday material practices through which merchants carried on the business of trade and constituted themselves as particular kinds of social subjects. I make this argument through an analysis of commercial and moral accounting in shops in Souk Jarba, where the House of Umar had long been based.

In her introduction to a landmark edited volume on the subject, Woolard (1998) sets out a charter for language ideologies as a field of inquiry. To set the stage, she first untangles various connotations of the term ideology. One approach to ideology, she notes, sees it as the shared beliefs held by members of society, which are capable of being explicitly verbalized. They are discursive "reports about the world" or "that part of consciousness that can be said" (Thompson 1984, 85, quoted in Woolard 1998, 6). Another strand, more influential in recent decades, sees ideology not as conscious or systematically organized but as the practical, prereflective meanings with which social practices are invested, similar to Bourdieu's (1977) conception of doxa—that is, naturalized understandings of the world that "rarely rise to discursive consciousness" (Woolard 1998, 9). The issue here is where is ideology to be found: is it in the explicit rationalizations offered by subjects, or is ideology mainly immanent in behavior, and therefore implicit and requiring the active construction and verbalization of an analyst?

A second issue Woolard addresses is the connection between ideology and power. Most uses of the term see ideology as "rooted in, reflective of, or responsive to the experience and interests of a particular social position" (1998, 6); thus an ideology is the view from somewhere and can be linked to the "material and practical aspects" (ibid) of social life and seen as in some way dependent on them. But some go further and see ideology as a tool of elites or would-be elites, those who inhabit or contest positions of power. Ideology in this conception is a set of ideas or signifying practices that form part of a struggle to acquire or maintain power, whether social, political, or economic. Woolard suggests that the great divide among scholars is between the first two positions: those who see ideology simply as a socially situated understanding of the world, and those who see it as a tool deployed in a struggle over positions of power. She suggests that the second of these uses is unnecessarily restrictive; even where there is no overt struggle over power, we can still usefully talk of the ideological aspects of cultural forms. This is because any signifying practices organize social relations, and "constitute social subjects," and are therefore connected to issues of identity and affiliation. Issues of power can be present in a diffuse sense, rather than only in a focused sense of some acutely identifiable struggle. She concludes that we can usefully define "cultural conceptualisations of language as ideological" not only when they are used to legitimate or contest the dominance of an elite group, but "when/because they are . . . politically and morally loaded ideas about social experience, social relationships, and group membership" (1998, 8–9).

The anti-clan discourses I discussed above are examples of ideology in the second sense. Members of Aleppo's commercial bourgeoisie construed powerful rural incomers as incommensurably different from them by characterizing their modes of commerce and speech as uncouth; they construed them as illegitimate power brokers by deeming their own modes of commerce as authentically urban, and their rivals' as out of place in the city. Ideological construals of commerce here are an explicit representation of the world and are deployed as part of an overt struggle over power and urban leadership. In the accounting practices I consider below, ideology exists in a different way. Merchants in Aleppo's bazaar could understand precise accounting both as a matter of inner orderliness and as an outer sign of respectability. Where credit and debt were being tracked, account books could also signify legibility and locus within networks of credit and accountability. Merchants could talk of such credit networks as defining the scope of the truly urban; and of the city as a domain of accountability and legibility threatened by the unruly behavior of outsiders. Ideology existed here at the level of practical, prereflective meanings of order, ruliness, and creditworthiness. Implicit in everyday interactions in the market, these meanings were not usually articulated as part of a struggle over power. Yet, even if they were not always made explicit and activated as part of an immediate struggle, ideas of urban order and legitimacy were latent in accounting practices.

Thus, the analysis tacks back and forth between the two senses of ideology that Woolard identifies. It asks questions about the relationship between explicit representations deployed in overt contests for power, and everyday practices that organize social relations and constitute social subjects. It argues that an affinity existed between bazaar merchants' anti-clan discourses through which they contested the legitimacy of regime-affiliated incomers in Aleppo's merchant chambers, and their accounting practices through which they constituted themselves as persons of credit, legibility, and respectability. Mundane accounting practices sustained the latent ideological resources that made possible urban merchants' contestation of the clans' legitimacy.

Ideology as Immanent in Material Practices: Commercial Accounting

When Fuad arrived at his shop in Souk Jarba, usually in the early afternoon, his adult son Hamdi would spring up from the seat behind the accounting desk. He would greet his father by stooping to kiss his hand—which Fuad would whisk away from him before receiving the kiss—and then cede to him the place behind the accounting desk. Fuad would take his seat at the heart (sadr) of the shop, from which he could survey the whole room. A copy of the Quran had pride of place, attached to the wall above the desk. Underneath it were stored the shop's account books—one ledger recording daily incomings and outgoings and the float, and another listing the business's suppliers and wholesale customers and their credits and debt payments. After taking his seat, Fuad would usually turn his attention to the account books, inspecting them to see which debts were falling due, checking the receipts tallied with the register of debts, and tallying the float against the record of daily transactions. These processes, rather than potential customers, absorbed much of his time and attention, as well as the collective attention of the shop. In the midst of his focused concentration, he called out to his son, or one of the two young teenage relatives: "have you recorded it? Where is it registered?"

It was a similar story in his eldest son's office. Salam ran an import business from a room in a block of the main alleyway in Souk Jarba. Twice a year, he traveled with his cousins to the Chinese cities of Yiwu and Guangzhou, where they placed bulk orders for household items for distribution within Syria. On his return from one such buying trip, I visited his office to find him surrounded by his younger brother and two assistants who sat on lower chairs looking up at him, waiting expectantly as he checked the accounts. Here, too, attending to his handwritten ledgers absorbed considerable collective attention. He issued me a perfunctory greeting, but otherwise remained absorbed in transferring figures from a scrap notebook into a neat account book. From time to time, he would break the silence to check with his staff whether a particular delivery or payment was duly recorded, reinforcing the critical importance of a precise accounting of the shop's credits and debts.

At one level it is not surprising that a trading enterprise would wish to keep accurate accounts.[8] But here, commercial exactitude was intertwined with other kinds of merit and discipline. As he sat behind the accounting desk checking the precision of his son's accounting, Fuad would also hold him to account for his ritual obligations: "have you prayed the afternoon prayer (sallait al-'asr)?" or "have you prayed the evening prayer (sallait al-maghrib)?" The process of commercial accounting could provide a platform for other forms of moral discipline. Fuad would tot up the daily revenue and outgoings that were jotted down on a separate sketch pad (misweddi), and check them against the notes he pulled out of the desk and tallied. When one of his teenage employees was accused of taking cash from the float, as well as persistent lateness at work, the young man was made to stand in front of the accounting desk. Fuad gave him a dressing down as he sat behind the accounting desk, with Hamdi, another employee, and an older relative standing in a circle around the accused. When Fuad was absent, one of his sons took the accounting seat and would subject younger employees to similar kinds of accounting. In Souk Jarba, where established families dominated, traders demonstrated their concern for everyday processes of moral discipline, noting that "in this market, you still see sons working alongside their fathers in shops, and the fathers educating and instructing them."

Other kinds of behavior could be held to account from behind the accounting desk. Fuad was trying to set up his youngest son Fadi with a retail stall nearby. Fadi was a well-built young man in his early twenties, who spent much of his time working out at the gym. One day he appeared in his father's shop wearing a tight T-shirt with the Playboy logo emblazoned on the front. Sitting behind his ledger, his father gave him a dressing down in public; it brought shame ('ayb) on the family that someone "bearing the name of Umar" would be seen in such a T-shirt. On another occasion, his father gave him a dressing down in the shop for being workshy and self-interested (awantaji), accounting for his value by saying, "the son who does not work has no value." He held him to account for spending all his time out with his friends, implying that he was visiting nightclubs. He invited me to follow him around; he said, "write about him in your books—you have notebooks? Do it, I don't mind!" envisaging ethnographic fieldnotes as a tool in the moral accounting of his son.

Various forms of accounting proliferated and intertwined in Fuad's shop. Alongside the inscription of the account book and the tracking of credits and debts, there was the holding of sons and others to account for the precision of their inscriptions. And then there was the holding to account for other things: honesty, ritual obligations, hard work, dress, and leisure time outside the shop. This indicates that the creditworthiness of the merchant family was more than a narrowly commercial matter; the factors that shaped it were moral as well as commercial, much as Christopher Bayly (1983) argued in his history of nineteenth-century merchants in north India, and James Laidlaw (1995) observed of the merchant community in Jaipur. The proliferation and intertwining of accounting practices also produced a sense of status distinction: merchants were a social group who were liable or responsible for their name in all domains of life. Among traders, the designation merchant (tajir) was a prestigious social status that could be distinguished from other social identities such as worker ('aamil), functionary or employee (mwazzaf), or peasant (fallah). A merchant was distinguished from these other categories by their status as an answerable person (dhimma) or whose liability for their debts was unlimited, and whose creditworthiness could be accounted for. Merchants could be referred to as the people who are answerable (ahl al-dhimma), in contrast to employees who had no name, honor, or liability for their actions. Among established merchant elites who voiced concern about the decline of honor-based forms of commerce and interaction, the idea of the dhimma was widely recognized and seen as central to what merchant life was about. One merchant said, "your dhimma is your whole person; it is your name in the market (ismak fi'l-suq)." Their sense of personhood was uniquely identified with their name, their publicly accounted reputation, which was said to be at stake in all interactions.

One way to express this status distinction, the unlimited liability of their name, was by publicly subjecting themselves to a rigorous accounting by self, family, creditors, and God. This is one way to read performances of precise accounting in the shop. Another way to express this status distinction was to publicly avow the ethos of self-accounting. In delivering mini-homilies in their shops, merchants in Souk Jarba could highlight that a merchant should "hold himself to account before others hold him to account" (hassib nafsuh qabl ma yhassibuh al-akhar). A prevalent theme in these homilies was the centrality of the Day of Accounting (yawm al-hisab) in Islam; one merchant simply told me, "Islam is the Account." As well as debts and prayers, speech was also construed as an accountable act in the market. Foregrounding the temptation to bend the truth when talking to customers or creditors, some merchants repeated the maxim that "in Islam you are held to account for every word that you say" (bi'l-Islam tithasib 'al-kalimeh), and that "a single word can make the difference between a halal profit and a haram profit." In shops in Souk Jarba, as among piety-minded merchants elsewhere in Aleppo, accounting was not just a commercial technique, but was also construed as a moral discipline and the basis for general moral personhood; Fuad, for example, said that he took care of his accounting so as to be an ordered (nizami) person.[9]

The construal of commercial accounting as a moral discipline could underpin claims that merchants were those who knew Islam best because they knew best what it meant to have their debts and actions carefully accounted for. In this view, merchants' constant tracking of credits and debts, and their unlimited liability attached to their name, made them more aware than most that all acts including speech had a morally irreducible weight. Scholars have often recognized that being a merchant is a high-status mode of livelihood in many societies. This is usually connected to the autonomy of their mode of livelihood, vis-à-vis the figure of the employee (see Marsden 2016; Laidlaw 1995). In Aleppo, autonomy was certainly one element of the status of merchant. One said that "a merchant is not a worker or a peasant, waiting for wages or living hand to mouth.

He has capital, he has a shop, he has trading relations." Yet mercantile status derived not just from their economic independence from employers but also from this ethos of accountability. Credit-based commerce, in which a person's honor and reputation were at stake, was understood as a model for developing moral discipline. Traders could talk about the figure of the merchant as an exemplar of general morality in domains beyond the market. One defined a merchant as someone "who is not a child, whose word is not two words"; another as "someone who doesn't lie, someone who is successful in life."

This sense of moral distinction between merchants (al-tjjar) and other social identities, cultivated through intertwining practices of accounting, could also be mapped onto a social distinction between the urban and the nonurban. I noted above that Alaa, a merchant from a pre-Baathist notable family, represented commerce as an urban heritage, and associated municipal employees by contrast with the rurally rooted Baathist state. Other merchants from old families (ailat 'ariqa) talked of reputational accounting as a vital structure that underpinned civic order in the city.[10] Anwar was a twenty-eight-year-old yarn importer from the House of Fayyad, a pre-Baathist merchant house related by marriage to the House of Umar, whom I had asked about the basis of trust and reputation in commerce. One afternoon as we were sitting in his office in the bazaar, he turned the conversation to civic order: "the son of the village (ibn al qarya) creates real problems. He is fine in his village. But in Aleppo, he creates problems, he creates most of the infractions (mukhalafat) in the city: he steals, misbehaves, because he is not known, there is no-one he knows who will talk against him. Here, I am afraid to misbehave because my brother will see me, and people will talk against me." Although we were not discussing commerce at the time, his comment cast rural incomers outside the bounds of the city proper on the grounds that they were not legible within a system of reputational accounting. There is an affinity between such a notion of beyond-the-pale rurality, and laments I heard in Anwar's social milieu about the decline of reputation-based commerce in the city. Such laments could construe the modes of commerce of clans rooted in Aleppo's hinterland as not fully urban because they did not entrust, trade on credit, or "have [any conception of] the accountable person (al-dhimma)." They were discourses about what it meant to be fully urban; to be an Aleppine merchant was to be embedded in relations of entrustment, in which one's person was recognized and accounted for by others who also lived by putting their honor/name at stake in the market. Anwar's comments expressed a similar social imaginary of the city: to be within the scope of the city proper meant to be legible and liable within networks of reputational accounting.

Mundane practices of accounting involved no overt evocations of anti-clan sentiment, and few explicit claims about identity or difference. I read them as ideological practices in the first sense that Woolard discusses, not as a tool in legitimating or contesting a social hierarchy, but as a signifying practice that constituted merchants as distinct kinds of social subjects. Immanent in practices of precise accounting and rigorous familial self-accounting was an ethos of being the people who are answerable, who live on our reputation, and transact on our honor. Yet these ideological constructions of identity formed part of the same fabric of meaning as the explicit ideologies of language and exchange considered earlier in the chapter. Bazaar merchants could draw sharp distinctions between civilized and uncivilized persons and modes of commerce in the context of acute struggles over the legitimacy of state-affiliated clans in domains of urban power. These anti-clan discourses were ideologies in Woolard's second sense: constructions and even distortions of social reality deployed by protagonists in a struggle to contest and acquire power. This struggle shaped what it could mean to be visibly embedded in networks of credit and reputational accounting.

Construing Authentic Urbanity through Commerce

Viewed purely in terms of geography, there was arguably little distance separating the House of Umar and the House of Asasneh. While Umar merchants publicly traced their origins to one of the seven gateways of the walled city, another less publicly avowed account went further back and located their origins in the rural lands east of Aleppo, in a village not far from the Asasneh origins. But in terms of their relation to the state, a gulf separated the two houses. The Baathist regime had disempowered older urban notables, while empowering minor rural clans as a state-dependent bourgeoisie. Its policy of recruiting minor clans from the steppe as state proxies and rivals to balance the existing commercial bourgeoisie created the conditions for politically charged identity discourses. Having entered the city around four generations earlier, the Umars now stressed their urban pedigree, for example by displaying images of generations of their forebears above the accounting desks in their shops. Meanwhile, among incumbent urban elites, the Asasnehs were figured as outsiders to whom urban forms of commerce and sociability were anathema.

It was in this context that particular social identities became recognizable in Aleppo through trade and discourses about trade. Commerce was one process through which notions of urban-rural difference were given substance, and clans figured as a threat to an urban social order, which incumbent merchants saw themselves as embodying. Exchange ideologies of urban-rural difference were located in the explicit rationalizations offered by subjects but could also be immanent in everyday interactions. They could be expressed in explicit verbalizations about urban pedigree that contested the power and legitimacy of the state and its proxies. But they were also diffusely present in tacit everyday practices such as accounting that constituted incumbent merchants as particular kinds of subjects—as persons of credit, legibility, and accountability. These latter everyday processes provided the raw material out of which explicit identities could be fashioned and political claims made regarding legitimate leadership in urban institutions. Exchange ideologies enable us to trace connections between the ways in which merchants constituted themselves as reputable subjects, and the conceptions of urban identity through which they sought to delegitimize social rivals and mobilize political support in elections to the Chamber of Commerce. Attending to exchange ideologies can reveal links between the everyday constitution of social subjects in the market and the contestation of positions of power and legitimacy in the city.

3

MERCHANT PATRIARCHY AND THE STATE

This chapter explores the role of the state in the reproduction of patriarchy among elite merchant families. It argues that state interventions supported exchange ideologies that figured the merchant as an economic patriarch. Among this stratum, the ideal of the socially respectable merchant was typically figured as a male elder, whose standing in society rested on his authority over sons. Respect for male elder" (ihtiram al-kabir)—sometimes described as the rule of the father (siyasat al-ab) by critically minded observers—was a dominant ideology of family and market relations. A patriarchal kin contract (see Joseph 1996a) defined social membership of the market largely through membership of patrilineal families. Yet rather than seeing this simply as a culturally ingrained model, the chapter explores the role of the state in supporting patriarchal authority, and in fostering this form of social membership of the market. It argues that the privileged status of male elders was reinforced by the ways in which state-merchant relations were institutionalized among this stratum. At the same time, because the state largely left the market to regulate itself, patriarchally oriented notions of reputation emerged to regulate access to credit and arbitration.

"Hajj Abdullah Can Do This": Predation, the Kin Contract, and Patriarchal Authority

The idea that urban merchants resolved disputes with peaceable Islamic civility—resorting to arbitration and saying, "may God hold you to account!" while tribal clans shouted and made problems—was an ideological oversimplification used to create and maintain urban distinction vis-à-vis the rural. It involved the "erasure" (Gal and Irvine 1995) from social consciousness of any information that did not fit the patterns underpinning hegemonic categories of identity. In practice even respected urban merchant houses resorted to other means when their rights were in danger. Here is another account of dispute resolution from a male importer and wholesaler of household items, also from the House of Umar, who sold on credit to several dozen customers. A heavily built man in his late forties, he sat one afternoon in 2009 on a plastic chair in the main alleyway of Souk Jarba sporting a multipocketed military-style gilet. When I asked him how he recovered bad debts, he replied, "If they don't pay, we tolerate them for up to four weeks. Then," he continued, crushing his fist into his palm,

> We go to the police and recover our goods by force. Except if the debtor is protected by the state (mad'um 'ind al-dauleh), a relative of a senior official, for example. In which case, for small amounts, one or two thousand dollars, we do nothing. But for large amounts, say fifty thousand dollars, we complain to the President's office. A senior merchant (tajir kbir), like Hajj Abdullah or Hajj Mahmoud, can do this. A small merchant, he will lose his rights, poor man. A high-ranking police officer's son recently stole sixty thousand dollars from a merchant here. We complained to the President's office. They got rid of that chief of police. He said, 'I am not responsible for my son!' But they got rid of him.

When it came to dealing with trouble, the House of Umar did not only speak in tones of Islamic civility, but also maintained relationships with regime elites and with the coercive arms of the state. According to this story, they did so not only on their own behalf, but also on behalf of those junior merchants in the market who appealed to them to stand up for their rights. Faced with cases of predation and theft, such interactions—between junior merchants and senior ones, and between senior merchants and the state—worked to uphold a patriarchal social order among Aleppo's merchants. It was the male elders of this house, and by extension of the wider merchant community, who were called upon to intervene with the state, to present petitions, and seek to reverse grievous cases of predation. Doing so consolidated their authority vis-à-vis younger men and women. It also reinforced the status within the wider merchant community of large, cohesive patrilineal houses such as theirs, whom the state regarded as large and influential enough interlocutors to be worth accommodating.

The theft in this story was also premised on a patriarchal principle—that the police chief's son would be protected—supported (madʿum)—by his father (embodying the state) and therefore able to act with impunity. It assumed a kin contract of citizenship (Joseph 2000) in which the state treats individuals as members of families, in particular through their relationship to their father rather than as bounded and autonomous individuals in their own right. The merchants who complained, and the regime authorities who removed the police chief, acted on the same principles, making the father responsible for his son. The father's attempt to override the kin contract by invoking a principle of bounded individual citizenship—"I am not responsible for my son"—fell on deaf ears, emphasizing the point that this is a story about the powers and responsibilities of fatherhood and male eldership. The kin contract, and the powers and responsibilities of fatherhood, ran from the marketplace into the state and out again, connecting all the players in this incident. The story then is told as a kind of battle of the patriarchs. The male elders in the House of Umar—the senior merchants—assume their paternal responsibilities to the juniors in their market who appeal to them; they ultimately prevail over the police chief, but not before he has tried to abnegate his own responsibilities as a father.

This chapter explores the reproduction and legitimation of patriarchal social order among Aleppo's merchants during the first decade of Bashar al-Asad's rule and asks about the role of the state in these processes. What were the mechanisms by which the rule of the father was enacted and naturalized in daily life? By patriarchal order I mean father-authority, drawing on Max Weber's ([1947] 2009) understanding of patriarchy as "a system of government in which men rule societies through their position as heads of households" (Walby 1989, 214). Feminist scholarship on Western societies often analyzes patriarchy as any form of domination of women by men, arguing that the social institution of fatherhood is a contingent rather than a necessary component of this domination (see, e.g., Walby 1989). But in the Middle East, "a region where family ties and kinship authority are particularly strong" (Weiner 2016, 13), father authority is particularly salient (Inhorn 1996), seen to run through and weave together many domains of society (Joseph 2005). It is a critical means by which women are rendered into subordinate citizens, and the authority of senior men over juniors (including junior males) is secured.

Merchants as Traditional Elites

Scholars of the Middle East noted the prevalence of patriarchal social structures in the region, noting that it is part of a "belt" of patriarchy (Caldwell 1978, 554), where "classic patriarchy" persists; that is, in which families are patrilineal and patrilocal, and maintain an ideal of endogamy (Kandiyoti 1988). Scholars argued that patriarchal forms connect societies with states in the region and persist even amid socially progressive states with trappings of modernity.[1] But patriarchal forms, albeit emphasizing male rather than fatherly authority, are also found across the West (Pateman 1988; Jones 1993; Phillips 1993; Eisenstein 1994).[2] And while father-authority is salient in the Middle East, I do not assume that patriarchy is either all-pervasive or invariant in Syrian society. Both family and patriarchy take many forms in the Middle East (Joseph 1996b; Tucker 1993; Schilcher 1985).

The House of Umar, like other large merchant houses in Aleppo, is a case of classic patriarchy.[3] Despite their efforts to assert distinction from the rural clans and locate their genealogical origins at the point of entry to the city, they represented a traditional elite (Moghadam 2004, 150), which continued to organize their families as patrilineal clans, much as farmers did, and thus maintained a rural-tribal social organization in the city (on tribes as an archetypal patriarchal form, see Caldwell 1978; Moghadam 2004). A patrilocal family, they foregrounded their size and patrilineal identity and maintained an ideal of clan-like organization and strength.[4] One member claimed, "We are around two thousand men, and we all came from one man in Nayrab Gate." They also foregrounded the ideal of elder privilege, claiming that their continued observance of it set them apart within their own society. They referred to this principle as respect for the senior man (ihtiram al-kabir); more sociologically minded observers called it "the rule of the male elder"[5] (siyasat al-hajj). This merchant house is also an example of "economic patriarchy" in which elder males were privileged through their control of economic resources, including labor, and in which patriarchal kinship provided economic security for most in the family, including women, younger men, and poorer relatives (Joseph 2005). They also enacted a kind of distinction vis-à-vis less wealthy families by instituting this form of economic welfare formally as a family fund (sunduq al-aileh) overseen by male elders, an arrangement that began in the 1990s.

So rather than taking the rule of the father (siyasat al-ab) as a ubiquitous, ahistorical, and ingrained cultural model of the Syrian or Arab family, I analyze how patriarchal authority was reproduced through mechanisms that were particular to Aleppo's merchant strata in this period. These included the ways in which the Asad regime intervened in the market, accepting petitions from influential networks, which tended to be those that had accrued capital and political support over generations through patrilineal family ties; and the role of large merchant families as a source of credit in the market made all the more significant because of the low level of generalized trust in banks and their low penetration of the market. Another mechanism was the critical function of reputation (suma')—implicitly family reputation—as a form of self-regulation, which also flourished because of the low level of generalized trust in state courts. I approach the House of Umar as an individual case that illustrates with particular clarity the workings of these more general mechanisms. As a large and cohesive merchant clan organized around the patriline, they had expanded their influence by maintaining capital and sons in the same sector over generations. They had also cultivated a family reputation for creditworthiness and impartiality as arbitrators. These factors enabled the lineage to regularly and successfully field candidates for the boards of the Chambers of Industry and Commerce, which in turn allowed its male elders to consolidate their political influence as petitioning channels to the regime.

Accessing the Market: The Patriarchal Kin Contract

The role of the state was critical in reproducing the hegemony of patriarchal families such as the House of Umar. This was despite the fact that the Baathist state had historically aligned itself with a progressive ideology that favored the empowerment of women and counted a women's union among its corporatist structures (Meininghaus 2016). On the one hand, direct interactions with political elites in the regime reinforced an extended kind of patriarchal kin contract of citizenship, in which individual merchants could represent their interests to the state through male elders in the community. On the other hand, the near absence of the bureaucratic-juridical state in regulating the market left the domain open to self-regulation on the basis of reputation. Since a merchant's name was implicitly and potentially a family name, the very notion of reputation assumed a framework of relations in which older males—fathers, brothers, uncles—were socially authorized to take responsibility for disciplining and vouching for younger ones.

It can be useful here, drawing on Suad Joseph's notion of a "kin contract" of citizenship, to think of a patriarchal kin contract of access to the market. An individual would often first seek access to the market by being introduced or vouched for (makful) by a senior male; they would then be known in the market as being from the side of (min taraf) that guarantor. In some cases the guarantor might be a senior member of the patriline, but it might also be a member of the matriline, or an affine, or simply a senior merchant or respected merchant (tajir muhtaram) who, while neither a blood relative nor an affine of the new entrant, created a kind of kinship with them by identifying themselves with their person. The liability which they assumed for them was said to be moral (ma'nawi) as much as material (madi) or financial; in other words, their junior's behavior would rebound on their own reputation in the same way as if they were related to them.[6] These bonds of kinship and created kinship, and the notions of reputation and forms of patriarchal authority and responsibility that they entailed were valued and cultivated as a counterpoint to the bureaucratic and juridical state that was seen either as apathetic and absent from the market, or as a set of corrupt relations encroaching on it.

These arguments contribute to scholarship that underlined the pervasive presence of "structures, moralities and idioms" of kinship throughout Middle Eastern societies, the role of the state in fostering them, and their effects of projecting hierarchies of gender and age through a variety of interconnected social spheres, from market and civil society to the state (Joseph 2005, 156; 1996b). Scholars underlined the effect of political idioms and leadership practices in sustaining patriarchal hierarchies, in practices such as dynastic succession through the male line; these were reinforced in Syria when the law was changed in 2000 to enable Hafez al-Asad's son to accede to the presidency despite his young age. Scholars of the region have also drawn attention to the role of law, especially family law, in sustaining the authority of fathers and husbands, in particular over daughters and wives.[7] Constructs of aged and gendered citizenship are also instituted through bureaucratic practice, when officials insist on speaking to fathers or male elders on behalf of other family members (Jad, Johnson and Giacaman 2000). Feminist scholarship focused on the effect on women; in a theoretical piece not concerned with the Middle East in particular, Walby (1989, 224) observed that women are often excluded from access to the state "because they lack power in the gendered political forces brought to bear on the state." At the same time, some scholars of the Middle East highlighting female agency described how women's networks in Cairo can also reach into the state.[8]

I argue that the mechanisms by which Syrian merchants were able to influence state elites tended to assume and reinforce hierarchies of "classic patriarchy" (Kandiyoti 1988) in Aleppo, reinforcing the status of men over women, older men over younger men, and older larger lineages over more recent entrants to the market. These modes of influencing the state were being threatened by the marketization of state-merchant relations (cf. Rabo 2005), as bribes or short-term monetary transactions were displacing the favors embedded in longer-term affective relations of friendship. The indignant reaction to this change among established families—the moral preference they expressed for economies of favor over the market in bribes—reflected hegemonic exchange ideologies by which Aleppo's merchants defined their identity vis-à-vis rural Bedouin. One effect of these exchange ideologies of urbanity was to sustain father-authority among elite Aleppine merchants.

"Friendship" among Fathers: Exchange Ideologies of Merchant-State Interaction

In the import and wholesale markets of Aleppo's old city, where large amounts of capital were concentrated, senior merchants sometimes displayed on the desks or walls of their offices framed photographs of themselves meeting the Syrian president Bashar al-Asad. Such strategies of visibility suggested that one was a protected (mahmiy) person. They were a warning to rival merchants not to play with them; they also offered a defense against harassment by state officials, ensuring that no one put an obstacle in their way. But if such photographs tended to record official events and meetings, merchants' narratives also foregrounded the level of intimacy they enjoyed with state elites. Some described their relations with particular officers (dbbat) or senior officials (mas'ulin) as those of friendship (al-suhba), speaking of their childhood associations stretching back to school or university. One young Umar merchant claimed that "the president and the prime minister know and like my father and uncle." Other senior merchants in the family made similar claims about themselves: "the prime minister knows me and likes me, from our university days." Some merchants belonging to other houses spoke of being invited to visit senior officials, such as the governor of a region, or senior officers in the army and security apparatuses. Others emphasized the private and intimate nature of meetings with officers and officials at their home, or some transgressive leisure they had passed with a senior officer in a forbidden pastime such as hunting.

The most valuable narratives inscribed relationships with state elites in a register of informality. The ability to move beyond formalities (ilgha' al-haleh al-rasmiyyeh) was a critical measure of influence; it implied the ability to access and mediate favors. An industrialist who could invite an officer for a simple plate of beans at his factory could claim more respect than one who needed to entertain him at a lavish restaurant. Such claims also moralized the connection to the state; the ability to make relations with one's personality (shakhsiyya) removed the relationship from the suspect register of transactionalism or socially unmoored interests (masalih). The personalization of business-state relations among this stratum was therefore not seen in negative terms of corruption, and was not represented as a demeaning form of clientelization, as Ismail (2018) argued. Rather, as studies of economies of favor have described, claims of friendship could be seen as ennobling and empowering particular social actors.⁹

These narratives of informality expressed an exchange ideology that defined the proper way to interact with the state. This exchange ideology of merchant-state interaction valorized the exchange of favors and sentiment embedded in long-term relations of friendship over short-term monetary transactions floating free of longer-term connection. This mirrors the exchange ideology, which described the proper way to conduct wholesale commerce. "We are like a family here," one wholesale yarn broker said, using an idiom of kinship to describe the ideal that trade should be embedded in relations of affection (mahabbeh). Another textile manufacturer said, "You see how I do things: social relations first, then business." According to this exchange ideology, instrumentalist transactions, based on interests, should be encompassed by relations of affective ease and intimacy. This representation of the normative forms of commerce closely reflected the dominant ideology of merchant-state interactions.

As in relations between merchants and officers, so in relations among merchants a value was placed on intimacy, on removing the state of formality between transacting parties. This was said to be achieved in relations of mawani, where neither party feels shy of the other (la yakhjalu min ba'd), and they were able to ask each other for anything (byimun 'ala ba'd). This was understood as a state of mutual, open-ended obligation in which they owe each other; it was also represented as one of mutual identification, where neither party kept track of the tally of favors so that "there are no accounts between us" (ma fi hsabat baynatna). Among merchants, the commercial form that corresponded to this ideal of mutuality was the line of continual credit (istijrar) or current accounts (hsabat jariyyah), in which a regular wholesale customer continually took goods on credit before they had fully paid off the previous consignment. This expressed an ideal of mutual identification between supplier and customer, in which what benefits one party benefits the other, and was said to amount to a kind of partnership (sharakeh). In relations between merchants and state officers, by contrast, the term partnership was demeaning rather than honorable, because it implied that the officers had a financial interest and that the merchant was in a dependent position, obliged to make regular financial payments in return for whatever facilitations the officer provided.

Nevertheless, merchants' exchange ideologies of wholesale commerce and of merchant-state interactions were remarkably similar. In both cases, a high value was placed on relations of mutuality, intimacy, and informality and the notion that these should encompass the transaction of interests. Merchants applied the language of friendship, affection, and informality to their interactions with state elites; and the language of mutuality (mawani), affection, and informality to their interactions with each other. Mawani indicated a kind of kinship or relatedness (Carsten 2000), which was said in some cases to surpass the closeness of formal kin; one broker explained that "it may be that there is mawani between two merchants but not between two brothers." Mawani suggested that the relationship was a long-term one, characterized by continuity (istimrariyya). But the reason that it was viewed in morally positive terms was that it implied that the parties were oriented to each other as human beings first and as transactors second; that the transaction of interests was properly encompassed by affective relations, expressing the parties' human capacity for mutual identification. This exchange ideology subordinated short-term transactional exchange to the longer-term reproduction of a social order of kinship.[10]

This exchange ideology could also be employed as a means of urban differentiation. The notion that affection should encompass the transaction of interests was sometimes claimed as a distinctively Aleppine and urban ideal, in particular vis-à-vis the Bedouin. Merchants could talk of themselves as maintaining friendship (suhbeh) with officers and making relations with their personality, in contrast to the Bedouin, the new businessmen who simply sought to buy off the security state—not realizing that once they had spent all their money, they would have no influence left. One younger merchant in the old city wholesale yarn market, who was an active participant in a Sufi circle, told me that "men here have affection for each other," claiming this as a specifically Aleppine ideal, uniquely associated with the city.

The Elder Bias of Economies of Favor

Because friendships usually formed between age contemporaries, and senior state officials tended to be older men, these exchange ideologies reinforced the status of male elders within merchant families. Whether or not it was true that the president and prime minister did actually "know and like" the father and uncle of the young Umar merchant quoted above, it is significant that he attributed this politically valuable friendship to his male elders. If the most valuable political friendships were archetypally rooted in childhood and schooldays, then only the family elders could be presumed to have been around long enough to have cultivated them with the current cohort of state elites.

At the same time, this economy of favors seemed to be under threat as officials increasingly demanded payment for their services. Annika Rabo (2005) observed that bribes were increasingly displacing personal relationships or mediation (wasta) as a means by which Aleppine merchants secured permissions to trade and other advantages from the state. Merchants from established families viewed this trend with disdain. Merchants in the House of Umar maintained relations with officials within the municipality who tipped them off about imminent raids, but also lamented that such individuals acted "not because of friendship" but because they wanted a kickback and had "interests in their pockets." One young Umar merchant said, "officers here eat your money, and then shit on your plate. The mukhabarat (intelligence services) came earlier today and just took all the boxes of goods that were outside shops. It is a disaster for some people. I know all the officers in Syria, but it is not friendship, it is just money. If you no longer have any money, they will kick you out of your place."

"They eat your food and shit on your plate"—the metaphor of hospitality invokes the intimacy of the hearth, holding up the realm of domestic intimacy as the proper mode of state-merchant relations. The problem is that the officers are bad guests; they shit on the assumption of mutuality and long-term exchange. The young merchant's indignation surely reflects not only the financial cost of bribing state officials, but the fact that it undermines a longer-established economy of favors and the social hierarchies and statuses upheld by that economy. These were hierarchies of age and gender, as I have argued, but also of pedigree. Marketization benefitted the nouveaux riches, opening the field for them to use their cash to bring influence to bear on the state, at the cost of the incumbents who had cultivated relations over the years. Because the marketization of state-merchant relations threatened the position of established families, the young members of those families voiced their indignation accordingly. These same responses, voiced by the young, also secured elder dominance within those families by reasserting patriarchal kinship as the proper basis of state-merchant relations.

Elections and Civic Sponsorship: State Support for Male Eldership

The ways in which relations between market and state were institutionalized—in this case through petitioning channels—were critical in reproducing father authority among elite merchant families in Aleppo. Though merchants often claimed that these channels of influence were rooted in personal liking and childhood relations, it is likely that the regime also identified interlocutors among merchant elites through managed elections to Aleppo's Chambers of Commerce and Industry (see Blaydes 2010). Scholars reported that these chambers were dominated by the state bourgeoisie—such as the clans discussed in the previous chapter and their clients.[11] Leading members of Aleppo's independent commercial bourgeoisie certainly criticized it for being a forum for individual self-seeking and the pursuit of state contracts rather than the representation of collective sectoral interests to policymakers. Yet members of the same families who made these criticisms were also successful in the elections to the boards. This suggests that the regime permitted managed elections to these institutions, and divided influence between rival state and commercial bourgeoisies. Managed elections enable authoritarian regimes to identify and coopt representatives of popular constituencies whom it is worth accommodating (Blaydes 2010). From the perspective of merchants, chambers were therefore arenas in which to prove the strength of one's faction. One Umar merchant who had recently stood down from the board, said of his time there, "I discovered the president of the chamber had taken money and used it for something he should not have. I sent proof of wrong-doing to someone [in the regime], to get him removed. That was four years ago. [People had thought] he was impossible to remove—he had even been received by the president." Managed elections permitted elders of such families to consolidate their influence as state-society relays and demonstrate their standing to their constituencies.

House of Umar candidates were regularly elected to the board because the size and cohesiveness of the lineage enabled them to mobilize voters across the extended kinship network and its associates. One measure that enabled them to consolidate patrilineal identification was the establishment of a family fund, which collected compulsory financial subscriptions from wealthier kinship members in order to channel them to poorer members. Overseen by male elders, this solidarity fund was started in the 1990s with the period of liberalization (infitah) when the state was allowing merchants increasing license to operate openly. This opening also incentivized them to organize themselves so as to make claims on the state, and therefore reinforced the value of patrilineal identity and patriarchal eldership. Another measure dating from this period through which the state reinforced existing structures of male eldership was invitations to civic sponsorship. This saw government ministers invite prominent merchants and industrialists to act as public sponsors of civic organizations and infrastructure as a mark of their pre-eminence. For example, one senior Umar industrialist was invited by a Syrian official to become a public sponsor Aleppo's Archaeological Society. He accepted; the merchant sponsors of civic organizations in Aleppo were widely understood to be able to ask Ministers for facilitations (tashilat) of their business interests as a quid pro quo and also to benefit by achieving a level of public renown (shuhra).

"The State Is Far from Here": Self-Regulation, Reputation, and Patriarchal Order

Scholars have argued that one way in which states promote patriarchy is by leaving territory to families; allowing the family rather than the state to provide services to their members.¹² This applied to welfare and social support in Aleppo. Merchants often commented, drawing an implicit comparison with the European welfare state, that "everything here is at your own expense" (kul shi hon 'ala hsabak); some noted that this placed a heavy burden on fathers. While these observations related to social welfare and provision, a similar observation could be made of markets. The state had largely vacated the role of regulating markets or providing access to viable financial institutions. As a result, informal commercial arbitration (al-tahkim al-tijari) and credit networks predominated in the market. This section argues that the concept of reputation that underpinned access to these often reproduced patriarchal authority. This is because one dominant understanding of reputation was as a potentially transmissible patrilineal asset. This authorized the intervention of older males to vouch for and discipline younger male relatives. Indeed, the common practice of vouching for others could often invoke male kinship loyalties and reinforce a common sense in which individuals could be located as part of patriarchally structured networks. In these ways, the absence of credible state-backed financial and judicial institutions had the effect of sustaining a patriarchal social order.

Distance from the bureaucratic and juridical state (al-dauleh) was said to define the market; as one yarn broker said of the wholesale market in which he worked, "The state is far from here (al-dauleh ba'ideh 'an hon)." Because state banks were not trusted and required high levels of collateral, and because private banks had been introduced only in the early 2000s, credit was typically provided by suppliers or within merchant networks, where reputation was assessed informally. Similarly, since state courts were seen as costly, unreliable, and—because of the association with bribery—morally tainting, merchants preferred informal arbitration. This was conducted either by reputable merchants or by religious scholars at the semi-independent Dar al-Ifta who would, in turn, seek the advice of reputable merchants. Most juridical powers were therefore exercised in the context of communal hierarchies. The Arbitration Law introduced in 2007 technically could allow for a mid-way alternative whereby the state underwrote the authority of any individual nominated and accepted by the disputing parties. But in practice, the law was either ignored or was liable to replicate preexisting communal hierarchies, since these determined which individuals disputing parties would regard as acceptable arbitrators.

This had the effect of reproducing the "patriarchal kin contract" (Joseph 2005), under which some form of male elder-dominated kinship structured social membership of the market. In the absence of credible state regulation and institutions, individuals accessed credit and arbitration through reputation, initially often by being vouched for by others.¹³ The institution of vouching meant that reputation was an asset or liability created and maintained within a social structure; this was often either a family or a patriarchally structured network. The power of this structuring of social membership of the market is seen in the fact that a rare female industrialist who had established herself as a yarn industrialist with EU funding also decided to form a close association with an older male manufacturer regarded as a respected merchant. He supplied her with raw materials, purchased most of her output, and vouched for her to others. She took the opportunity to visit her guarantor when she could, extolled his reputation, and referred to him as like gold (mitl dhahab). As she drove me to her factory outside of Aleppo, in the town of al-Bab, she explained her need for a guarantor:

> I knew one person, B., a rich merchant, who had a million dollars to play with in his current account. His son gave me bad quality thread. I went to see his father, he told him off, told him "this kind of thing hurts your reputation, if you have a bad name (ism taʿban) in the market, it is not good for you." I didn't have a name, so when I complained, it doesn't carry any weight. People say, Umm A., who is she, what does she know? I had no documents, no witnesses, just swearing on my honor (hilf al-yameen) but without a name, what does that count? But if you have someone to back you up, someone with a good personality (nafsiyyatuh ndifeh), it helps. So you need to know someone with a name in the market, someone known to be honest, to support you.

To the extent that reputation was overseen by male elders, market entry implied membership of a network structured by patriarchal authority. In this instance, the yarn manufacturer made use of this principle herself, pressuring her opponent by appealing to his father. That understandings of reputation were often embedded in a patriarchal social order can also be seen in the connections that several merchants drew between reputation in commerce and in marriage. Commenting on the institution of asking about (saʾl ʿan) others' reputations before entrusting goods to them on credit, one merchant said, "We ask about them first. It is exactly the same for marriage. If they have a bad reputation, we won't intermarry with them. Would you entrust your daughter to a thief?" There are echoes here of the Levi-Straussian view of women as pawns exchanged in male alliance strategies. The homology that several merchants drew between commerce and marriage suggests that their notions of reputation were embedded in the structures of the patriarchal family. Whether the men of substance are asking about to whom they should entrust goods on credit, or to whom they should entrust daughters in marriage, reputation was the same. In this understanding, reputation was a concept of the person that became salient in relation to the patriarchal family and its reproduction.

Patriarchy and Connective Personhood

Kinship was a hegemonic way of thinking about personhood and agency in the market—that is, one that was taken for granted and hard to question. At one level, merchants could seek to locate others acting in the market as part of a particular kinship group, enquiring about their identity by asking "part of which house (bait min)?" or they could locate them by identifying their guarantor (kafil) whose sponsorship was understood as a kind of moral relatedness. But I am not saying that reputation was always family reputation. Not all parts of the market were dominated by large families; trades were not always passed on from father to son; and new entrants without an established family name could be important players. Even where sons had inherited a trade, it was recognized that one brother might be good and another might have a tired personality (nafsiyya ta'baneh). Nor again should the institution of vouching for others be overdone; once a merchant was known (ma'ruf) in the market, vouching was less relevant. Merchants were then responsible for themselves; one might intervene with their father in the case of a dispute, but it was recognized that fathers might not take responsibility for their sons. I am not making an argument about the ways in which merchants actually evaluated the reputation of particular persons, and the relevance or irrelevance of family name to these. Rather, my claim is that (i) it was widely recognized that reputation governed social membership of the market; (ii) dominant representations of reputation reinforced the patriarchal kin contract, the notion that persons belonged to the market through the patriarchal family; and (iii) these dominant representations of reputation entailed particular understandings of proper family relations, and of personhood within the family, which also made patriarchal authority appear natural and normal.

Abdurrahman Umar usually sat overseeing business from behind the accounting desk in one corner of his cavernous store, one of the largest wholesale outlets in the market, issuing directions to his adult sons and other employees on the shop floor. On the wall above an alcove directly behind Abdurrahman's seat, a series of framed photographs displayed, to anyone who looked up, images of the previous owners, offering a kind of visual genealogy of this branch of the family. The display of such photographs offered an image not just of ancestors and bygone fathers, but of current father-son relations: of the present owner sitting under the father, observing filial piety (and directing his own sons). Such images and displays were relatively common in Aleppo. Where a business had been in the family for more than one generation, the business owner might hang a framed image of his father, or another male ancestor, who had founded or previously owned the business and passed it on to him. This pattern was observed in shops and offices in Aleppo's old city markets, and elsewhere in the city. These were usually positioned on the wall above the accounting desk. In part, this was a way of identifying the son and ensuring that the patrimony of the shop—the father's network of customers and creditors—was transferred from one generation to the next. In the old city markets, in particular, such images could anchor rituals of respect and remembrance—whereby those who knew him recited the fatiha for the deceased on the anniversary of their death—which could also keep the clientele of the father attached to the shop.

The display of the image in itself was also an act of remembrance, of re-presenting or making present and visible the agency and personhood of the father. Asked why he kept the image there, one wholesaler of textiles in the old city markets said, "It is because of his hand in the success of the shop"; in other words, to credit his agency. Conversely, his neighbor, who sat across from him in the caravanserai in a small office in the market displayed no image of his father or any other ancestor, despite the fact that he was a member of an old merchant house. Apart from a couple of old rolls of fabric, he displayed no stock and never seemed to have any customers visiting. His father, he explained, had been overly generous in his hospitality; what little he had left him, his brother had lost in a bad investment. Both neighbors arguably displayed the same understanding of reputation and intergenerational relations: reputation was a good that properly flowed down the patriline, and in exchange credit was properly attributed in the other direction.

Explicit discourses about reputation could also convey normative understandings of the proper relation between fathers and sons. It was common for traders in the old city to talk about the markets there as a site of moral formation akin to family life, saying, "I was brought up in the market" (trabbait bi'l-suq). Talking about his own upbringing in the market, Taher, a broker in his early thirties in the wholesale yarn market, said,

> My father worked in fabrics (nasij), manufacturing them. We were close to yarn, we knew the trade, and we had a good reputation. My father gave us this. Some people complete (kammil) the work of the father, some people cut it off. [Paul: how did you enter the market?] My father said, "he is with me" (huwwi 'indi). My brother, who is two years older, entered before me. I went around with him, learning. A brother was the boss (al-mu'allim); he sent me to do errands for him. He entrusted (amman) me a bit of his work, not all of it. I learned the trade—how to deal with people. I entered the market in 1995, and things really took off in 2000. That is when my brother left the work to become a merchant.

In this case, the father worked in manufacturing and the two sons in yarn brokerage. The speaker acquired his practical knowledge of brokerage largely from his older brother. What was passed on to him from his father was not the trade (his father was a manufacturer, he was a yarn broker) but knowledge of yarn and reputation. Reputation is what he was referring to when he said, "some people complete the work of the father, some cut it off." The metaphor of cutting off implies that reputation is a substance that connects father and son through organic growth; that this kind of connection between father and son is as natural as the growth of a tree. Father and son were also connected through a guarantorship that gave expression to this natural relationship; the father identified morally with his son by acting as his guarantor. "He is with me" meant they shared liability rather than work; morally they were a single unit.

This represented one influential way of thinking about reputation in the markets. It was patrilineal; reputation was a good that was always potentially transmissible down the patriline. And it was patriarchal; the father was the source of the good, authorized to initiate relations of moral identification, to claim sons as extensions of his own moral identity: "he is with me." The yarn broker's narrative is a classic case of patriarchal family dynamics, in which the father is the source of reputation and market access, and the older brother has delegated authority to cultivate the younger one through progressive acts of entrustment. There were other modes of entry into the market: a person might benefit from the reputation of matrilineal relatives, affines, or others to whom he had apprenticed himself; or he might conspire to create a reputation for himself. But the patriarchal model of reputation was hegemonic, seen as the norm from which others deviated. The transmission of moral identity from father to son was able to be represented as a process of natural organic extension.

In such narratives of market access and displays of father images in shops, reputation was construed as a potentially transmissible patrilineal good. Moreover, fathers and sons were seen to be connected through this transmissibility; sons were construed as extensions of fathers. These understandings expressed normative ideas of personhood, agency, and relations between generations. They did not determine how a person might assess the reputation of particular merchants. They did not require a person to believe that if a merchant was good, his son would be so also; or that a father would always assume liability for his son; or that a son who respected and credited his father was necessarily a good person with whom to do business. Rather, they meant that where a business had success, the sons should properly attribute it to the founding father, rather than claiming it as an expression of their agency as bounded autonomous individuals. And they meant that if a father had been well regarded and a son was not, the son was guilty not just of earning himself a bad reputation, but of cutting off the reputation bequeathed to him by his father. In other words, while the son was responsible for himself, he entered the market not as a bounded individual but as an extension of his father.

Such ideas expressed a system of family relations that Joseph (1993, 1999), writing about Lebanon, called patriarchal connectivity. Connectivity is a "culturally specific notion of the . . . self" common in the Middle East that "constitutes the self as a person with relatively fluid boundaries." Connective selves "experience themselves as a part of significant others" and emphasize "relatedness, rather than boundary, autonomy, separateness, and difference."[14] Connectivity "invites and requires persons to be involved with each other in shaping selves" (Joseph 2005, 155,156). Patriarchal connectivity is a system of family relations in which the privilege of males and elders is expressed through connective relations. It "entails the production of selves with fluid boundaries organized for gendered and aged domination"—selves "who respond to the involvement of others in shaping the self"; thus, "[w]omen and juniors expect seniors and elders to have authority in their lives (even though they may resist that authority), and seniors and elders expect to have responsibility that entails their authority toward women and juniors (even though they may not carry out those responsibilities)" (Joseph 2005, 156).

In Aleppo, constructs of connective personhood were naturalized through discourses about reputation. These asserted that sons did not exist as bounded individuals in their own right but as extensions of seniors. This can be seen in the commentaries on father images, which construed the father as still present in the shop, in the success enjoyed by the son, or even in the person of the son. When I commented to one merchant that he resembled the image of this father, he received it as a huge compliment. Character, agency, and likeness were not contained within bounded individuals. Representations and claims of connectivity were patriarchal; it was the father who was honored, his agency privileged and made visible. The ideology of patriarchal connectivity can also be seen in the aphorism about the son's responsibility in completing or perfecting (kammil) what the father has planted; if the son's reputation is good, this notion privileges the father over the son as the source. If his reputation falters, he is guilty not just of bad behavior, as a bounded individual person might be, but of cutting off the merit of his father; he is the father's extension who has failed to properly extend the father.

Such notions naturalized father authority, leading sons to expect and invite intervention and discipline from their fathers. We saw this in the previous chapter in the accounting and moral pedagogy and discipline in Fuad Umar's shop. Widely shared understandings of reputation as a shared transmissible substance licensed senior males in the patriline to vouch for and discipline younger ones. The hegemony of these ideas meant that those who embodied them, as the House of Umar claimed to, could claim social honor. If reputation was a potentially transmissible good whose value was comprehensible primarily in the context of patrilineal succession, then a lineage that had nurtured reputation successfully over the generations was a glorious thing, an exemplary expression of the value on which the wider market depended. The yarn broker who invoked the ideal of completing his father's legacy was not himself a member of a large family and had relatively little claim to pedigree (asl wa fasl). But his notion of reputation legitimized the precedence of those who could make such claims. The House of Umar merchants foregrounded their distinction on these terms, stressing that "this is one of the few markets where you still see fathers working alongside their sons, instructing them."

The state reinforced patriarchal authority in Aleppo's markets not only through maintaining petitioning connections with male elders from influential families, but also by leaving the space of regulation and credit to actors within the market. In the absence of credible and trusted juridical and bureaucratic state institutions, the main means of regulating access to credit and arbitration was reputation. While a person's reputation was neither subsumed nor determined by their family reputation, kinship provided the idioms and structures for thinking about reputation. Both within and alongside markets, father-dominated families were understood as the primary context within which it made sense to think about personhood in terms of reputation. Dominant ways of thinking about reputation established patriarchal hierarchies as a norm. Although not all merchants had family relations or an extended patriline in the market, hegemonic understandings of reputation conferred social precedence on those who could claim membership of the market through patriarchal and patrilineal families.

4
ECONOMIC PATRIARCHY AND CONTESTED MODERNITIES

One bitterly cold January morning, Hamdi Umar sat behind the desk at the back of his father's shop in Souk Jarba in the old city. A few meters away the doors were opened wide to encourage passing shoppers to wander in from the souk. There was a small bar-heater by his feet, and he was wearing fingerless gloves, but Hamdi was still rubbing his hands together for warmth. He looked tired; he had opened the shop early this morning and had been kept awake the previous night by his two young children. A lone customer approached and made a small purchase. Hamdi took the cash and returned some change to the customer with the words "God is the Provider." I had come to see Hamdi's relationship with his father as a model of unquestioning filial respect and loyalty. His younger, tearaway brother, not yet married and usually pumping iron in the gym, was known as an awantaji—someone always skiving off, looking out for his own advantage, not the family's. But Hamdi was different: quiet, uncomplaining, hardworking, and loyal. Then he turned to me and said, his breath condensing on the cold air, "if this shop were mine, I would close it during the winter months and go on holiday." "But," he added with a rueful smile, "it is not mine."

This chapter discusses the relationship between economic patriarchy, speculative modes of apprehending the future, and wider debates about modernity in Syria. Hamdi desired more autonomy and speculated on what he might do if he owned the shop outright. Yet because he expected one day to inherit the business, he also accepted his subordination within the shop for the time being. His willing subordination illustrates the logic of what Suad Joseph (1996a, 15–16) calls economic patriarchy: "the privileging of males and elders in ownership and control over wealth and resources." These resources include labor; "[e]conomic patriarchy gives men and elders control over kinship labour; they can call upon others for services and labour (paid or unpaid) more than women and juniors can," because their possession of wealth means that they are usually in a better position to reciprocate (Joseph 1996a, 15). As both Joseph and Valentine Moghadam (2004, 156–57) argue, economic patriarchy underpins patriarchal authority within families, as it provides male elders with the resources to offer economic security to other kin. Along with the state's minimal role in formal welfare provision, this made kinship networks often the chief source of economic security and wellbeing for citizens.

Scholars have observed that in many Middle Eastern states, economic patriarchy has been reinforced by inheritance laws and customs that favor sons over daughters. It is often sanctified by religion and buttressed by state welfare policies. And its significance is amplified by the tendency to concentrate entrepreneurial ventures within family structures, and by the use of kinship terms and idioms in workplaces outside the family (Joseph 1996a). Conversely, it has also been challenged by demographic and socioeconomic changes, notably the spread of higher education, urbanization, and industrialization (Moghadam 2004). In Aleppo under Bashar al-Asad, economic patriarchy was reinforced by a commerce ideology promoted by established merchant lineages in Aleppo, which construed a respected merchant as a patriarch with moral authority over sons, and as a pedagogue responsible for their moral instruction. The patriarchal authority enjoyed by merchants worked through structures of connective selfhood which bound fathers and sons together.[1]

Although family dynamics of patriarchal connectivity were hegemonic among Aleppo's wealthy merchant families, they could be evaded or worked around in domains of speculative activity at the margins. This chapter explores three such speculative, conjectural domains and their different relations to structures of patriarchal authority and control.[2] The first was Hamdi's imagined future ventures in the shop, which projected a domain of autonomy away from the father, while remaining firmly embedded in structures of patriarchal connectivity and the expectation of inheriting the privileges of economic patriarchy in the future. The second was under-capitalized speculative trading on yarn futures in Aleppo's stock market in wholesale yarn. These trades happened outside the bounds and terms of economic patriarchy and were therefore denigrated and marginalized by the patriarchal exchange ideologies of wealthier yarn merchants. The third was an educational venture by a social entrepreneur in Aleppo who established a training institute in a speculative challenge to patriarchal structures in economy and society.

The social entrepreneur's initiative was emboldened by a debate about the validity of economic patriarchy in public discourse during Bashar al-Asad's first decade in power. This debate was part of a wider contestation of Syrian modernity after the death of his father Hafez al-Asad, and was connected to Bashar al-Asad's promotion of an entrepreneurial, technocratic modernity and his sidelining of Baathism as a public ideology. Although Bashar was presented to the Syrian people as a modernizer, his regime continued to support a structure and culture of economic patriarchy in Aleppo in an attempt to win over influential merchant families in the city. The social entrepreneur who railed against economic patriarchy as an obstacle standing in the way of technocratic modernity saw himself as operating from the margins. Other merchants in the bazaar, at the economic center of the city, represented economic patriarchy as a valued form of Aleppine heritage, or as the basis of an efficient economy and moral society. The figure of the economic patriarch was at the heart of contestation of Syrian modernity in Aleppo in the late Baathist period. While many accounts of contested modernities in the Middle East have focused on domains of self-consciously cultural production and consumption, this was a contestation in which Aleppo's entrepreneurs and merchants engaged as cultural actors in their own right.[3]

Speculating from the Accounting Desk

Most mornings, Hamdi was up early to open the shop. He would oversee the business and look after customers until his father arrived in the early afternoon, whereupon he would spring up, offer his father a respectful greeting, bowing as if to kiss his hand, then briefly kiss his own hand and touch it to his head. Hamdi was the middle of three sons; his older brother was now established in a wholesale office of his own, and his father was trying to establish his younger brother in a steady job in his own stall nearby. Hamdi had worked in the shop since childhood, first for pocket money, then for a small wage, and now for a share of the profits. Now he was in his mid-twenties, an adult man with children of his own. But still he had only a minority share of the shop—his father owned the majority share—and Hamdi could only speculate about what he might do in the future. While his father called traders who inflated their margins deceitful (ghashashin), Hamdi talked of his desire to innovate by finding some new item unknown in the market and charge a fortune for it. This was not ideal, he admitted, but "Islamically permissible" if the items were nonessential ones. Even when he speculated on what he might do with more freedom, he did so in a way that maintained notions of Islamic rectitude. He was similarly deferential toward patriarchal hierarchy in the way he staked out domains of autonomy in the present. He stacked his packet of Marlboro in his sock whenever his father was nearby, out of respect (min al-ihtiram). As the cigarette packet invariably formed a bulge visible to the world, it was less an act of concealment than one of veiling, which publicly displayed deference toward his elders (Abu-Lughod 1986; Meneley 2016).

Hamdi's speculations about the future, and deferential domains of autonomy, were no challenge to the structures of economic patriarchy.[4] On seeing his father arrive at the shop, he sprang up to cede his place behind the accounting desk. In acknowledging this as his father's natural place in the shop, he also recognized his prerogative as a father to hold him to account within the structures of patriarchal connectivity. To repeat Joseph's notion drawn from the study of working-class families in Lebanon, patriarchal connectivity is a system of family relations that "constitutes the self as a person with relatively fluid boundaries" who expects and invites the involvement of male elders in shaping and directing the self (2005, 155–56). The moral pedagogy dispensed from Fuad's accounting seat enacted these structures. When he was absent, Hamdi took on the role, maintaining the principle of male seniority. Patriarchal connectivity was one component of the family reputation; for merchants of this lineage, it was a matter of pride that "in this market, you still see fathers working alongside sons, instructing them." The prestige that this ostensibly conferred on the family name gave Hamdi—who had a share in the respected name of his lineage—an interest in his own subordination within the family.

The place behind the accounting desk was the seat not just of authority but of the shared liability of the family name. To sit in it was, symbolically at least, to assume responsibility for the shop's debts. A close male associate outside the family invited to sit there could joke, "do you expect me to pay your debts?!" Fuad engaged in moral pedagogy in the name of that shared liability; he sought to inculcate Islamic values—commercial precision and orderliness (nizam wa tartib), honesty (sidq), and regular prayer—but under the authority of family reputation rather than as part of separate individualized projects of piety. If attending to the account books represented the ineluctable relationship between a merchant and his reputation, transferring the accounting seat between kin enacted relations of connectivity within the family, the tie between reputation and family. Accounting practices enacted close ties between account book, personal liability, reputation, and family. These ties formed the matrices of connective personhood, within which family members acted out relations of care and control, even as they also carved out domains of autonomy and quietly speculated on the future.

Speculating from the Margins

If the forms of commercial, ritual, and moral accounting in this market described in chapter 2 enacted structures of patriarchal connectivity and authority, traders in another part of the bazaar openly contravened the ideals of patriarchal connectivity and operated outside the bounds of economic patriarchy. Aleppo's open-air stock market (bursa) in Taiwanese yarn was one in which—uniquely, it was said—sons competed against their fathers.[5] Wealthy yarn merchants emphasized that the open-air market contravened the Islamic principle that people should not sell what they do not own, referring to it as Islamically unlawful (haram). But they also referred to all the participants in the market as children lacking in stature and authority; their trade was empty chatter rather than the authoritative words associated with men of creditworthy weight (wazn) and patriarchal authority. Islamic morality and language ideologies of economic patriarchy intertwined in their denigration of this speculative trade. That a form of trade contravening the principles of patriarchal connectivity and authority could flourish only at the margins of social and economic power, and only in an Islamically questionable speculative mode, suggests that Islam, capital, and economic patriarchy intertwined as a structure of power in the yarn market.

Aleppo's wholesale yarn market was headquartered in the Khan al-Oulabiyya caravanserai. The caravanserai was one of several in the heart of the city's complex of historical markets. It comprised some fifty offices, including some of the wealthiest merchants in the old city markets. Operating as sole traders, family businesses, or partnerships, they organized the trade in yarn, Aleppo's most important commodity, supplying the city's textile factories which account for the bulk of the city's industrial output and employment. Some offices represented local yarn manufacturers, who had been growing in strength since the early 2000s because of government policies of import substitution; but importers were still a significant presence in the market, bringing in shipments from Malaysia, Indonesia, Taiwan, China, India, and Turkey. Other offices housed merchants—wholesalers and semi-wholesalers—who purchased from producers and importers; and some, like Taher, were brokers, who did not purchase any yarn but toured textile factories around the city each morning, bringing back orders and living on commission.

Because of the significance of yarn to the city's industrial sector, significant sums of capital flowed through these offices, which explained the security cameras outside Taher's office and the pistol which he kept in his desk.[6] One type of yarn in particular—Taiwanese intermingled (mta'aj)—was in high demand because it was a common component of polyester fabrics. But it was not only traded in the offices of importers and merchants; it was also bought and sold in the stock market in the courtyard of the caravanserai. Every afternoon, after the 'asr prayer, up to fifty men gathered on the stone paving in front of the offices of Aleppo's largest yarn manufacturer to haggle on the price of imported Taiwanese.

Office trade has finished for the day, and the sandwich maker is packing up to go home; a metal grill makes a loud roar as it is pulled down in front of one of the offices. The men of the stock market—the bursajiyya—have gathered in the courtyard. Most of them appear to be in their forties and fifties; a few are in their late sixties. Several of the men look slightly unkempt: rumpled shirts, heads hanging forward. A few look well off: cleaner, pressed shirts, an upright posture, polished shoes. Then there are the younger men: around ten of them, in their twenties and thirties, all dressed in jeans, trainers, and a T-shirt or a polo shirt. Men pushing food trolleys enter the caravanserai, like stagehands changing a set. One is selling sugar-coated candies and pistachios. One of the middle-aged men takes a couple of pistachio nuts from the trolley as he wanders past. He does not pay. A man is begging; he looks old and haggard and grabs the arm of one of the stock marketeers, who shakes him off. Sometimes the mood is boisterous, with sarcastic price offers being shouted; men rush at each other in horseplay, or they kiss their interlocutors on the cheek suddenly and forcefully. "Three thousand boxes at forty lire!" one man proclaims loudly to another, accompanying his joking offer with a theatrical flourish of his arms.

During the day, inside the merchant offices, the atmosphere could not have been more different.

Abu Samt is praying when I enter. Kneeling on a prayer mat on the floor, he senses my arrival and invites me in with a single word—strih, have a seat—before returning to his prayer. He intones the fatiha, the first chapter in the Quran, in a barely audible whisper, as I take a seat on one of the comfortable leather armchairs in front of his desk. Directly in front of me, in a framed photograph prominently displayed on the wall, he is shaking hands with the president of the Syrian Arab Republic. On his desk are two calculators, a telephone, and a large ornate Quran housed in its own box. Calligraphic inscriptions of Quranic verses hang from the wall behind his large desk. Opposite them is a large television screen which is switched off during the prayer but which, I remember from a previous visit, had been showing stock market and currency news on al-Arabiya channel. It is five in the afternoon, and we are alone in his wood-panelled office. Abu Samt, in his mid-fifties, is one of the richest wholesale importers of yarn in Aleppo. He finishes his prayer, rises to his feet, and returns slowly to his desk. From inside the quiet wood-paneled and air-conditioned space, we can both hear the combative shouting and joking of the crowd outside.

Like most of the merchants in the caravanserai, Abu Samt was dismissive of the stock marketeers. Their noisy bluffing and apparent frivolity were not the reasons he disapproved of them. More to the point, most of the yarn which they were so noisily discussing was mostly imaginary (wahmi). The deals were highly leveraged; they were selling boxes of yarn they did not own and could not afford to buy if they had to. By making only verbal promises, without any collateral, each person ensured that he bought as many boxes as he sold in each thirty-day period, and then made or lost money on the price differences at the end of the month. Although they bought and sold thousands of boxes of Taiwanese yarn at a time, for Abu Samt they were children who had at most fifty boxes to trade; the market was just chatter (haki). Worse than that, it was a type of betting (qimar), forbidden in Islam. Another reason to disapprove was its association with usury, also forbidden in Islam. One way to lend money was to sell a notional quantity of Taiwanese yarn to a customer with payment delayed for six months, and immediately repurchase it at a lower price for cash. To add a veneer of legitimacy, another courtyard broker could repurchase the notional yarn as a third party. Immediate repurchase for cash was known as flipping yarn (qallabeh). Structuring the arrangement through a third party could be construed as two separate trading transactions rather than a single financial one which was illegitimate in Islam. But for most office traders, this was right at the edges of acceptable practice, legitimate only if the yarn physically existed and changed hands in two unrelated transactions.

Alaa al-Din Tufayl was one of those who speculated on the stock market. A twenty-six-year-old studying for a master's degree in plant sciences at the University of Aleppo, he hoped to study for a doctorate in Germany the following year. He was also planning to get married and worked part-time as a broker to finance himself through his studies. He had been introduced to yarn brokerage through his brother-in-law, an older man who had acted as his guarantor. He made commission on sales of real Taiwanese intermingled yarn, as well as a range of other natural and artificial yarns and threads bought and sold in the caravanserai. At the same time, he also tried to make money by speculating in the stock market. It was fun and easy to fit in around his studies. The fact that trades were largely notional enabled those without resources to participate in the market and on equal terms with the wealthy merchants. "There is no big boss (mu'allim) in the stock market," he said. "A student can make money out of (yarbah) a merchant who is worth millions." It was also a frame in which individual autonomy and bounded individuality were licensed; the logic of patriarchal connectivity did not apply: "everyone works on his own. Sometimes, you kind of work in a team. But one month they are in your team, the next month they are your enemy. Sometimes a son might even compete with his father (yunafis abuhu); that is something special to the stock market."

The stock market was a domain in which normal hierarchies of patriarchal authority, and merchant capital, did not apply, and could even be reversed; a poor student could get the better of a millionaire merchant. In this space, participants were not expected to observe the rules of patriarchal authority, to respect their elders; they could indulge in the verbal play, mock-fighting that, when taken to excess, as Michael Gilsenan observed of Lebanon, "was not fitting for male assemblies, particularly if persons of rank were present" (1996, 208–9). And it was a space in which men were not expected to act as patriarchally connective selves seeking the direction of their fathers; they could act as separate, bounded, individual egos, even seeking to get the better of their fathers—to make them lose (khassir). It was open to men who did not hail from wealthy families, whereas the sons of office merchants would have risked their reputation by entering into it.

Given the stock market's reversal of patriarchal family norms, it is not surprising that the moral idioms of that world were arrayed against it. The stock market was described from the merchant offices as a form of chatter (haki)—a term that was often used in the collocation empty talk (haki fadi). This derogative term implied contrast with the men of substance or weight (wazn), who possessed word (kalimeh), and whose word was heard (kalimatuh tusma')—that is, who had authority and were obeyed. In the merchant offices, participants were described as children, in contrast to the father-like figures who sat in the offices; and as day-traders or mercenaries (murtaziqa) who were living hand-to-mouth on each day's proceeds. Their speculation could also be denounced as un-Islamic betting. Merchants' denunciations invoked notions of obedience, authority, generational position, the possession of capital, and Islam—the structures and moralities of economic patriarchy. It was because the stock market dissolved the social hierarchies premised on capital and patriarchal connectivity that the moral armory supporting these hierarchies—Islamic discourses and merchants' ideologies of speech and commerce—were turned against them.

Because the stock market ignored or reversed the logic of economic patriarchy, it is significant too that it was tightly bounded in time and space. The structures, relational dynamics, and performativity of this market were enacted within a tightly circumscribed arena. The stock market began only when the serious offices closed: the grills were rolled down, and the sweet-sellers arrived. It was bounded in space as well as time, confined to the northeastern corner of the courtyard of this caravanserai. The rules of the game—that the futures contracts be settled every fifteen or thirty days, or three or six months—also cut the transactions off from the less predictable temporalities of yarn import and production and the much more significant flows of capital they attracted.

These forms of censuring and the bounding expressed the hegemony of Islamic morality and economic patriarchy and their close intertwining. According to many of the office merchants, the stock market contravened the principles of Islam, because it involved selling something one did not own. Taher expressed an opinion common among his clients: "What happens there is the cause, even though on a very small scale, of the global financial crisis. It is not correct trade (tijara sahh), because they have nothing to sell. It is betting. It is just chatter, just air (hawa'). It is not the Islamic way." But the stock market was also free from the ideals and constraints of the patriarchal family order, and open to those who did not hail from wealthy families. It emerged at the edges of the flows of capital controlled by economic patriarchs, and at or outside the edges of Islamic morality, entangled in usury and betting. That it emerged only at the edges suggests that the patriarchal family, capital, and Islam intertwined to structure and regulate the social and economic hierarchies of the yarn market. Their intertwining stigmatized certain forms of commerce and pushed them to the margins, where they clustered together outside the bounds of economic patriarchy and the claims of Islamic rectitude.

In both the examples above, the ownership of capital, actually existing wealth, was bound up with the structures of economic patriarchy. Attempts to evade the grid of patriarchy were necessarily speculative, in the sense of conjectural and sometimes fanciful imaginings of the future: Hamdi speculated about what he might do with more freedom; Alaa speculated on yarn futures. In both cases, speculative evasions had to tread carefully around notions of Islamic normativity. For Hamdi, charging as much as one could get away with was not ideal in Islamic law (bi'l-shara'), but it was tolerated. Alaa suggested that there were different opinions regarding the Islamic question; in answer to the charge that theirs was an un-Islamic form of betting, some speculators objected that the whole stock market was based on commitment (al-iltizam) to one's promises—invoking a moral quality that has come to be valorized in movements of Islamic piety (Schielke 2015).

Speculating against Economic Patriarchy

I now consider the third case of speculation which, unlike the first two, sought to overtly challenge patriarchal social structures and took a self-conscious stance against them. This was a construction venture and educational project launched by a former textile trader turned social entrepreneur in Aleppo; I analyze it as a speculation on the future of the Syrian nation. In establishing his training institute for school-leavers in a well-to-do suburb of Aleppo, this social entrepreneur faced what he saw as the constraints of patriarchal mentality in Syria's security-minded bureaucracy, but persevered because he saw it as his mission to challenge patriarchal attitudes and structures in the economy. He also recognized the speculative and conjectural qualities of his venture; it was a risky undertaking that, taking on deeply rooted patriarchal structures and mentalities, might fail at any hurdle.

I met Saad Ibrahim in a well-to-do suburb of Aleppo on the premises of a small property development and real estate agency firm where he was the managing partner.[7] Then in his forties, he had an MSc and a PhD in international relations. Through the 1990s he had worked in a large textile manufacturing enterprise, working his way up to become general manager, the right-hand man of the owner. After disagreements with the owner's inexperienced young son, he resigned. After a brief stint as an independent wholesale trader in the bazaar, he found a new position as general manager of another industrial conglomerate, where he battled for over a year to institute a more efficient corporate structure before resigning and opening a property development business. In 2008, he was in the process of opening an entrepreneurial training institute to equip school-leavers with the business skills needed to flourish in a job market where the state no longer guaranteed employment for all. An advocate of the management and development of human resources (idara wa tanmiyyat al-mawarid al-bashariyya), he railed against what he called the politics of the father (siyasat al-ab)—the tendency to concentrate all decision-making in a single patriarchal authority. With building work going on around him, he passionately critiqued the old-fashioned way of running businesses in which the male proprietor is the be-all and end-all (al kill bi'l kill). For him, this critique was part of an intensely felt personal mission to build a bridge to the new Syria, still a decade or two away. Syria's future, he said, was a modernized business culture and structure, where authority was not hoarded by the figure of the father-owner but delegated to professionally trained young executives.

The first time I met him, I stayed for three hours, our conversation broken only twice, when he went into the adjoining room to pray. We sat in his small, air-conditioned office:

> I want to set up a training institute to prepare people for work, so it is not a surprise when they reach the job market. I believe in the Syrian people: eighteen million in the country, but as many outside the country—skilled, successful, hardworking. However, it is difficult. The mentality here, especially in Aleppo, is behind: people don't see the point of sitting in a room listening to someone talk. What do they benefit from it, they think. They don't see the point of paying for it, especially when businesses are family businesses where the father doesn't trust anyone to run the shop or the factory. Even on his day off, his staff call him fifteen or

twenty times just to ask permission for very simple things. Often the new generation are modern thinkers, but with their fathers around aren't allowed to express it.

At the moment, people in Aleppo have a simplicity, a goodness, but perhaps they can be naive (sadhej) too. They have old ways of doing things: religious heritage (mawruth dini), traditional heritage, and political heritage. The problem is that many businesses are family businesses. Companies are in the control of a single man, the father, he controls the stock, the accounting, the buying and selling, everything. He doesn't trust any members of his family or other staff. It is all centralized, so when he is away, nothing happens. He runs his factory according to the old mentality that he knew in the 1960s and 1970s; he presses down on staff, doesn't pay them much, and has them run after him. He doesn't develop them, train them, encourage them. We are trying to improve the business culture—we are in an important period of change. In 2003 we started modernizing the business culture; by 2025 things will be different. We are the bridge.

Businessmen running larger enterprises won't pay to train their staff either; it is not in the mentality. The only reason people pay is to get the certificate to put on the wall—they stop caring as soon as they have the certificate: it is just for prestige. This will be a problem when Syria starts free trade with Europe, which will happen soon: the Association Agreement is about to be signed in the next few days. So we need to change the culture... There will be a demand for a modernized workforce when Syria brings in more foreign investment. At the moment, this has not happened a great deal; investors need to go into partnership with the state, which takes the lion's share or even steals money. Turkey, however, has made great leaps forward. Ten years ago, Turkish people came to Syria as poor people looking for work. Now, they are rich, getting ready to enter the EU.

At the moment there is no demand for training, so I am not rushing to finish the renovations; they cost a lot of money. And it is very difficult to get permission from the Syrian administration to set up a training institute. There are lots of rules, and no one knows what the process is. And the security people are afraid of anything where people gather together, they want to know that it is not political or religious activities; they are very afraid of this. Sometimes I lose hope and think there is no hope for this project. But I believe the country needs it, and in twenty years' time business will be modernized here.

Saad saw himself struggling against what he called the old mentality, those in society who could not open their mind to the new, who would not listen to others, whose minds are like stone ('aqlhun tanihh). He saw this mentality in old-fashioned interpretations of religion, who did not see that the principles of modern human resources were found in the Quran and hadith. He also saw it in the conservatism of Syrian bureaucracy, in family businesses, and in larger conglomerates presided over by a single dominant figure who could not see the value of modern corporate structures. Across these domains, the problem was the same: the rule of the father, repressing the innovative energies of the young. In this analysis, father-son relations in family businesses were not intimately connective but domineering and unsuitable for the kinds of economic subjectivity required in the new era. The solution was to cultivate open-mindedness (infitah al-'aql) that would accept science and innovation. This was needed because of the free trade agreements that were coming into force; indeed, the term he used for open-mindedness corresponded to the term for economic liberalization (infitah). He cast economic liberalization as a cultural process—as the opening of minds, not just markets or borders.

Technocratic Modernity

Saad's frustration with the obstacles put in his way by a security-minded state was sincere. But its conditions of possibility were the regime's own discourses of technocratic entrepreneurial modernity. His critique of economic patriarchs as old-fashioned was aligned with a vision of Syrian modernity that was being promoted by circles within the government. Soon after the accession of Bashar al-Asad in 2000, a group of reformers around the young president sought to accelerate the liberalization of the economy. In 2005, the regime published a new Five-Year Plan, shaped by the Deputy Prime Minister for Economic Affairs Abdullah al-Dardari, which proclaimed the need for new entrepreneurial "mentalities" (Selvik 2008). Sidelining Baathist ideology, the government increasingly championed entrepreneurial values such as personal responsibility and initiative, addressing citizens as potential job-creators rather than job seekers. They espoused technocratic modernity, in which the solution to problems of economy and politics was not democracy but putting skilled professionals—such as the economist al-Dardari—in charge.

These moves were far from politically liberalizing. Bashar al-Asad was presented in the early 2000s as a young reformer, surrounded by technocrats, battling an old guard of securocrats inherited from his father Hafez al-Asad.[8] The first family supported associations to develop entrepreneurial initiatives and business skills among young people. The first lady Asma al-Asad became a patron of entrepreneurial training camps, while Bashar al-Asad championed internet and computer skills (maʿlumatiyya). Although entrepreneurial associations and youth-training organizations afforded a modernizing image, they constituted a politically compliant civil society while autonomous forms of civil society continued to be repressed (Terc 2015). Large companies setting up corporate structures were often owned by figures close to the regime. Like such corporate enterprises, the entrepreneurial institutes that functioned as their training ground offered opportunities for middle classes and urban elites, but did not empower the masses or provide a forum for formulating independent political demands (Hinnebusch and Zintl 2015a). As Lisa Wedeen (2019) has argued, the cult of the entrepreneur inculcated fantasies of market-oriented success and individual self-realization, which were premised on obedience to the regime and support for the status quo.

Entrepreneurial modernity was also being promoted by the former presidential adviser I had met in Damascus:

> The traditional traders and their ways of doing business are dying out. Syria is modernizing; with President Bashar al-Asad, they are trying to make it part of the world economy. The deputy prime minister for economic affairs is working on this. So it is good that you study the traditional ways, but then you should consider issues regarding the future of Syria. Now we are being globalized, or we are globalizing. Traders have globalized ethics. They are modernizers and you are traditional, looking for traditional social anthropology material. You should speak to the modern traders and entrepreneurs like Mr. Haykal of al-Haykal publishing.

Abussalam Haykal, the businessman behind Haykal Media and owner of *Forward Magazine*, was the son of a shipping magnate from Tartus.[9] He had studied in Beirut and London before becoming a founding member of the Syrian Young Entrepreneurs' Association (SYEA), an organization that sought to "create a new economic environment where young entrepreneurs contribute on the basis of science and modern management techniques" (quoted in Selvik 2008, 42). As Kjetil Selvik observed, this ambition mirrored "Bashar al-Asad's call to modernize the Syrian economy and society" (2008, 42–43). Haykal's *Forward Magazine* promoted a program of politically compliant reform; its website stated that "it does not distort facts, however, nor does it falsify realities. Simply, it looks at the bright side of things, while pointing to the shortcomings, with the objective of change and reform, rather than criticism" (quoted in Selvik 2008, 43–44).

Selvik again observes that this echoes Bashar al-Asad's call for "constructive" rather than "destructive" criticism (2008, 44).

Saad's critique of economic patriarchy was aligned with this reform program. Although I had met him through a different route, he knew the political adviser in Damascus and described his encounter with him as "a turning point in my life." His critique of the "old mentalities" of those whose "minds were like stone" echoed a discourse circulating in Syria's politically conformist Parliament, which blamed the nonentrepreneurial mentalities of lazy workers standing in the way of the nation's economic success (Selvik 2008, 47). He said of the courses he delivered at Syria's new private schools that he aimed to move students away from a traditional (taqlidi) mentality where they were mere functionaries (mwazzafin), to taking responsibility and innovating. His critique of the politics of the father also echoed the adviser's contrast between the thrusting, dynamic, technologically enabled merchant faxing Shanghai, and the traditional merchant sitting in the bazaar—a phrase that implies laziness and inactivity, by analogy with the phrase sitting at home (barik bi'l-bayt), an idiom for being unemployed.

Patriarchal Forms as Authentic Modernity

Fuad Umar, sitting behind his accounting desk in Aleppo's bazaar, did not remain mute in the face of these notions of Syrian modernity. While reformers figured the patriarchal merchant in the bazaar to be an obstacle on the path to national development, he championed patriarchal Islamic modernity, holding up father-son relations of discipline and moral pedagogy as a model of economic efficiency, trust, and authenticity in social relations. Critically minded intellectuals and politicians spoke of patriarchy or the politics of the father as a social problem and an object for reform, while merchants in the Umar family spoke of respect for male elders (ihtiram al-kabir) as a valuable principle, an ideology of social relations which they consciously sought to preserve in the market. They deliberated on the value for wider society of the father-son relations of moral pedagogy and deference which they enacted in the market. In this way, like intellectuals and political figures, they engaged in contestations of national modernity.

The House of Umar was a pre-Baathist merchant lineage. In 2008, its senior merchants still spoke nostalgically of the forms of commerce and society that had been displaced by the Baathist state in the 1960s. Having removed Syria's urban notables from power, the early Baathist regime promoted a form of socialist modernity, dismantling traditional forms of authority, and reorganizing society around state-approved categories such as workers, women and peasants (Pinto 2017, 91). While Hafez al-Asad oversaw a period of selective economic liberalization in the 1990s, he continued to promote Baathism as state ideology. Under Bashar al-Asad, however, private entrepreneurs became figures of modernity, and even deputies in Syria's conformist Parliament criticized state functionaries for lacking their drive. In Aleppo, members of the House of Umar also voiced criticism of socialist modernity. But rather than championing the youthful entrepreneur who was breaking with traditionalism, they promoted patriarchal authority as both modern and authentic.

Fuad asserted the efficiency of economic patriarchy, credited by Japanese scientists: "researchers came from Japan to study how businesses like this could be controlled by just one man. The answer is that they are family businesses." He developed the theme as a critique of socialist modernity as bankrupt, producing workers without commitment: "There was one business run by five families, just five men, it was known as 'the company of five' (al-khumasiyya). When it was nationalized, they put in five hundred employees. It did less than before, and with the wage bills it failed!" Other senior men in the family lamented the loss of paternalistic religious scholars, who had looked after merchants like their children. They saw the postcolonial state's takeover of independent religious endowments (waqf, plural awqaf) as leading to a loss of this authentic religious leadership. Since the takeover, the Ministry of Awqaf had used the endowments to appoint its own religious scholars who were little more than functionaries. Abdurrahman's cousin Ahmad, an éminence grise who had previously been elected to the board of the Chamber of Commerce, remembered that

> fifty or sixty years ago, there were only a few shaykhs. Traders would go to shaykhs, listen to their Quran and hadith lessons, and ask their advice: "I have done this or that wrong, what should I do?" Or "how can I solve this problem?" Then the shaykhs were trusted. Now they are not trusted so much. In those days, they had money—they were funded by their family or by the waqf. The shaykhs used the money to look after them, like their children. For example, the Umar shaykhs in Hadid Gate . . . Once, Aleppo was known as the city of waqfs. Then, shaykhs were good; they worked from their inborn disposition (min al-fitra), from their nature (min al-tabi'a). Now very few are honest . . . These days there are no morals. Morals come from religion . . . But true religion these days is less, and so morals are less. There is no decent upbringing (tarbiyya). That is why there is a problem in the market [with trust].[10]

Fuad and Ahmad were both making a similar point: that the social forms introduced under the aegis of Baathist modernity had led to a loss of authenticity in economy and society. By contrast, in systems of economic and religious patriarchy, company employees and religious scholars worked from the heart, so these were the basis of authentic modernity. State employees who inspected and regulated the market were further evidence of the loss of authenticity in society; they were derided as self-serving bribe-seekers (rashwa'iyyin). Even state employees who tipped them off about forthcoming raids were guilty of inauthenticity; they did so not out of friendship but because they had interests in their pockets. As well as lacking moral authenticity, such functionaries also lacked the urban authenticity of families of pedigree. On one occasion, when market inspectors had confiscated one of his neighbor's goods, a senior Umar merchant complained that "these functionaries (mwazzafin) come along, no pedigree (la asl wa la fasl) to them, no culture, and close the shops. It is a travesty! The Chamber of Commerce do nothing, they should be standing up for merchants, but they are just concerned with their own pockets."

In each case, they associated patriarchal forms—father-run businesses, shaykhs who cared for their children, families of pedigree who stood up for merchants—with the possibility of authentic social relations. Patriarchal forms were the antidote to corruption (al-fasad), which was understood in Islamic terms as a pervasive spiritual state, manifested in the prevalence of false intentions in social relations throughout society. Traders who made false claims about their goods, bureaucrats who ate bribes, arbitrators who acted with interests in their pocket, religious shaykhs who gave rulings for wrong motives—all were expressions of the same spiritual malaise. The accusation you are not authentic (ma nak asil) could also be leveled at employees who took money from the float or shirked off work while claiming to be running errands for the shop. The solution was to cultivate sincerity (sidq) and pure intentions through a Sufi discipline of rigorous self-accounting (muhasaba). It was for this reason that they placed a high value on father-son accounting, discipline, and moral instruction in their shops.

Authenticity, Aleppine Heritage, and the State

For Umar merchants, patriarchal moral accounting was a bulwark against corruption; as a legacy of waqf paternalism, it was also a way of preserving Aleppo's heritage. Lamenting the dissolution of the independent waqf system and its authentic moral instruction, Ahmad emphasized that the system had given Aleppo its name; it used to be called the city of waqfs (madinat al-awqaf). Authenticity was another value strongly associated with the city. Within Syria, Aleppo more than any other city was known for its traditions of urban prestige and for retaining an "old-urban culture" (Hachimi 2012, 325), with authenticity being its watchword. Other epithets of Aleppo were the city of authenticity (madinat al-asala) and the mother of sincerity (umm al-sidq) (Shannon 2006). By formulating economic patriarchy and patriarchal moral pedagogy as solutions to the problem of insincerity, they cast them as authentically Aleppine forms of commerce and society.

As Jonathan Shannon (2006) observes, notions of cultural authenticity had been current in public discourse since the late nineteenth century and had been central to Arab nationalism. After the Arab defeat of 1967, intellectuals wrestled with the crisis of modernity, the thwarted ambition to overcome the legacy of colonialism and achieve economic and political sovereignty. Some advocated a turn to heritage (turath), arguing that the path to modernity was not to mimic the West but to maintain a connection to an authentic past. Shannon argues that in 1990s Aleppo, these ideas were articulated not just in explicit discourses of politicians and intellectuals, but in the ways in which musicians and their audiences valorized Oriental (non-European) sensibilities of emotion and sincerity. The old cities of Aleppo and Damascus, merchant gatherings, and Sufi zikr ceremonies were all construed as sites of authenticity. While modernists, especially Marxists, had opposed the return to heritage since the 1970s, states responded to it by posing as preservers of Arab-Islamic authenticity. As Patricia Kubala (2007) suggests, tourism and world music economies, long used to trading in Orientalist tropes of the traditional Islamic other, also played a role in commodifying Easternness for consumption by Western audiences.

Christa Salamandra (2004) observed that in 1990s Damascus, the valorization of authenticity by middle classes and urban elites was not only tied to resistance to Westernization or the commodification of Easternness in tourist economies; it was also part of a competition for distinction among rival social elites. Authenticity was claimed by old urban elites seeking to differentiate themselves from new competitors who had humble rural roots, but privileged (often sectarian) connections to the regime. Ten years later in Aleppo, much as Salamandra observed in Damascus, urban merchant elites valorized authenticity in an attempt to delegitimize those who encroached on their power and territory: agents of the rurally rooted bureaucratic state and powerful rivals in the state-dependent bourgeoisie. But they also did so at a time of intensified economic liberalization and ideological change amid a fray of competing discourses of modernity. Reformist circles within the regime were championing technocratic entrepreneurial modernity, casting the bazaar as old-fashioned and thus potentially in need of reform. In this context, claims of authenticity and critiques of insincerity were a way in which Aleppo's established merchant strata could assert the value and integrity of their own forms of commerce and society. These claims and critiques positioned the patriarchal merchant-cum-moral-pedagogue not as an obstacle to development but as a pillar of authentic modernity.

The regime played contradictory roles in these contestations of modernity. On the one hand, it championed technocratic entrepreneurial modernity that figured the economic patriarch sitting in the bazaar as an obstacle to national development. On the other hand, as it moved away from Baathism, it also sought to co-opt Aleppo's traditional merchant elites by sponsoring the city's Arab Islamic heritage. As well as hosting the UNESCO festival "Aleppo, capital of Islamic culture" in 2006, it also celebrated the city's traditions of artisanal production, showcasing Aleppine heritage to visitors in an annex located between the city's bazaar and its historic citadel. Most shops sold postcards, carpets, and other artisanal products aimed at tourists, but one booth housed a weaving workshop. Saif al-Din, a man in his sixties, was a master craftsman. While a younger man sat at a traditional wooden loom, hand-weaving a carpet with an intricate design, he sat nearer the edge of the display, embodying patriarchal authority as Aleppine heritage:

> I learned from my father, he learned from my grandfather, and so on. I am the master (al-muʿallim), the person in charge of the trade (sahib al-maslaha). I have several weavers working under me. It is a long-term relationship: they become like members of the family, they eat with me, and I help them with many things. I teach them not to cheat customers, even tourists. [Paul: The financial crisis is putting people's pensions in danger.] In Syria, old people don't have to worry, because they can take the income of their children. My father died recently, but when he was alive, he could come to my shop, and if he saw a piece of work I had done that was not good, he could strike me in front of everyone—even when I was in my fifties, and a grandfather myself! I couldn't say anything. He could take all the goods in my shop away for himself, and I couldn't say anything. We have a verse in the Quran that says: "saying oph (complaining) to your father is forbidden." We have to carry out our fathers' orders without grumbling, except if he tells us to do something irreligious.

By showcasing Aleppo's authentic artisanal production, the state was undoubtedly catering to a tourist economy. But in siting the display next to the citadel, often seen as the symbolic heart of the city, it was also positioning itself vis-à-vis the city's merchant bourgeoisie as a protector of traditional social and economic forms; in this case, as voiced by Saif al-Din, patrilineal transmission, economic patriarchy, and filial piety.

Liberalization under Bashar al-Asad was not only an economic process, much less one that was as predictable as suggested by notions of crony capitalism and neoliberalization. It also involved unpredictable cultural contestations of the nature of modernity and, in particular, the relationship between patriarchy and modernity. On succeeding his father as president, Bashar al-Asad was popularized as the herald of a new era in Syria. His accession opened up space in public debate for the question of generational change and, in particular, the place of the father in economy and society. The technocratic modernity promoted by the regime enabled a critical discussion of patriarchy or the politics of the father as standing in the way of Syria's future. At the same time, the way in which the regime managed relations with Aleppo's merchant bourgeoisie reinforced patriarchal social structures. Its sponsorship of Aleppo's heritage and urban traditions also emboldened those who saw in economic patriarchy the possibility of a more authentic modernity. Senior members of elite merchant families spoke not of the politics of the father but of respect for male elders. Their commerce ideologies figured the respectable merchant as an economic patriarch and moral pedagogue whose authority over sons conserved a vital aspect of the city's heritage. The regime's sponsorship of Aleppine heritage emboldened them to contest discourses of technocratic modernity which denigrated the traditional merchant, instead construing the patriarchal merchant-cum-moral-pedagogue as a pillar of authentic Aleppine modernity.

As Moghadam (2004, 148–49) and others argued, state policies on patriarchy can be contradictory; for example, when governments open higher education to women but maintain patriarchal Islamic family law. This chapter has described similar kinds of contradictions. The Syrian regime's championing of technocratic entrepreneurial modernity unleashed critiques of economic patriarchy, while its institutionalization of state-merchant relations and sponsorship of Aleppine heritage continued to privilege father authority. Bashar al-Asad was promoted as a youthful modernizer; however, his accession to power embodied the principle of patriarchal succession, and required a change of law to enable him to succeed his father at such a young age. The result was that despite the desires of reformers, economic patriarchy remained hegemonic among merchant strata in Aleppo's bazaar. Those who sought to operate in the market outside of economic patriarchy and its ideals of patriarchal connectivity had to do so in a marginal and speculative mode. Cultural reformers who sought to realize technocratic modernity as an institutional reality were also in a sense speculating from the margins.

5

THE HOSPITALITY ECONOMY

Six kilometers northwest of Souk Jarba, near Aleppo's urban periphery road, lies the suburb of Ghirba. Like Souk Jarba, it was to become a front line in the fighting after 2011, which left it largely destroyed. But there was little to suggest this destruction in 2009, when it was a quiet and largely industrialized area. Wide avenues lined with four—and five-story buildings housed textile and printing factories. A bus line, served with brand new Chinese vehicles, brought an influx of workers and customers from transport hubs in the center of the city every morning. If, one morning, you had alighted from one of these bus stops, crossed the road and walked a further fifty meters, and stopped just outside a four-story stone-clad building, you could have glimpsed a hive of activity behind the factory gates. Male workers in red overalls milled around, loading up Suzuki trucks with two-meter-long rolls of stretch fabric, ready to be driven off to wholesalers' warehouses in Aleppo and Damascus. Others were destined for the port of Lattakia with the fabric then shipped further afield to Dubai. Inside, on the second floor, the polished stone floors were stacked high with hundreds of boxes of yarn imported from Turkey, India, and Malaysia. Hundreds of tons of fabric rolls—knitted stretch fabric for T-shirts, vests, and leggings—were piled up, ready for loading onto trucks. On the floor above, twenty industrial knitting machines, watched over by attentive technicians in white overalls, turned the yarn into fabric. The next and uppermost floor of the factory was as yet unfinished: the owner, still in his mid-thirties, was planning a new enterprise here, making clothes and underwear, building a supply chain that was vertically integrated.

At the center of this image of plenitude and prosperity sat Mohannad Sanub, an ambitious young entrepreneur whose name was increasingly being heard across the city. Mohannad no longer supervised machine labor directly; instead, his work every day from around 10 a.m. onwards was to welcome a stream of visitors to his factory office. This room, set in one corner on the third floor of the factory, was known as his "place of hospitality" (madafa). It was furnished as an executive office-cum-salon, with leather sofas and armchairs, as well as an executive desk with live CCTV footage from across the factory fed into a computer screen. Most days the madafa offered a picture of fullness: morning and afternoon, Mohannad's customers, suppliers, friends, and associates gathered here to drink tea and coffee, talk, renew acquaintances, exchange news, place orders, and pay debts in wads of 500-lira notes or 100-dollar bills. As Julia Elyachar (2010, 454) argued about coffee houses in Cairo, it was a hive of conviviality where men came to "settle disputes, arrange deals," and learn about customers, suppliers, and employment and investment opportunities. Mohannad was a consummate host; he would greet newcomers, listen to and contribute to the talk, sit next to one guest then another, and order rounds of drinks from his assistant. In the midst of the flow, he would take and make telephone calls, skype an agent in the Far East, summon the factory foreman to relay brief instructions, or inspect the color and quality of a batch of yarn. Sometimes, he would move the madafa to another location—to his fashionable modern office, all glass and metal, in the showroom in an adjacent building, or to a table and chairs placed on the wide pavement by the road in front of the showroom, displaying the dense sociability of the madafa to anyone who passed.

This chapter explores two themes emerging from the madafa or place of hospitality in Mohannad's factory. The first part addresses the relationship between hospitality and economy—between the practices and understandings of guest-host relations and Mohannad's commercial activities and fortunes as a merchant. Several scholars explored the significance of hospitality in Middle Eastern societies, but most work focuses on hospitality as a domain of political rather than economic action, as Magnus Marsden (2016) observes; analyses of the relevance of hospitality to commerce focused on the commercialization of hospitality and tourism.[1] By contrast, this chapter considers the salience of hospitality to commerce by analyzing the intertwining of guest-host relations and credit-debt relations. It argues that the arena of hospitality was one in which a skilled social actor such as Mohannad could engage and address the ambivalences in both sets of relations and assert an exchange ideology in which credit relations were construed as a kind of kinship. The second theme is the relationship between hospitality, market, and the state. For those who participated in it, Mohannad's madafa structured social membership of the market, affording them access to multiple goods—commodities, credit, information, opportunity, and arbitration. But it was also a node of political economy, since in exchange for access to these goods, participants were expected to show political loyalty to the central figure and support him electorally in his ambitions to insert himself into patron-client relations with political elites in Aleppo. Analyzing this space of hospitality therefore brings an ethnographic perspective to the question of how authoritarian regimes manage to retain political control while permitting a kind of economic liberalization or the organization of markets outside the purview of state economic planning.[2]

The Tensions of Hospitality

Mohannad Sanub did not hail from an established merchant house, let alone an old notable family like the Umars. His father had owned some commercial buildings in the southern end of Aleppo's old city, which provided the family with a rental income. At sixteen, Mohannad started as a manual laborer in the gold-smelting business. After military service he took an accounting course and moved through a series of positions in tailoring workshops in his early twenties. He then formed a profit-sharing partnership with Nasir, a university lecturer and textile trader who had done well in the textile boom in Aleppo in the 1990s driven by export to newly independent Russia. At first the two worked out of Nasir's wholesale shop in the old city's covered markets, importing and buying rolls of fabrics from factories and supplying tailoring workshops which then produced T-shirts, suits, and women's clothes. Each year, they reinvested the bulk of the profits in the business. As they expanded, they moved to a larger shop in the new city. In 2001 the business had accumulated enough capital that they moved to industry and the city's periphery. Having negotiated a cheap lease on the Ghirba factory, they purchased several circular knitting machines for producing stretch fabrics. They sold these fabrics to clothes manufacturers in Aleppo as well as to wholesalers in Dubai. By 2005 the Aleppo Chamber of Industry had awarded their level of output as excellent, which entitled them to a larger quota of tax-free yarn imports.

Mohannad cut a markedly different figure from the Umar merchants in Souk Jarba, many of whom regarded public frugality as a component of their creditworthiness. Fathers in the Umar lineage could demand an account from their adult sons when they saw that they had purchased fashionable new clothes for Ramadan and could criticize customers who insisted on purchasing only European products as if this alone was a guarantee of quality. By contrast, Mohannad displayed his wealth by sporting expensive consumer items and European brands. Not yet forty years old, he drove a top-of-the-range imported German car with a cream leather interior and wore French designer clothes—Lacoste and Pierre Cardin. Not hailing from a large or well-known family, his social world was also configured differently from the established merchant houses; he socialized and developed business associations within a smaller circle, consisting mostly of generational peers rather than under the watchful eye of a patriarch and extended networks of relatives. Yet he was determined to make a name for himself. He co-owned the knitting enterprise on the second and third floors with a financial partner, whose name was on the goods alongside his, but the enterprise on the fourth floor would be his alone. Already, the hospitality which he was known for dispensing to his guests at the factory every morning was said to be a testament to his generosity rather than his partner's, and the regular guests were said to belong to Mohannad's gathering (jama'at Mohannad).

While merchants who were not bound to the temporality of machine production could afford to sit on goods and wait for the right customer and price before selling, Mohannad and his partner needed continual sales to fund the purchase of new raw materials and keep their machines operating at full capacity. They therefore needed to foster long-term relations with their customers and did so in large part through the hospitality dispensed in the madafa. Credit was central to these relationships. Mohannad had somewhere over twenty customers who visited him regularly, mostly the owners of clothes workshops in Aleppo, or wholesale textile merchants supplying the central bazaar. The closest of them maintained permanent lines of credit. Guest-host relations were also bound up with credit. Most of Mohannad's customers were close to him in age, in their thirties and early forties. They talked of him as a generous host, not only keeping an open madafa during the day, but hosting dinners five nights a week. His generosity (karam) was also seen in the substantial amounts of debt forgiveness (musamaha), which he offered regular customers each year.

Why would Mohannad invest resources and time in holding a madafa? What have hospitality and generosity—both components of the Arabic term karam—got to do with commercial credit? One broker in his circle observed that his generosity meant that he had "less problems with customers not paying." So one explanation of the madafa is that it created a generalized sense of indebtedness: an obligation to reciprocate that was manifest as customer loyalty.[3] The broker also observed that the madafa expressed Mohannad's status as one who is big in the trade (kabir fi sana'tuh), giving him a kind of symbolic capital that arguably made him a harder person to cross. While these explanations have merit, they are also somewhat circular. For all his generosity, Mohannad remained vulnerable. When times were hard and debts were not being paid, the madafa could offer an image not of social plenitude but of emptiness. Then the mood of the factory office shifted from light-hearted banter to one that was more forlorn. The same broker observed after a rather somber visit to Mohannad's factory office, which we found uncharacteristically empty, "Mohannad is sad. No-one is paying their debts (la ahad 'am yidfa'). But what can he do? If he pressures them, they will just run away from him (yahrubu minhu)." Mohannad's authority as a creditor, and his status as a host, were contingent on the presence of customers and the repayment of debts. The idea that generous hospitality created indebtedness and fostered loyal custom therefore begs the question. If the debtors don't consent to be guests, what is the source of their obligation?

We need another explanation for Mohannad's madafa, another account of the relationship between hospitality, commerce, and credit. The relationship between hospitality and commerce is however relatively underexplored in anthropological scholarship. As Marsden (2016) observed, while some have focused on the wide-ranging commercial activities of khanjis or caravanserai owners, and others on the role of hosting in building trust within mafia organizations, most studies of hosting as a domain of economic action have focused on the commercialization of hospitality.[4] Commercial hospitality—the provision of food, drink, and accommodation for profit—has long been associated with migration and trade (Walton 2000), in part because it enables traders to avoid burdensome obligations to hosts (Goitein 1999). Yet for the same reason, commercial hospitality is often distinguished from "true hospitality" (Heal 1990; Herzfeld 1987). As the anthropologist Tom Selwyn (2000, 35) put it, "the rules and principles of hospitality stand at one remove from the principles and procedures of the market place."

Yet for Mohannad, the dynamics of hospitality were integral to commerce. Marsden (2016, 233) also observes that among Afghan traders, hospitality was "central to commerce." Guest-host relations underpinned the processes through which commercial partnerships were continually being made, broken, and remade. In particular, hospitality enabled skilled actors to forge a shared moral universe, despite their different ethnic, religious, and ideological backgrounds. Often they did so through reflexive and ironic commentaries on the very tensions inherent in guest-host relations. Following Marsden, I theorize the connection between commerce and hospitality in Mohannad's madafa in relation to the tension between intimacy and formality inherent in guest-host interactions. I draw on both Marsden's (2016) and Herzfeld's (2012) observations that hospitality provides social actors with opportunities for the skilled use of irony. What I add to these studies is a consideration of structural parallels between host-guest and credit-debt relations, and of the socially productive ways in which skilled creditors could make use of the homology between hospitality and credit. It was through this homology that hospitality became integral to commerce. The sociability of Mohannad's madafa expressed and rendered tractable the ambivalences of credit-debt relations, while also inscribing them in a discourse of kinship and subordinating them to expectations of long-term mutuality.

Anthropologists have often drawn attention to the ambivalent nature of hospitality.[5] Andrew Shryock (2004, 2008) observes that for Balga Bedouin in north Jordan, hosting implies sovereignty over a given space. At the same time, hosts also remain vulnerable to guests once they depart, since it is never certain whether they will remain loyal or alternatively speak against the host. Among his Jordanian hosts, awareness of this vulnerability was expressed in the proverb, "The host must fear the guest. When he sits [and shares your food], he is company. When he stands [and leaves your house], he is a poet" (Shryock 2004, 36). Anthropologists have also often understood the unstable interplay of amity and enmity to be central to hospitality. For Julian Pitt-Rivers (1963), this was because hospitality served to incorporate into a community the stranger who, being unknown, was always potentially hostile. It was a rite of passage that transferred the visitor from the status of a stranger, whose intentions were assumed to be hostile, to that of a guest, whose hostility was "laid in abeyance." Rather than eliminating conflict, hospitality merely prohibited its expression by replacing it with the duty on both guest and host to exchange honor (Pitt-Rivers 1963, 25). Following these observations, studies of hospitality in the Middle East and North Africa have often dwelt on the capacity of hospitality to express and control relations of antagonism, by providing a forum for social competition in which the honor of the parties is at stake.[6]

Hospitality has also been seen as an ambivalent form of sociality in that it confronts participants with a tension between unbounded openness to the other, and the need for separation and strategic interaction (Candea 2012). For the Balga Bedouin, "hospitality is not calculation" but a transcendent value in which generosity can properly be taken to excess (Shryock 2008, 406). Yet as Annette Weiner (1992) argued about gift exchange, there are always things too valuable to be given away. As Shryock (2004, 36) notes, "Throughout the Arab world, houses are marked by a strong desire to receive visitors and, at the same time, to safeguard their own interiority, which is often described as hurma, as 'sacredness' or 'inviolability.'" Hospitality is constituted in the tension between drawing outsiders into the bosom of the house, while also keeping them at a distance through the formalities of greeting, special food, and cutlery. Scaled up to the level of the nation, hospitality has since the 1990s inspired political theorists in Europe to call for an openness to immigrants—mainly Arab and Turkish Muslims—that goes beyond political calculation.[7] Yet while valorizing themes of sacrifice and the transcending of politics, Jacques Derrida also conveys the tension at the heart of hospitality, arguing that "we need to condition this unconditionality"[8] and that hospitality is neither assimilation of, nor occupation by, the Other (Derrida and Bennington 1997).

The Ambivalence of Being a Creditor

These ambivalences that constitute guest-host relations—between sovereignty and vulnerability, amity and enmity, openness and boundedness—found parallels in the dynamics of creditor-debtor relations between Mohannad and his customers.

Sovereignty and Vulnerability

Mohannad could emphasize his position as a sovereign, one who chose whether or not to admit a customer to his circle. He told one visitor and potential client in the madafa, "I don't take anyone off the street. I maintain a select group of customers." While this was no doubt partly flattery designed to entice a potential client, the expectation of principal merchants to provide credit for their regular customers meant that their clientele were a selected and somewhat exclusive group. Although private banks had recently been established in Syria, they remained inaccessible to many. This meant that a principal merchant-creditor such as Mohannad could place himself in the position of a sovereign, defined by Carl Schmitt ([1922] 2005, 5) as "he who decides on the state of exception." In describing his relationship with his customer-debtors, Mohannad portrayed himself as the one who decided on exceptions to the rule of exclusion or "not taking anyone off the street." But with sovereignty came vulnerability. The rapidity with which Mohannad could be transformed into a forlorn figure awaiting the call of his debtors in an empty madafa resonates with accounts in anthropology and related disciplines of the debtor as a powerful social position (Roitman 2005) and of the creditor as a vulnerable one (Akin 1999; Brison 1999).

Mutuality and Estrangement

In a review of the anthropological literature on credit and debt, Gustav Peebles reports the pervasiveness of the folk theory that credit is "beneficial and liberating for the creditor" while debt is "burdensome and imprisoning" for the debtor (Peebles 2010, 225; see also Gregory 2012).[9] But discussing his relations with his customers, brokers in Mohannad's madafa could emphasize the credit-debt dyad rather than the separate statuses of creditors and debtors. Mohannad maintained relations of permanent credit or running accounts (hisabat jariyya, or istijrar) with the closest members of his gathering. These customers regularly bought from Mohannad, and him alone; they made regular weekly payments but enjoyed a permanent line of credit which enabled them to take more goods before they had finished paying off the previous order. According to the cash they had at their disposal, they might also pay off all their debts and put credit on their account, leaving Mohannad in their debt. The principle was to remain bound in a credit-and-debt relationship that both parties ensured was never settled. Such relations were not established immediately; they were built up gradually over time; the establishment of a permanent line of credit was designated as a point of trust and intimacy, of mutual interaction (al-taʿamul), deemed beneficial to both parties.

This accounting relationship expressed an ideal in which the fortunes of two persons were bound together. Ongoing credit-debt relations could be represented as a valued form of mutuality and moral proximity; a broker in the madafa observed that "merchants like to remain tied to each other (mawsulu maʿ baʿd) through their accounts, hoping for good fortune through the relation." He also likened running accounts to a quasi-partnership (mitl sharakeh) in which "what benefits one party also benefits the other." His understanding expressed Marcel Mauss's (2002) notion that relations of indebtedness are socially productive, creating moral solidarity through mutual identification between the parties. This broker evoked a folk theory in which creditors and debtors who maintained running accounts with each other were often bound in a relation of mutual indebtedness. He described these as mawani relationships, which meant that two parties owe each other. As Pitt-Rivers observes of the obligations inherent in guest-host relations, their "mutual obligations are unspecific, like those between spiritual kinsmen or blood-brothers" (1963, 26). Mawani relations could be invoked in parting comments between a merchant and a customer at the end of a transaction, through the phrase "you are dear to me / you have mawani with me" (inta bitmun ʿalayya), which meant "there are no barriers between us—don't be shy of asking me for anything."

In practice there were limits to how far the principle was tested, but mawani was said to be common between merchants, especially those bound in istijrar relations of credit and debt. Mawani expressed an ideal of mutual identification of one person with another, in which either party could speak for or act on behalf of the other, and use their property as if it were their own. It implied a moral identification between two persons: one could act as if there were no barriers (ma fi hawajiz) between them; as one broker said, "You can use his car, or enter his kitchen and raid his fridge, as if it is your own." By contrast, to say "he has no mawani with me" (ma iluh mawneh ʿalayya) implied social distance and a rejection of intimacy. Ideals of mutuality between merchants could be invoked through idioms of kinship—the notion that they were like a family and bound in relations of affection (mahabbeh). Yet mawani relations were said to be stronger in some cases than the bonds of kinship since sometimes brothers do not even visit each other.

Yet a permanent line of credit, while signifying a mutual identification of persons, never fused creditors and debtors. Mutual identification was always also mutual exposure, in which two potentially separate entities encountered the unpredictability and unknowability of others. Alongside the readily accessible discourses of mercantile relations as a kin-like affection was a secondary discourse, expressed in a proverbial register, which recognized the danger of ta'amul relations. These evoked the lurking possibility that a customer and visitor to the madafa might not keep the affection (hifz al-widd). A debtor was free to abscond, and might even be calculatedly building up trust to abscond with a larger amount of credit. The underside of relations of mercantile mutuality was acknowledged in proverbs such as "It is not every time that a dropped vase remains intact" (mu kull mara taslim al-jarra)—you might be lucky nine times and find your fortunes smashed the tenth time. The danger of relations of mutual indebtedness was also recognized in proverbs about hospitality, such as "The one who ate with us betrayed us" (akal nakkal). This interplay of primary and secondary discourses about ta'amul relations shows that the credit-debt dyad comprises an unstable mix of openness (mutual identification) and boundedness (the unpredictable assertion of self-interest).

Informality and Calculation

Officially, those bound in mawani relationships were party to relations of intimacy and informality. Members of the madafa would sometimes say that they were "not shy of one another," invoking the ideal of mawani in which the "state of formality has been removed" (ilgha' al-hala al-rasmiyya) and in which no party should feel hesitant in making requests of the other. This ideological construction of relationships made the madafa into an arena in which varying levels of intimacy could be put on display and social stratifications enacted. Mohannad would sometimes move from behind his executive desk to sit next to a particular guest, pausing to confer with him in low tones, displaying their closeness. At meals he hosted in the evening, he would sometimes call particular guests to move to the center of the table to sit next to him. Abu Zaki, a regular visitor and close friend of Mohannad's, displayed the degree of intimacy which he enjoyed with Mohannad by occasionally sitting in his seat, using his computer, or directing his employees to run small errands for him. On one occasion, he instructed Mohannad to turn the electricity generator off, since the noise was disturbing him. Mohannad complied immediately, directing an assistant to turn the engine off while they enjoyed the tea. This kind of intimate presumption on the host was a gendered ideal: proper men were not shy in front of one another. Mawani could be described as sociability of being just among men (bayn al-shabab); the presence of women was said to add a note of formality.[10]

Mohannad sometimes telephoned absent guests inviting them to come and hang out (nitsalla) and enjoy the shared leisure. Yet the ideological construal of social relations in the madafa as informal, and as governed by ideals of mutual identification, also introduced unspoken constraints on behavior. One morning in the madafa, Mohannad sat at his desk conferring quietly with Abdullah, a stocky man in his late thirties. Abdullah owned a tailoring workshop, and was one of Mohannad's regular customers, buying only from him, and enjoying a permanent line of credit with him. Abdullah sat close by Mohannad's side, leaning into him. I sat on a couch chatting with Abu Zaki; otherwise, the room was empty. Abu Zaki and I had recently returned from a holiday on the coast; he had driven, and I owed him 2,000 lire (around US$40) for the petrol. Remembering this suddenly, I took the money out of my pocket and handed it to him. He waved it away as if I did not owe him anything. I insisted, but he still did not take it, so I dropped the cash on the sofa next to him. Abdullah broke off from his conversation and stared at me. Abu Zaki discretely put the money in his pocket, removing it from sight. Later that morning, as we visited another factory, Abu Zaki took me aside and said, "I want to tell you something. When you settle accounts (tahsub l-hisab) between friends, you should not do it in front of others. It should be private (khass)." When I asked him why this was, he thought for a moment and said, "otherwise people might think there is some [commercial] dealing (al-taʻamul) between us. If there are work accounts to be settled, it can be done openly, but if there are personal accounts, it should not be done in front of others." It was taboo to settle personal debts in front of others.

While anthropologists have shown that the notion that true friendship is unconnected to the domain of interests and calculation is not a universal one, Abu Zaki's response suggests that it may not just be a Western ideology either.[11] Friendship needed to be publicly performed as a relation free from calculation, in which there are no accounts between us (ma fi hsabat baynatna). In reality, friends did keep track of the balance of obligations. Abu Zaki expected the petrol money to be repaid, and used his account book to keep track of whom he owed a visit. But like the misrecognition at the heart of gift-giving, in which a gift depends on concealing from view its obligatory nature (Bourdieu 1977), friendship depended on concealing from public view the tracking of credits and debts. Merchants bound in mawani relations, similarly, could say, "there are no accounts between us." This invoked a mutual but nonspecific indebtedness in which, as Pitt-Rivers observes of spiritual kinship between hosts and guests, "each should accede to the desires of the other" (1963, 26) without stopping to calculate whether or not the exchange was a balanced one.

Managing Ambivalence: The Skills of Hosting and Lending

Like mawani relations and guest-host relations, permanent credit relations too depended on invoking the ideal of pure mutuality, of unbounded openness to the other. They were relations in which what benefits one party benefits the other. Abdullah was one of Mohannad's closest customers; the mutual identification between them was expressed both through hospitality—his physical proximity to the host—and through the conventions of permanent credit relations. It was difficult for Mohannad to chase up debts from Abdullah, and from any customers bound to him in mawani relations; to do so could be considered shameful ('ayb). Where he did chase up debts within regular members of his gathering, he was careful to deploy tact and humor in order to respect the ideology of mutuality between the parties. Telephoning an absent customer, he used gentle irony to remind him of his obligations and invite him to the madafa: "you were supposed to pay us yesterday, no? Tut, shame on you." Listening to the response, he broke into a small smile. "You'll pay us today, no? Certain? Ok, I'll be waiting for you." Because credit was equated with intimacy, calling in debts was a delicate task; a lapse of manners could endanger Mohannad's reputation as a host and creditor. Brokers said they could shun suppliers who chased late debts ungracefully. As Marsden (2016) and Herzfeld (2012) observed of host-guest relations, skilled social actors could use irony and humor to manage the ambivalence of credit-debt relations in socially productive ways.

This recognition of the power of the broker-debtor to sully the reputation of the creditor recalls the observation recorded by Shyrock (2004) that guests become poets on their departure from the scene of hospitality. In Aleppo, the ambivalent position of the creditor—sovereign yet vulnerable—reflected that of the host. Relations between creditors and debtors, and hosts and guests, were homologous—founded on the same ambivalence of being together yet apart. Credit-debt relations combined informality and calculation; Mohannad could claim "there are no accounts between us," yet was bound to his customers through their accounts. In the madafa, there was to be no shyness to ask for anything; yet Mohannad needed to tread carefully in chasing up debtors lest they left and never returned. Credit-debt relations were construed as mutual identification and benefit, yet harbored the intrinsic possibility of estrangement. The madafa was a domain in which to engage and manage these tensions through skilled performance. Hospitality involved many of the same tensions—between sovereignty and vulnerability, intimacy and estrangement, informality, and formality—as credit-debt relations. The salience of the madafa, for Mohannad, was not simply that it created a general sense of indebtedness and loyalty among his customers; but that it provided a forum in which to engage and manage the tensions of credit-debt relations.

As a host, Mohannad's role was partly to foster a sense of mutuality and informality. The way he dispensed rounds of drinks signified a mutual identification between all those in the madafa, as he offered the choice of beverage—tea, coffee, herbal tea, or juice—to one guest, and then applied the choice to all. Close guests knew that they were permitted to sit behind his desk, use his computer and even direct his staff, identifying themselves with him by assuming rights over his property and subordinates. When he was called away on business, he invoked the universal motto of hospitality—feel at home—as he parted the madafa: this place is your own place, gents (al-mahall mahallkun ya shabab). The designation of his factory office as a place of hospitality after the Bedouin tradition (al-taqlid al-badawi) also invoked the principle of mutual identification, since a madafa was traditionally, as well as a guesthouse, the gathering place of a clan (Slyomovics 1998).

Yet Mohannad's skill as a host was, while invoking a sense of mutuality, to tacitly elicit the subordination and discipline expected of guests and debtors. When he needed to remind guests to attend, or to observe the proper forms once they had arrived, he usually sought to do so obliquely. I made sure to smarten up my appearance after once arriving in a sweat-stained shirt and experiencing nothing more than his lingering gaze. Only occasionally did Mohannad choose to rupture the sense of mutuality explicitly. Once, in the middle of winter, when the factory office was full of guests, a visitor in his late thirties, perched on a small seat directly in front of Mohannad's desk, was trying to amuse the crowd by relating a story about a lecherous shaykh at a mosque in Aleppo. Suddenly, Mohannad intervened to make it clear that he had overstepped the bounds of informality: "Don't repeat that story, you cannot generalize from one example." The visitor tried to continue but had been cowed and lowered his voice. Mohannad spoke over him again, "This is unpleasant talk. If you insist on continuing, this talk (haki) is between you and him only!" After he had left, Mohannad commented on this person's habit of inappropriately heavy joking (mazh ti'il). Despite the ethos of informality in the madafa, there were boundaries of propriety, but only occasionally did Mohannad need to assert his authority overtly and make explicit where they lay.

Mohannad managed the tensions of credit-debt relations in the same way. When a debtor was late in paying, he might gently and indirectly remind him where the contours of propriety, the limits of mutuality, lay. But at a certain point, when he deemed that the bounds of mutuality had been not only stretched but breached, he asserted his authority and spoke of cutting off relations. One morning in the madafa it transpired that one of his customers was refusing to pay back a debt of 1,000,000 lire (around US$20,000). His customer was a merchant who owned several clothes shops in Damascus. Abu Zaki called a childhood friend, the Director of the Chamber of Industry in Damascus, and set up a call for Mohannad to make after eid. Mohannad did not seem angry but pensive and disappointed. The jokes in the madafa had stopped, and he was not talking much. His financial partner also seemed sunk in his own thoughts. Mohannad told me that his customer "will not do business again in Aleppo ... I will talk to my friends in Damascus, three or four bigger merchants, and they will put pressure on him. He will respect them ('be shy of them') and pay me back." While in this case Mohannad had no choice but to follow the logic of rupture, most of the time his skill was to elicit subordination and discipline from guests and debtors without overt compulsion.

Mutuality and Kinship: The Ideology of Exchange Relations in the Madafa

It was as a host, then, that Mohannad managed the tensions inherent in credit-debt relations. The madafa allowed him to anchor the tensions of credit-debt relations in a sociability that was officially designated as one of mutuality and unbounded openness. It transformed the business of chasing debts into the practice of inviting guests; it inscribed commerce in a discourse of mutuality, kinship, and continuity.[12] Hospitality was the performative arena that made it credible to construe credit and debt as a form of mutuality. The meanings of hospitality were well-established; it was a form of welcome that incorporated strangers, bringing them into an arena of solidarity and kinship. After I had attended Mohannad's madafa for several months, Abu Zaki told me, "You can ask us anything you like. You have become one of us (literally: 'of us and among us' [minna wa fina]). If you have any problem, anywhere in Aleppo, you can just call one of us, and we will call someone to go and stand alongside you." Again, the designation of Mohannad's factory office as a madafa, and of the madafa as a "Bedouin tradition," gestured toward such solidarity; as Slyomovics (1998, 141), drawing on El-Barghuthi (1924, 179), observes of Palestine, madafas had historically been meeting places geared toward "communal self-defense in the case of attack." What we might call the exchange ideology of the madafa—what it meant to give and receive hospitality—was clear: it was to be mutually identified. By embedding credit relations in host-guest relations, Mohannad attributed the same meanings to credit and debt, articulating an exchange ideology in which credit was construed as kinship.

Through these notions of what it meant to give and receive hospitality and credit, commerce was construed as a form of mutuality and kinship. This understanding of commerce enabled ruptures to be situated within broader expectations of continuity. Abu Zaki and a business partner whom he knew from Mohannad's madafa had sold Abdelhadi, a manufacturer of sofa and armchair fabrics, an industrial engine over a year earlier. They had sold it to him on credit for 400,000 lire (around US$8,000), but now he had stopped making repayments. Instead, he had sent Abu Zaki a gift of a roll of velveteen fabric which Abu Zaki was planning to use to cover the sponge mattresses in his apartment. As we sat on these sponge mattresses in one corner of his salon, Abu Zaki told me, "He has delayed (ta'akhkhar 'alayya) one year. I am angry with (za'lt min) Abdelhadi; I'm not talking to him anymore." Anger or upset was an idiom of rupture familiar from the domains of amity and kinship. It could imply an underlying continuity despite the ups and downs of relationships. Abu Zaki told me, "one day we will look back and remember this fondly, the times we spent together, the times of anger (za'l) when we fell out." Though he had fallen out with Abdelhadi and stopped visiting his factory, he also envisaged an ongoing relationship with him, telling me, "I won't take any interest from him when he pays the money back. Everything on mawani and trust (thiqa)!" Casting the bad debt in these terms meant that the rupture remained within the ambit of kinship; it implied an ongoing relatedness amid the estrangement. Abdelhadi's gift similarly kept the relatedness going despite the alienation.

This is not to say that the exchange of gifts and hospitality created amity on which credit and trust then depended. Rather, credit too was a way of making kinship. Before Abdelhadi defaulted, Abu Zaki had taken me on one of his regular visits to Abdelhadi's factory and told me, "I lent have him money (dayyantuhu), and now I can call him up like a friend and ask him for things." One of the things he had requested, and Abdelhadi had granted, was to use his factory as storage space for a container load of massage chairs, which he and a business partner had imported from China. He had reassured his business partner at the time, "Abdelhadi has affection for me, there is trust." Friendship then was not construed simply as a domain separate from calculation and instrumentality; rather, it was a domain created in the context of commercial interaction and simultaneously deemed capable of containing the vicissitudes of those interactions.

Hosting also enacted Mohannad's dominance over his guests, and thus engaged an ambivalence at the heart of commercial and credit-debt relations: who was the dominant party and who needed whom more? This ambivalence is manifest in English in the designation of a customer both as a client and as a patron of the shop. As a creditor to his customers, Mohannad was both a dominant and a dependent figure. Hosting addressed this ambivalence and asserted his dominance. While hosts were recognized as vulnerable to betrayal by their guests, a more prevalent discourse established hosts as sovereign, preeminent and respected figures; Abu Zaki said that Mohannad kept a madafa, "which is a Bedouin tradition by the way—because of two conditions: first, he is an important person in the trade (kabir fi sana'tuh) with customers always coming; and second, because he is generous," Hospitality both recognized and stabilized the ambivalence of credit-debt relations, asserting that Mohannad as host, was the patron of his customers. This echoes a dynamic observed in Michael Herzfeld's (1987) account of hospitality between Greek hosts and flea-ridden European hippie tourists. While the visitors came from the politically dominant societies of northern Europe, patrons within the international political system, the notion of hospitality enabled the Greek hosts to reverse their political positions. The hosts' patronizing stance toward unwashed and penniless guests enabled them to maintain self-respect while benefitting materially from their visitors.

As with credit, critical accounts of hospitality recognize that hosts are dependent on their guests for their status. In Mohannad's circle, it was sometimes acknowledged that he was dependent on his customers for his position, as when Abu Zaki said that a condition of the madafa is that "he always has customers coming."[13] Yet the notion of hospitality-as-generosity opened up a space of ideology in which it could be asserted that the source of his position as a host was his own character. Abu Zaki observed that Mohannad might benefit materially from his generous hospitality, yet he offered it first and foremost because he was naturally generous. He was a person of charisma (karisma, hudur) who was naturally able to gather others around him. Tamar, a fabric manufacturer in his early twenties who was at the edge of Mohannad's social circle, also attested to Mohannad's natural charisma and generosity, describing him as a "beautiful personality" (shakhsiyya hilweh): "I believe that this is something given by God. Some people tell such silly jokes, they never shut up, it is always chatter (al-haki) that never ends. Mohannad is definitely a personality." In these accounts, Mohannad's dependence on his customers and guests was obscured as his preeminence—his status as a personality—was attributed not to his guests but to his God-given generosity and charisma. It was these qualities that drew customers and guests to him, rather than vice versa. In this way, the ambivalence at the heart of hospitality and credit—who depended on whom—could be resolved in favor of the host.

The Madafa as a Site of Arbitration

So far I have argued that the madafa was an arena in which the ambivalences of credit relations could be engaged, handled, and ultimately absorbed into overarching notions of kinship, mutuality, and the dominance of the host. These overarching notions can be seen in the widespread understanding that the regular participants in the madafa constituted Mohannad's gathering. A gathering was understood as a network of peers constituted around a dominant central figure to whom duties of loyalty were owed. The relationship between members and especially between each member and the central figure was understood as one of qaraba (literally: proximity, but often translated as relatedness or kinship).[14] The sources of kinship in the madafa could vary and overlap, including friendship and affection (mahabbeh) as in the case of Abu Zaki, as well as shared interests (masalih mushtarakeh) in the case of customers who maintained running accounts. Mawani relations of mutual identification were central to these forms of extra-familial kinship; while they varied in strength from one member to another, Mohannad was said to be able to presume on (byimun ʿala) each member of his gathering for loyalty and support. Every merchant was said to have a gathering (jamaʿa) of loyal customers who were obligated to attend his events and vote for him if he stood in elections to Aleppo's Chambers of Commerce or Industry; and the bigger the jamaʿa, the more influential the merchant. Mohannad understood the ability to gather (jamʿ) customers, capital, and supporters around him as an integral part of being a merchant (tajir); a merchant was someone who "knows how to count, has good relations, knows how to gather, understands the trade and has capital" (byaʿrif yahsub, iluh ʿalaqat kwayyiseh, byaʿrif yajmaʿ, byifham biʾl-maslaha, wa iluh rasmal).

One way in which Mohannad sought to constitute his authority as a host and as the central figure of a gathering was in the field of commercial arbitration. As I discussed in chapter 3, informal commercial arbitrations were a common way of addressing disputes, much preferred to state courts. Mawani relations were said to be critical to this form of dispute resolution, as commercial arbitrators were expected to be able to "prevail on" (byimun ʿala) the disputing parties, to ask for favors from each side to reach an agreement. The authority of the arbitrator was understood to be less formal or official than that of the judge or policeman, based not on legal office but on dynamics of connectivity. One merchant said, "he [the arbitrator] must be able to say: I have mawani with you" (bimun ʿalaik). This means there are no barriers (ma fi hawajiz), I can ask you something, and you can ask me." A lawyer who worked in the field said, "some people have the wrong mentality, the mentality of the judge (qadi), which is the mentality of the government (sulta). It is someone who says, 'I am in charge [his face becomes harsh and supercilious], do this, do that.' But there is a difference between a judge and an arbitrator. The judge is like a policeman—he blows his whistle and orders people around in his job. But he shouldn't behave like this when he goes home to his wife!" Arbitration then was spoken about as premised on forms of authority that were in contrast to those of formality and the state, and as depending on dynamics of connectivity, intimacy, and informality. The lawyer said, "The arbitrator is not like a judge . . . he has been chosen by his friends, people he knows personally. He must act with affection. He has the power of a judge, but he doesn't act in a very formal, official way." These dynamics were by no means always effective; it was not unusual to hear stories of merchants who had refused to be bound by a ruling they found unsatisfactory. In 2007, the government sought to address this problem by passing an arbitration law, based largely on similar legislation in Italy that combined state and community-based sources of authority. The law allowed the parties to a commercial dispute to nominate their own arbitrators and temporarily conferred on them the authority of a state judge. This meant that the ruling could in principle and if necessary be enforced by a state court; the arbitration therefore depended on forms of authority and reputation embedded within merchant networks but was also licensed and endorsed by the state. Under the law, it was normal for three such arbitrators to be appointed: one nominated by each of the disputing parties, with the third agreed upon by the other two appointees.

In 2009, Mohannad acted as an arbitrator under this law in a dispute between Mr. Selim Nashar and the NUR company. Selim Nashar was a fabric manufacturer and friend of Mohannad's who had rented factory capacity from the NUR company over a three-week period in 2009 in order to weave cotton sheets. However, he had not received the share of the NUR company's cotton import quota that he had been expecting, and so had been forced to buy extra cotton on the black market at higher rates, which had substantially reduced his profit margins. At the end of the three-week period, he had secured a quittance note from the NUR company stating that he had paid for the manufacturing costs as agreed. In reality, he had not paid for the electricity which he had consumed, which amounted to a considerable sum. The quittance note he secured had effectively awarded him a discount on his electricity input costs, which more than outweighed the loss he had incurred in having to purchase his cotton inputs on the black market. Recognizing that he had gained overall, he was willing to accept that the NUR company had a claim against him for the difference, but he was unwilling to accept liability for the total electricity costs that the NUR company lawyer wished to claim.

Both sides agreed to arbitration. Selim Nashar nominated Mohannad, a previous customer and now a tenant of the NUR company, as one of the arbitrators appointed to look into the case; the NUR company nominated a lawyer familiar with the company; these two in turn agreed to nominate as the third arbitrator and chair of the panel Mukhlis Sabbagh, a former military police inspector who had managed one of the NUR company's factories before establishing himself as an independent merchant exporting clothes to Germany. Of the three, Mohannad was the wealthiest and most influential within Aleppo's broader merchant networks. Unlike the other two, he had the highest Chamber of Industry grade—a ranking that determined import quotas and was an important marker of capacity and status. As well as running the most extensive manufacturing operation, the large and well-known madafa, which he maintained at his factory gave him a social profile among merchants and industrialists which the other two lacked.

Mohannad moved quickly at the first hearing to activate this advantage. During the first sitting, he insisted on changing the venue from the anonymous lawyer's office where we met to his factory in Ghirba where he wished to host the proceedings. The legal clerk appointed by the court protested that this was against the rules: the initial venue agreed by all parties could not be changed in mid-process. Mohannad overrode these objections, insisting that his factory was closer and more convenient for all parties. The other two parties agreed, and the subsequent three hearings were held in his own factory office. Smoothing over the move in the face of the clerk's objections, Mukhlis joked that it would guarantee a better standard of hospitality. In fact, Mohannad had hosted the other two arbitrators in his factory office outside the arbitration: Mukhlis had frequented his madafa from time to time, and Mohannad also hosted the arbitrator nominated by the NUR company. By embedding the proceedings within these guest-host relationships, he positioned himself as the first among the equals of the three appointed arbitrators. By the third session of the arbitration, the three arbitrators agreed to reduce Selim Nashar's electricity costs in a way that effectively compensated him for the extra costs he had incurred on the black market.

Mohannad's authority as an arbitrator depended in theory on the voluntary consent of the nominating parties, and the sanction of state law. But in reality it went beyond state law and surpassed the authority that was vested in the other two nominated arbitrators. Mohannad activated his position as a host by moving the proceedings to his madafa. The move was against the letter of the arbitration law, but it was accepted because it was in line with the forms of authority on which arbitration was understood to rest. As I observed above, the nature of authority, which an arbitrator was said to wield, paralleled the dynamics which were said to obtain between Mohannad and his regular guests: an authority based on proximity. The authority of the arbitrator, like that of the host, was understood to rest not on the official or the legal but on what was necessarily informal. This informality was well-suited to the circumstances of this dispute: the case rested on understandings which, while they may have been inadmissible in a court of law, nevertheless needed to be tacitly acknowledged in order to reach what would be seen by the parties as a just outcome. These included the understandings that factories routinely sold their cotton quotas and merchants hiring factory capacity could expect this as part of the package; that resort to the black market for cotton was a common rather than culpable practice; and that possession of a quittance acknowledged to be inaccurate might nevertheless be a legitimate bargaining chip.

Practitioners contrasted the informal dynamics of arbitration to the coercive nature of state authority, and the proximity of the arbiter to the moral distance of the state. Yet, as I argued about the patrilineal merchant clans, the madafa in Mohannad's factory office cannot be understood in isolation from the state. Madafas—traditionally guesthouses or special meeting places in which an extended kinship group assembles and receives guests—exist across the mashreq or Arab East region, offering participants a social arena outside the control of the state (Slyomovics 1998). As Susan Slyomovics (1988) noted, some observers had predicted that they would die out in the postcolonial period with the advent of strong central bureaucratic states and authoritarian rule. But far from dying out in industrialized urban settings, madafas—meeting places that appeal to traditional ideals of kinship solidarity and tribal generosity—have often flourished in the mashreq (Arab East) region (Slyomovics 1998). Known by a variety of names across the mashreq (madafa, diwan, mudif, diwaniyah), madafas serve a variety of purposes, including recreation, information-sharing, and dispute resolution (Slyomovics 1998; Antoun 2000). They have been actively encouraged by governments in traditional states—those which govern through idioms of tribal leadership—such as Jordan and Kuwait.[15]

The Madafa Economy: Market, Civil Society, and the State

Scholars have debated the reasons why states might support madafas (e.g., Slyomovics 1998), and the relationship between the madafas, the state, and civil society. In some cases they foster a civil society capable of meeting needs beyond the reach of the state (Slyomovics 1998). Richard Antoun (2000) argued that as forums for dispute resolution, madafas function as a grassroots civil society in Jordan, fostering trust and cooperation in ways that are often more effective than the civil society organizations envisaged by international NGOs. Others have emphasized that as sites of kinship-based hierarchies, madafas forestall the formation of more radical, class-based and profession-based forms of association. Ali Hussein Qleibo (1992) argued that Palestinians under Israeli occupation preferred to resort to traditional forms of dispute resolution than to seek redress in the Israeli courts; but the result was to foster divisive tribal forms of political organization, which prevented the emergence of a strong national government. Al-Hasbani (1994) argued that the Jordanian state had promoted a madafa-based civil society in order to forestall the development of effective political parties which might address the needs of urban middle-classes and call the legitimacy of the regime into question. Still others question the extent to which the madafas are inevitably archaic and regressive. Fatima Dazi-Heni (1994) drew attention to the role of the madafa (or diwaniya) in fostering political discussions beyond the limits set by the state and thus in constituting a nascent civil society.

This critical literature has focused on madafas in traditional monarchical states such as Jordan and Kuwait, and on the madafa as a site of civil society and political deliberation. Relatively less attention has been paid to madafas in Arab republics such as Syria, and to their role as sites of economic activity and organization. Yet Mohannad's madafa did flourish as a critical site of commercial enterprise in the Syrian republic. It did so in the context of renewed authoritarian control and politically managed economic liberalization overseen by the state. Analyzing the connections between Mohannad's madafa and these processes adds a new perspective to the question of authoritarian upgrading—how regimes modernize and liberalize economically while retaining political control.[16] Much analysis of authoritarian upgrading in Syria has focused on the co-option of economic elites through economic and trade policy, and on the formation of narrow networks of privilege joining state elites and business elites in newly privatized sectors into a state-dependent bourgeoisie.[17] But it has not yet considered the way authoritarian upgrading intersects with the social forms and practices of the wider commercial bourgeoisie.

The dispute described above was resolved in Mohannad's madafa under the Law of Commercial Arbitration (qanun al-tahkim al-tijari) passed by the Syrian Parliament in 2007. One plausible factor in the Syrian government's decision to introduce this law was to strengthen grass-roots judicial institutions which might support a growing industrial economy in Aleppo, without instituting an independent judiciary or the rule of law that would have threatened the prerogatives of the regime. Merchants often preferred to avoid state courts because of their lengthy delays, and their association with bribery which made them unreliable and morally tainting. Mohannad's relatively informal madafa was well suited to this case for other reasons too, since the case rested on factors that could not easily be admitted in a court of law and therefore required a form of authority that was less official than that of a judge. State-backed informal arbitration in this case provided a forum for a dispute that would not have reached the courts but which may not have been resolvable without state sanction.

Mohannad's madafa also served to incorporate an enterprising middle class in Aleppo into a political economy tied together at the top by patron-client relations with the regime. Abu Zaki was one of the regular attendees at Mohannad's place of hospitality. In his early forties, he cut a tall, jovial, and imposing figure, and easily commanded the attention of those around him. Unlike most of the men in the madafa circle, he was not a customer of Mohannad's. He styled himself as a businessman rather than a merchant, and maintained a portfolio of different activities, making his living as a part-time broker, a manager-for-hire, and an occasional investor and importer. He was not of merchant stock: his father had been a civil servant, but he had trained as an accountant in the 1990s, and had later risen to become the general manager of a dyeing factory owned by the NUR conglomerate, which was situated on the ground floor of the building underneath Mohannad's factory. He prided himself on being enterprising (nashit), and having left the dyeing factory, now made a living in the interstices of the networks of principal industrialists like Mohannad. He acted as a broker, putting the principal industrialists and merchants in touch with one another and taking a commission on any deal.

Abu Zaki's livelihood depended on his insertion into these jamaʻa networks. He sometimes pooled capital with other entrepreneurs in Mohannad's factory circle to finance ad hoc import deals, distributing the goods through his own extensive social networks. He was therefore keen to hear about new opportunities and ideas and the latest happenings in the market. He said that he attended Mohannad's gathering "for pleasure (li'l-mutʻa). It is like you switch on the TV, and get a panorama for one hour of the news. You learn what things are new in the market, and which merchants have lost people's trust (faqid thiqatuh)." He also regarded the gathering as a kind of exhibition (miʻrad) in which he needed to market himself to possible employers and business partners looking to put together a deal. He attended the factory gathering "to say 'I am here', so that they remember me, when they are thinking of a deal, or of going on a trip, or looking for a manager." As well as providing access to information, investment, and employment opportunities, Mohannad's gathering was also a market. Abu Zaki had bought a car there, which he used on his daily rounds of visits from another member of the network; it was not uncommon for cars and real estate to change hands within the gathering.

While the association between madafas and dispute resolution procedures has led some scholars to think of it as a civil society, arbitration rights were only one of several goods transacted in Mohannad's madafa. Abu Zaki came to listen to the news (to access information) and to be remembered (to be included in economic ventures).[18] Mohannad's customers came to access credit and commodities. Because multiple goods were transacted in this domain, we can think of it as a madafa economy, in which market and civil society overlapped. Mohannad's madafa structured access to credit, commodities, information, opportunity, arbitration, and commercial rights.

Regular participation in this domain also involved an exchange. If attendees could presume on Mohannad for credit and inclusion in the market, he could presume on them for their loyal custom and their votes at election time. In 2009, Mohannad launched a campaign for his election to the board of the Aleppo's Chamber of Industry. Abu Zaki served as his campaign manager, basing himself at Mohannad's madafa. Many mornings, the two sat next to each other at the factory office, poring over lists of target voters and seeking to identify the wider constituencies that they might be able to mobilize in his favor. Abu Zaki emphasized that members of Mohannad's clientele were under an obligation to support his candidature: "If Mohannad puts himself forward for an election, and you are from his jama'a, you have to go and vote for him. Even if you are traveling and away from Aleppo, you have to be there at 7 p.m. at the reception. There is no choice." As well as targeting Mohannad's customer base, he also sought to prevail on them to deliver their own constituencies. He saw interlocking jama'a networks as forming a potential electoral base, if they could be mobilized by a charismatic figure and his lieutenants. Over several weeks, they sought to persuade the face-to-face networks of Mohannad's jama'a to reach wider groups of merchants and invited a wider-than-usual array of visitors to the madafa.

The madafa was therefore a site of exchange, in which attendees were admitted as Mohannad's clients on the condition that they patronize his political ambitions. Because election to the Board of the Chamber of Industry could help Mohannad to insert himself into patron-client relations with the regime, the madafa was a site where aspiring middle-classes like Abu Zaki were indirectly incorporated into a clientelistic system overseen by the regime. Although members of the madafa such as Abu Zaki did not directly receive rent from state elites, they constituted Mohannad's electoral support base. If Mohannad sought the patronage of regime elites, his middle-class clients came to depend on him for access to the market and its civil society. The madafa economy incorporated members of aspiring economic strata who were not part of extended families into a political economy that was structured by patron-client relations with the regime. In this sense, it forestalled demands for other forms of incorporation, such as through class-based organizations—independent sectoral and professional associations—which might have constituted a challenge to the regime.[19]

Thus the madafa economy and the forms of kinship on which it was premised cannot be understood in isolation from processes of politically controlled economic liberalization and authoritarian upgrading. The madafa both structured access to market, and incorporated attendees into a political economy sanctioned by the regime. This quid pro quo also subordinated participants to the norms of authoritarian civility. Mohannad occasionally needed to enforce authoritarian norms of speech in the madafa, intervening as the host to censor politically sensitive speech. One evening in 2009, he invited me, Abu Zaki, and a business partner of Abu Zaki's to the lounge of a five-star hotel in Aleppo. Abu Zaki and Mohannad were exchanging some anecdotes about members of the business elite connected to the regime, and at one point, Abu Zaki said, "power is always corrupt." Possibly mindful of my presence, Mohannad replied sharply, "not always, there are ten percent of them who are not." Abu Zaki apologized, and Mohannad repeated his rebuttal of Abu Zaki's charge. The latter replied, "You know the rule of double jeopardy. I already said I am sorry, you can't try someone twice for the same thing!" In intervening to correct Abu Zaki, Mohannad spoke as a host and drew on the hierarchy of host-guest relations established in his factory madafa. Being Mohannad's guest could mean being disciplined according to authoritarian standards of proper speech. In his madafa, the social practices of Aleppo's commercial bourgeoisie were imbricated in processes of authoritarian discipline.

Drawing on Mauss's (1990) analysis of the gift, Mohannad's hospitality can be seen as a form of gift-giving that created prestige and status for the giver, and a general sense of indebtedness among his clientele which bound them to him with regard to solidarity and loyalty. But as Weiner (1992) argued, gift-giving can also be an ambivalent practice, as much concerned with retention or not-giving as with exchange and moral relations.[20] This chapter approached hospitality in that light, as sociability characterized by tensions and ambivalence. It is that ambivalence, rather than simply a capacity to generate status and loyalty, that made it relevant to Mohannad's commercial operations in Aleppo. His space of hospitality provided a forum in which he could engage the tensions and contradictions at the heart of his credit relations with his customers, while also inscribing them into overarching notions of mutuality. Through skilled hosting, he managed the balance between openness and boundedness, formality, and informality in his relations with debtors. By designating his factory office as a madafa, traditionally a space of clan solidarity, and his clientele as a jama'a, a term that implied extra-familial kinship, he subsumed these tensions into a discourse of moral proximity and relatedness. Practices of commensality and debt forgiveness also emphasized mutuality as the principle of his exchange relations with his clientele. In all these ways, he established mutuality as the overriding exchange ideology of his relations with his customers, construing the giving and receiving of both hospitality and credit as forms of mutual identification and obligation.

This is not to argue that the intertwining of hospitality and commerce is a uniquely Eastern or Arab form of market relations. Notions of mutuality can underpin commodity exchange in a variety of social and cultural settings. As Caitlin Zaloom (2006) reports, even on the trading floors of Chicago, in the supposedly socially disembedded heart of US capitalism, stockbrokers create expectations of reciprocity with one another through their market trades. Far from being a traditional form of Arab culture, Mohannad's madafa economy flourished as part of broader processes of politically controlled economic liberalization in Syria. It provided a basis for extra-familial trust and cooperation—organizing credit relations and regulating disputes—that did not require a framework of individual rights that might have challenged the arbitrary power of the regime. And as membership of the madafa also implied subordination to a single dominant figure who was himself seeking patronage from the regime, this social form also incorporated aspiring economic elites into a structure of patron-client relations which forestalled class mobilization. Attention to the social forms of the market in a time of economic liberalization adds a new perspective to the question of authoritarian upgrading: how regimes modernize and selectively and partially liberalize economic life while retaining political control.

6

CIVIC PATRONAGE

"You are doing an anthropology study and you don't ask about the color of the tablecloth?" One evening in 2009, I attended a dinner in Aleppo hosted by Mohannad Sanub. Mohannad had invited a dozen of his circle, most of whom were around the same age as him, in their thirties and forties. As we sat down to the meal, one of Mohannad's friends teased me about my incuriosity; I had not noticed that while all the other tables in the restaurant were all laid in white, the cloth covering our table was blood-red. Red was the color of Aleppo's famous football team, Union Club (Nadi al-Ittihad), and Mohannad's devotion to the team was well-known. Since 2007, he had been one of its major sponsors; in return for his substantial donations, his image appeared under the caption members of honor ('ada' al-sharaf) in the team's promotional literature, and his name was mentioned at its matches. He also displayed his association with the team at his factory, clothing his workers—the dozens of men who manned his machines and loaded his trucks on the streets below—in blood-red tunics, with his own name and that of his business partner emblazoned on the back. Football sponsorship extended Mohannad's name into new arenas; it was said to bring him popularity (sha'biyya) and fame (shuhra). Talk in the madafa often revolved around football sponsors who were gaining a name, through their patronage of the team, amid its thousands of supporters.

Analyses of the sociopolitical investments and orientations of Syria's merchant bourgeoisie have often focused on their proximity to Sunni religious scholars (ulema) rather than their attachment to sports and sporting institutions. Thomas Pierret's 2013 study of the Sunni religious establishment in Syria shows that middle-ranking merchants have traditionally been an important funding base for ulema and hail from the same social milieu.[1] He highlights their proximity in cultural outlook, citing a Syrian merchant who observed in 2007 that "the two main values of Damascene society are: to have money, and to have a shaykh" (Pierret 2013, 144). In an account of different varieties of civil society in Syria, Raymond Hinnebusch (1993) also highlighted the similarity in sociopolitical outlooks between traditional merchants and religious scholars in Syria. Describing the merchant-ulema nexus as a center of resistance to the regime's modernizing and secularizing politics in the 1970s and early 1980s, he identified "the traditional urban quarters and the suq" as the site where "religious institutions and the trading economy came together." He described the souk as a site where religious sensibilities remain "deeply rooted" (Hinnebusch 1993, 249–50). And as Kjetil Selvik and Thomas Pierret (2009, 598) observed, the "ulema-merchant nexus" has remained an important social actor under Bashar al-Asad, becoming the backbone of a largely autonomous Islamic welfare sector with which the regime entered into an uneasy partnership.[2]

Yet under Bashar al-Asad, some merchant elites preferred to associate themselves with the sporting establishment (al-mu'assasa al-riyadiya) rather than the religious establishment (al-mu'assasa al-diniya). Moreover, political elites were known to encourage donations to sports clubs and cultural institutions; prominent merchants were said to have become sponsors of such associations at the invitation of the Syrian prime minister. This chapter considers the motivations and meanings of this philanthropy: why merchants chose to become sponsors, and why the regime invited donations and made them public. One distinctive feature of these invited acts of patronage is that they were directed at associations that promoted Aleppine identity or heritage. Sponsorship of such associations established donors as patrons of the city. The first half of the chapter argues that patronage of sporting institutions promoted civic rather than explicitly religious expressions of urban identity and enabled the regime to balance Islamic discourses of urbanity. The second half of the chapter considers the paradox that even civic acts of patronage could be elicited and directed by political elites. It argues that invitations to civic patronage were one way in which the regime managed economic liberalization, by establishing a politically subordinate merchant notability, and fostering competition among rival elites for preferment within the regime's patron-client networks. These arguments contribute to a body of work on recombinant authoritarianism, which understands authoritarianism not as an archaic disposition that persists through apathy and coercion, but as an institutionalized mode of rule that is flexible and adapts to emerging conditions.[3]

Giving to the City: Modern Euergetism

Studies of religious giving and endowments by merchants have often emphasized their role in creating status or standing in the community and in legitimizing claims to political leadership.[4] In Aleppo, too, merchants' financial support for prominent religious figures could boost their public standing and their electoral prospects. And public support for sports clubs was seen in analogous terms as providing a symbolic resource that could underwrite political ambitions as well as offer a type of social insurance. Abu Zaki described endorsements from both the religious and the sporting establishments as a kind of advertising (diʿaya):

> The shaykhs have a following (jumhur), they give a Friday sermon every week. It would be enough for one shaykh to say, such-and-such merchant buys yarn from Jewish merchants; in other words, if you buy from him, you are supporting Israel. Or, such-and-such merchant is a philanthropist (muhsin), he helps us. That helps the merchant if he is looking for votes, if he is standing for the Council of the Old City (majlis ili mdineh), the Parliament, or the Chamber of Commerce or Industry. Or it helps him if he has suffered some catastrophe and lost money: merchants will come and offer him money in support. This happens at the Union Club too.

It may seem strange to understand sponsorship of a sports team conferring an "elevated moral status" (Ismail 2013, 123) in the same way as an endorsement by a religious authority might. But both were said to lend their financial supporters a popular support base: a following, fanbase, or public (jumhur). The Union Club was said to inspire a strong sense of moral identity and solidarity; fans would "cry if you say something against the team." To be identified as a sponsor was to be in solidarity—to be one of us, one of our group. Abu Zaki said,

> Everyone talks about football here. Mohannad supports Union Club financially. He has a fanbase of twenty thousand people who love him. In two years, he will have fifty thousand people. Then 200,000 people. He doesn't do it to advertise his company. But for the future—if there is an election to the Chamber of Commerce or the Parliament, it will help him. It won't help Nasir Tabkhi [his financial partner], just Mohannad. He is building a presence (hudur), his charisma. The club will say, "he is one of us," he is one of our group (huwa minna, huwa min shillatna).

In Abu Zaki's account, then, the religious and the sporting establishment were not necessarily mutually exclusive attachments, but were rather alternative routes to the same goal of acquiring a popular support base, which might be useful in electoral contests. And while the two establishments did not, in principle, represent mutually exclusive orientations, Mohannad and several members of his social circle did implicitly distance themselves from the religious establishment. Mohannad said that "Islam doesn't need to be something public, in the street. It can be something in the home: you can pray at home, you can go to the mosque on Fridays, that is it." Some of his guests said that they found the milieu of the bazaar uncongenial, with one commenting to the others, "I don't know about you, but I didn't find myself in the old city" (ma la'ait hali bi'l-imdineh).

Founded in 1949, the Union Club was Aleppo's largest football club. Its nickname, People's Aleppo (Halab al-Ahli), reflected its status as a popular club (hala jamahiriyya), one that was not part of the top-down apparatus of the state but a civic organization. While the regime usually permitted only public gatherings, which it had itself orchestrated, popular sports clubs provided spaces for gatherings, which did not depend on centralized authorization. The descriptor jamahiriyya indicated that the Union Club was one such place where crowds of people (jamahir; singular: jumhur) could congregate outside of the state's initiative. The Union Club was one of several institutions that the regime invited leading merchants to sponsor. Others included the city's second largest football team, basketball team, and Archaeology Society, which promoted and conserved urban heritage. In addition, some prominent merchants and industrialists were invited to finance the building and reconstruction of urban infrastructure such as roundabouts in the city center. What all had in common—whether sports clubs, heritage, or infrastructure—was an association with the city of Aleppo. They offered the publicly named donors an opportunity to acquire the honors of the city. By giving to them, merchants were giving to the city and becoming urban patrons.

These forms of sponsorship therefore bear comparison with the phenomenon of euergetism in the ancient Greco-Roman world described by Paul Veyne ([1976] 1990) and others.[5] Veyne coined this term to describe contributions by the wealthy to public funds in Hellenistic Greece and the Greco-Roman world. Such donations were used to fund both entertainment and public buildings; in other words, to provide goods for the benefit of all citizens, not only for the poor or for a particular group of clients. Euergetism was therefore distinct both from charity and from gifts dispensed within networks of patron-client relationships. Euergetism was performed willingly but was also a duty expected of the wealthiest; it was characterized by a mixture of freedom and obligation, but was always in some aspect voluntary and therefore distinct from taxation. It was performed by a class of notables who ruled the ancient city; euergetism was not a feature of democratic early Greek city-state but emerged in Hellenistic Greece when the political community was ruled by a status group of notables whom "public opinion recognized as possessing the right to govern and the duty to perform patronage" (Veyne [1976] 1990, 71). Veyne observes that a distinct form of euergetism emerged later, during the imperial era, among Roman oligarchs. Among the oligarchs, a small group of men involved in elite politics, euergetism was intended to influence electors—those who could vote them into public office. Donations to support public entertainment and buildings in this case were understood to reinforce the dignitas or political honor of these elite competitors.

Veyne argues that this form of "private liberality for public benefit" (1990, 10) was a feature unique to the ancient world. However, the concept of euergetism brings out several features of invited sponsorship by Syrian merchant elites during the period of economic liberalization. These, too, were contributions of funds by the wealthy to support public entertainment and building works. Here we see a mixture of voluntariness and compulsion; sponsorship was offered at the "invitation" (doubtless hard to refuse) of the regime in some cases, but not in all. Mohannad, for example, was acting on his own initiative, perhaps hoping to come to the attention of political elites. Rather than thinking in terms of coercion, merchants suggested that those who publicly sponsored the Union Club and other sports associations were motivated by fame (shuhra) or did so simply because they were allowed to—as in an earlier period of Baathist rule, public expressions of status and wealth distinctions had been taboo. Such wry observations also suggest an understanding that the desire to extend one's name through space and time into new arenas of circulation (see Munn 1992) is intrinsic rather than forced, needing only the removal of political constraints in order to be expressed. Finally, the association of football sponsorship with a status distinction of notability also echoes the forms of euergetism described by Veyne. In Mohannad's case, association with the Union Club was said to give him a public, popularity, charisma, and presence. These were currencies in potential electoral contests, qualifying him as a credible candidate in the eyes of other members of the Chamber of Industry who might vote for him. As such they corresponded to the political honor, which recommended Roman oligarchs to the electors in the ancient world.

In his account of religious giving by Jain merchants in contemporary Jaipur, James Laidlaw (1995) also describes as euergetism large-scale donations by the heads of the wealthiest merchant families to their community's temples. Like Veyne, Laidlaw distinguishes between euergetism and charity, between the provision of goods to the temple and the donation of funds to the poor, observing that Jain merchants put more emphasis on the former. Because these donations were "collective goods," they did not create patron-client ties, but rather served to "create and sustain a distinct public realm" (Laidlaw 1995, 144). In the Syrian context, too, mercantile euergetism partially created and sustained a public realm. We might think of this as a civic domain, consisting of the sporting and cultural institutions founded outside the Syrian state, the merchants' donations to these institutions, and the popular followings appended to the clubs and their donors.

This civic domain was not a politically muscular one or a counterweight to the state[6]. After the regime repressed the Damascus Spring civil society movement in 2001, the limits of permitted ambitions were clear—at most election to the Chambers of Commerce and Industry, or accession to the conformist national Parliament. Nor should it be collapsed into the civil society of government-organized nongovernmental organizations, which were dependent on the patronage of the regime that established and funded them.[7] Its associational base consisted of popular organizations (hai'at jamahiriyya) such as sports and cultural clubs, which typically predated the Baathist regime and remained outside the structure of Baathist Ministries and state-controlled unions and professional associations. It was a space of exchange with the regime in which donations and political compliance were exchanged for business facilitation and fame. In part it was fostered by political elites as a stepping-stone to success in regime-managed elections, in which the Syrian security apparatuses vetoed candidates they saw as undesirable. But it also emerged in part from the bottom up as an expression of merchants' desires for renown and status.

Ideological Constructions of the City: The Civic Frame

What interest did the Syrian regime have in permitting and even inviting such a civic domain? Why should it encourage public gifts to the city? The gifts may have relieved some pressure on public funds, but this does not mean that their purpose was only or primarily fiscal. Sports and cultural associations in Aleppo provided a framework for expressing civic identity, by which I mean one that foregrounded attachment to the city and in terms that did not directly empower religious authorities. Aleppo was well-known within Syria as a religiously conservative city. During the events of 1979–82, it had been one of the centers of Islamist mobilization against Baathist secularizing modernizing reforms. After the crushing of the uprising in 1982, the regime had repressed Islamists but saw public attachment to Sufi expressions of piety grow and become mainstream through the 1990s in Aleppo as across Syria. In the mid-1990s, hoping to ride the wave of public piety, the regime allowed some space for Islamic welfare and preaching organizations (Stenberg 2015). In Aleppo, the regime made moves to win over the city's Islamic bourgeoisie. In 2005, Bashar al-Asad appointed the Aleppine scholar Ahmad

Hassun as the Grand Mufti of Syria. And in 2006, after the city was named the capital of Islamic culture by the Islamic Educational Scientific and Cultural Organization, the government sponsored the festival, displaying images of Bashar al-Asad alongside those of Aleppo's religious heritage (Pinto 2011).

Alongside these strategies of co-option, the regime also sought to promote other forms of attachment to the city. The Union Club was a well-known icon of the city, its logo and nickname "the red citadel" (al-qala'a al-hamra') indicating its association with the city's most famous historical monument. In the aftermath of the civil war, the regime has been keen to promote the team as an icon of Aleppine identity, foregrounding it in upbeat social media videos promoting the relaunch of the city and the renovation of its old city markets. But the regime had been promoting the club as a framework for urban identity by directing mercantile euergetism since the 1990s. On the face of it, the club might be seen as an arena in which urban populations can relate to the city in ways that do not foreground sectarian identity, much as Kristin Monroe (2016) argued that ecotourism projects in Lebanon had provided arenas in which urban populations could move beyond sectarianized geographies and experience a sense of national territory. Yet the sports clubs to which the regime directed mercantile euergetism were widely associated with particular sectarian, ethnic, and class identities. As the owner of a small sweets factory near Aleppo's bazaar put it, "the Union Club is known for being [associated with followers of] Islam. It is the most popular club in Aleppo. The Hurriyeh [football] club is for Kurds. The Jalaa [basketball] club is for Christians." Other merchants confirmed these ethnoreligious codings of civic clubs and added a class dimension: the Union Club was associated with merchants, artisans, and laborers; the Hurriyeh club was for professionals and for Kurdish seasonal migrant workers from Aleppo's northern hinterland; "the shoeshine boys (boyajis) you see near the bus station waiting for a job," as one of Mohannad's guests put it. As elsewhere in the region, sports clubs were one of few arenas in which it was permitted to expose these identities.[8] But they also kept such identities within a putatively civic frame, in other words one that was not explicitly religious, and which did not directly empower religious authorities vis-à-vis the state.

For the regime, then, sports associations were an instrument for construing the city ideologically, for defining the kinds of urban identity that could be spoken in the public sphere. They provided a framework for attachment to the city that was civic rather than explicitly religious. They did not suppress ethno-sectarian identities, but designated the permitted framework for their expression and kept them within a formally tacit register. Sectarian and class identities were present implicitly and even fostered through these institutions, but were also contained, directed, and steered away from domains in which they might be consolidated and mobilized under the aegis of religious authority. Sports clubs offered the regime an alternative kind of urban association to those that empowered religious authorities. By tacitly fostering sectarian divisions, they arguably also heightened the value of social peace (al-aman)—especially the prevention of sectarian conflict—the provision of which underpinned the regime's claims to legitimacy.

The value to the regime of civic frameworks of urban identity needs to be understood against the backdrop of its attempts to manage and control Islamic iterations of civil society and urban space. Having repressed preaching and charitable activities in the aftermath of the uprising, the regime began to license some again in the mid-1990s (Pierret and Selvik 2013, 596). While allowing an Islamic civil society of nonpolitical preaching and welfare associations, the regime also managed the potential threat they posed to its own legitimacy by imposing periodic limits on the expression of public piety and charity; for example, bringing shariah institutes under Ministerial purview in 2008 (Stenberg 2015). In these accounts of the fraught relations between the Syrian regime and Islamic civil society actors since the 1979–82 uprising, Islamic civil society is analyzed as a domain constituted through preaching and the provision of welfare.[9] In other academic accounts of Islamic civil society in Jordan and Egypt, the provision of welfare has been understood to recruit the recipients' loyalties and build the donors' political legitimacy through patron-client networks; or alternatively to foster horizontal middle-class networks of solidarity.[10] And in influential theorizations of Islamic piety movements and counterpublics in Egypt, preaching has been analyzed as shaping moral identities and commitments through projects of self-formation and through inculcating sensory dispositions in which political subjectivities are grounded.[11]

One dimension of Islamic civil society that has been less emphasized is the spatial, the ways in which religious identities and commitments are imbricated in processes of emplacement. Emplacement has often been seen as an adaptive response to displacement, as the "social processes through which a dispossessed individual builds or rebuilds networks of connection within the constraints and opportunities of a specific city" (Glick-Schiller and Çağlar 2016, 21), and Sarah Tobin (2020) analyzed the relevance of emplacement to moral identity among Syrian refugee women in Jordan. But the significance of emplacement arguably extends beyond contexts of displacement to the ways in which religious identities are mediated in spatially specific ways, through particular buildings, streets, monuments, neighborhoods, and landscapes, as well as through the attachments that individuals develop to these in their routines of circulation and exchange, and through practices of giving. Viewed from this perspective, the preaching and welfare that constitute Islamic civil society are not only processes of network formation and ethical self-cultivation but also of place-making and emplacement.

Euergetism could play a critical role in these processes. Among Aleppine merchants, religious giving often left its mark on the urban landscape; a water fountain inscribed with the name of the donor and given to the old city markets—described as a form of sadaqa jariyya or perpetual charity, said to earn the donor salvific merit whenever it was used—was also a gift to the city. For all that it might be conceptualized as a source of arithmetically measurable salvific merit, religious giving was not an abstract, un-emplaced activity, but one that expressed an attachment to particular locales and often created a particular claim to urban identity and status.[12] Fuad's branch of the House of Umar had built two mosques in the city, one of which, he told me, "still carries my name." When he drew my attention to the images of their forebears affixed to the wall of his cousin's shop, he emphasized these were not simply religiously learned men but "the religious scholars of Aleppo" ('ulema' Halab); for the current generation, they were in part a claim to *urban* prestige; a prestigious attachment to the city. As Paulo Pinto (2009) observed of a lineage that entered Aleppo in the late Ottoman period at the same time as the House of Umar, to affiliate oneself with a network of Sufi scholars was a way of negotiating entry to the city and claiming a place in urban networks of power.

For the House of Umar, religious endowments continued to be a way of creating urban status and articulating claims to social leadership in Aleppo. One of Fuad's older brothers had been well-known as a fundraiser who had helped to build a prominent mosque in an upmarket district of Aleppo, which was now a landmark of the city; and he had started to build the hospital which stood next to it. Fuad recalled that he had gathered substantial funds from merchants, both rich and poor, in the souk, giving each donor who contributed 10,000 lire or more a glass memorial and their name above a room in the hospital. He had also traveled to Saudi Arabia to solicit a large donation. He died shortly after the Islamist uprising of 1979–82, and twenty-five years later, the hospital still lay unfinished. Such philanthropic endeavors were in part gifts to the poor and, for their donors, one of the keys to salvation. But they also expressed a sense of Aleppo as an Islamic space. Another of Fuad's cousins, who had held a senior position in the Chamber of Commerce, recalling that Aleppo had once been known as the city of waqfs, lamented the intervention of postcolonial governments since the 1950s to transfer control of the funds in these independent religious endowments to the state, seeing this as an encroachment on the authentic Islamic character and space of the city.

Euergetism in support of civic sporting and cultural associations therefore created an alternative mode of urban attachment and status to those offered by explicitly religious associations and forms of giving. By awarding public honors for the sponsorship of other kinds of urban attachment, the regime contested the hegemony of Islamic civil society and urbanity. This is not to say that the religious and the civic were always opposed to one another as sectarian to nonsectarian forms of citizenship and urban identity, nor that the regime's strategy was simply to balance one against the other. The interplay between the two could be more complex. The civic—and the related notion of heritage—could be ways of configuring and formatting the religious. The government's decision to sponsor the festival "Aleppo: Capital of Islamic Culture" in 2006 is one example. Pinto (2011) interpreted the government's sponsorship as an attempt to engineer a rapprochement with the city's traditional Islamic bourgeoisie, but he also noted that these moves were received with some ambivalence by members of the Islamic bourgeoisie. One reason for this may be that the sponsorship of the city's Islamic traditions consigned Islam to the category of heritage. Acts of heritage-making are ambivalent in that they assign value to whatever is designated as collective patrimony (Pinto 2007), but also locate it in new frameworks of regulation, meaning, and value, such as the consumer preferences of the tourist economy (Shannon 2003b; Wynn 2007) and associated norms of national and international governance. As Petra Kuppinger (1998, 2006), Yasser Elsheshtawy (2006), and others (Willams 2006; Salemink 2016, 2021) argued, such moves can disempower local populations, transfer control to distant elites, and sever what had previously been living relationships between local communities and urban spaces and objects.

Like heritage-making processes, the category of civic patrimony has a similar capacity to reorder meanings and disconnect people from their environments. After repressing Islamic civil society and welfare institutions in Aleppo, the regime had invited a leading House of Umar merchant to become a public sponsor of Aleppo's Archaeology Society (jama'iyyat al-'adiyat), a putatively independent association that organized tours of Aleppo's old city and visits to sites of historical interest. The choice was appropriate in one way, as the Umars were a religiously oriented family who were already patrons of a Sufi lodge and two mosques in the old city and surrounding districts. But by inscribing Aleppo's Islamic infrastructure within the ambit of archaeology, this move framed it as an object of historical interest rather than as a source of identity and continuing moral commitment. By inviting an established merchant family to become patrons of the city in this mode, the regime both opened to them the renewed possibility of urban notability, and foreclosed the meanings of their euergetism and the kinds of urban identity and prestige that it could afford them. This may be one reason why the Umar merchants seemed to be less keen to talk about the donation to the Archaeology Society than their association with the mosque that already bore their name.

The Revival of Merchant Notability under the Baathist State

The regime was probably keen to elicit euergetism from the House of Umar; as a respected merchant house, their sponsorship lent credibility to the civic domain. But this strategy ran up against a paradox; in Aleppo, a city proud of its autonomy from the state, credibility depended on retaining a critical distance from the regime. Umar merchants embodied this paradox; they were, on the one hand, proud of their proximity to political elites but, on the other, harshly critical of the inauthenticity of the bureaucratic state. This ambivalence expressed their position in the Baathist polity of merchant notability. In Albert Hourani's (1968) analysis, notables are intermediaries between state and society whose influence rests both on proximity to authority and on an independent power base that gives them a position of natural leadership. Notability is one way of structuring state-society relations by enabling social groups to present petitions to the state; as Raymond Hinnebusch (2015) argued, it became more important in rural areas of Syria after Bashar al-Asad hollowed out the Baath party as a system of patronage, leaving local populations with no other channels through which to make demands on the state.

The House of Umar had long been associated with notability. When the Umar forebears left Aleppo's hinterland at the end of the nineteenth century and sought to establish themselves in the city, they entered a political domain ruled by urban notability. The notables were grand families with traditions of learning and positions of social leadership in cities of the Ottoman Empire (Gelvin 2006). Economically, their position was based on ownership of land or merchant capital and sometimes control of religious endowments. They acted as mediators between local populations and the Ottoman rulers, cultivating personalistic patron-client relations that enabled them to represent dependent local populations to the imperial state. After entering the Ottoman bureaucracy in the late nineteenth century, they were sometimes appointed as local governors (Lapidus 1967; Hourani 1968; Khoury 1990). As provincial notables, the Umar negotiated entry to these networks through affiliating their Sufi order to one associated with a leading Aleppine family. Having established a foothold in the city, the family had pursued other urbanizing strategies. In the early twentieth century, they were able to acquire a mosque in Hadid Gate, a popular district to the east of the Citadel, where they have since presided over a Sufi following. Around the same time, and in a further move to prominence within the urban domain, an Umar trader and grandfather of the man who managed the shop up to the start of the 2011 uprisings purchased a commercial property in Souk Jarba near the city's covered bazaar. He bought it from a family of Ottoman notables who owned most of the market, tracing their lineage back to the 1700s (Meriwether 1999).

Acquiring this property, which dated back to the seventeenth century, from such a prestigious family also confirmed the arrival of the Umars as urban notability.

The French mandate authorities reinforced the power of Syria's urban notables in exchange for their political loyalty, but the Baathist revolution of 1963 removed them from power. The Baathists sought to bridge social divides—of class, sectarian identity, and urban-rural cleavages—through mass party institutions. When Hafez al-Asad came to power in 1970, he also sought to stabilize the regime by building an alliance with the merchant class in Damascus and permitting a measure of economic liberalization (Hinnebusch 2008). As class divides widened, the regime revived structures of merchant notability but in a politically attenuated and controlled way. Merchants were admitted to the Syrian Parliament as independent deputies in the 1970s during the first period of economic liberalization; and were admitted in greater numbers, from Aleppo as well as Damascus, starting in the 1990s. As Christa Salamandra (2004, 2013) observed, discourses of notability were expressed openly in Damascus in the 1990s, in the context of status competition between new and old socioeconomic elites.

In Aleppo discourses of notability were common among merchants under Bashar al-Asad. Leading merchants were referred to as noble (akabir), and members of older families claimed pedigree (asl wa fasl). Echoing the Ottoman association between grand families and traditions of learning, the Umars in 2008 advertised their urban notability through visual genealogies that displayed their historical association with the city's leading religious scholars. And echoing the Ottoman connection between grand families and political leadership, Fuad Umar described his lineage in terms of political notability and influence: "My father was a tall imposing figure—you would say [that he was] a governor to look at him. Now, if I stand by someone, give him my status (wajaha) and dignity (karama), it will help him when he stands for office." Ambitious new entrants without pedigree, such as Mohannad, sought to attain a preeminent status by cultivating popularity. The possession of a public, too, set a merchant apart from his peers; as Abu Zaki put it, "every merchant has a loyal gathering (jama'a), but not every merchant has a public." They could also be described as formidable personalities (shakhsiyyat)—persons of preeminent authority and influence.

These idioms of distinction need to be understood in relation to the ways in which the regime organized relations between itself and leading merchants. These fostered competition between different elites, and engineered a politically circumscribed but not totally neutered form of urban notability. As well as admitting leading merchants to the national Parliament, the regime allowed elections to be held to the Chambers of Commerce and Industry. Far from an autonomous domain, the merchant Chambers were penetrated by the regime (Hinnebusch 1993; Haddad 2012), which vetoed unacceptable candidates and ensured a balance between different power bases: old merchant families, new industrialists, and the clans of the state bourgeoisie. The chambers were arenas for expressing status distinctions. Members of the Chamber of Industry were ranked according to their production capacity, and their grade was printed on their membership card. Mohannad's card showed the highest ranking, of excellent (mumtaz), which entitled him to purchase a higher quota of cotton from state factories. A high-status ranking was also seen as a qualification for leadership of the chambers; the list of candidates standing for election to the board always displayed the rank of each candidate alongside their name. Board members could sit on arbitration panels and approximate Max Weber's notion of notables—those citizens whose economic position afforded them the prestige and leisure to undertake oversight of community affairs.

The regime had the power to annul the candidature of individuals whom it regarded as undesirable and to appoint individuals alongside the elected officials (Daher 2020). Elections to the boards of the chambers were also a measure of the size of the constituency behind each candidate, and therefore enabled the regime to determine which figures were valuable enough to draw into its patron-client networks, as Lisa Blaydes (2010) argued about the use of competitive elections by Egypt's authoritarian regime. In Aleppo, political elites opened petitioning channels with candidates who had proven their popular backing in this way, as it did in the case of the House of Umar (see chapter 3). This conferred a status of notability on successful candidates as intermediaries between state and local populations, and could lead to a competition for influence between rival bases.

Euergetism was understood as one strategy for building a popular base in advance of an election. As Abu Zaki said, "Mohannad supports Union Club financially. He has a fanbase of twenty thousand people who love him . . . if there is an election, to the Chamber of Commerce or the Parliament, it will help him." Since his donations to the club did not create any patron-client ties with dependents, this suggests that euergetism was in itself a way of attaining and expressing preeminence, reflecting Veyne's understanding of notables as outstanding citizens recognized by public opinion "as possessing the right to govern and the duty to perform patronage" (1990, 71). But unlike in the ancient Greco-Roman world, in this case the regime took an active role in eliciting euergetism from particular individuals; in doing so, it invited merchants to compete for the status of urban notability. As expressed in electoral success, then, merchant notability rested to some degree on popularity from below; but it was also elicited from above by the regime through invited euergetism and through the opening of petitioning channels with selected merchants and merchant houses.

Unlike urban notability in the late Ottoman state, merchant notability under the Baathist state did not imply any significant political power. To the frustration of some scions of the pre-Baathist notability, the Chambers of Commerce and Industry were not places to govern or defend class interests, as Laidlaw also notes of arenas created by euergetism by Jain merchants in Jaipur. Although the ability to petition political elites undoubtedly conferred some honor on the House of Umar, these channels were mainly used to object to predation by other arms of the state. Petitioning by merchant elites, and predation that kept merchants in a state of vulnerability, were two sides of the same coin of merchant-state relations. Euergetism, for its part, conferred some public honor on donors as patrons of the city; their names were read out at matches or inscribed on roundabouts in the city center. But to the extent that it was performed at the invitation of the regime and known to be given in exchange for business facilitation, donors were also publicly subordinated as clients of the regime.

Limits on Merchant Notability

During periods of economic liberalization—in the 1970s and again since the 1990s—the regime created politically attenuated forms of merchant notability. Merchants may have been permitted to develop fame or popularity—for example, by paying for trains and a free lunch for fans traveling to matches, but they were not permitted to develop large constituencies that were politically or economically dependent on them. In rare cases where such relations of dependence did start to develop, the regime intervened to prosecute the businessman and disband his following. In this section, I recount one such episode in Aleppo's history. These events illustrate the limits the regime set on merchant ambitions, and show the active role of political elites in shaping and managing hierarchies of Aleppo's merchant notability.

One summer in the early 1980s, a high-school mathematics teacher, recently returned to Aleppo from a posting in northeastern Syria, was searching for a screw to fix his son's bicycle.[13] He visited the hardware market on Khandaq Street in downtown Aleppo, not far from Souk Jarba. Here he was greeted by one of his students who happened to be working in one of the shops. As he recounted the episode to me in Aleppo some twenty-five years later, Muhammad K. said that his student offered him, too, a summer job working alongside him. He took up the offer, and having succeeded in learning the trade in forty days, he decided then to establish his own business. His rapid success, he said, enabled him to purchase a car when all his teacher colleagues were still riding bicycles. The shift from bicycle to a car was also a potent sign of the profitability of his business which, he said, encouraged others to invest money with him. First among the ranks of his depositors were his teaching colleagues. Stagnating public sector salaries and the rising price of real estate meant that the loans that they were entitled to take out from the Baathist state's Teachers' Union no longer enabled a family to afford housing. Instead, they took out the loans and passed them to Mohammad K. to invest for them. As his business grew, he offered them a regular monthly return on their investment—a predictable 3 percent per month. The monthly returns were so regular and predictable that one newspaper later observed that they functioned "like a salary."

During the late 1970s and early 1980s, Syria's model of state-led economic development stalled, resulting in a foreign exchange crisis. Rapid currency devaluation severely diminished the purchasing power of salaried workers, threatening the regime's core base of public sector workers (Boissiere 2005). Those with access to hard currency were able to resist the effects of devaluation, but the fact that this often depended on access to export and import licenses multiplied opportunities for bureaucratic corruption. To address the shortage of hard currency and in a move to attract foreign capital, the government passed regulations making it easier to import raw materials and machinery, which created opportunities for new entrepreneurs in industries with relatively low capital thresholds such as clothes manufacturing. Muhammad K. was one such entrepreneur to emerge in this shifting economic landscape (Boissiere and Anderson 2014, 355).

At first, his investors were drawn from his family, neighborhood, and professional networks. The business then took the traditional form of a profit-sharing partnership (sharakat li'l-arbah), in which restricted networks of investors or partners (shuraka') known personally to the entrepreneur financed small projects. Muhammad K. recalled that this form was common at the time: "There was no trader in the old city who didn't take money from his in-laws and his family, giving them a share of the profits at the end of the year." Yet Muhammad K.'s ability to pay out regular returns every month, at a percentage of the original deposit, gave the form a renewed importance at a time of economic crisis when the value of public sector salaries had declined sharply. The returns he paid earned him a reputation as an effective entrepreneur, and other businessmen soon introduced new investors to him, acting as investment brokers and moral guarantors. The enterprise captured the public imagination at a moment of social and economic transition. Regular annual returns of 36 percent drew both salaried workers striving to keep up with inflation, and small business owners who reportedly sold their productive assets to invest in the scheme.

Muhammad K.'s reputation also spread after he became a patron of Aleppo's Union Club. As the circles of his depositors widened, he established a range of factories for the manufacture of screws and nails (1989), circular saws, T-shirts, and underwear (1990), jeans that were sold in Italy (1990), ready-made clothes marketed under European labels (1990), fridges, fruit juice (1992), cotton yarn (1993), and polyester yarns (Boissiere and Anderson 2014, 358). The weaving factories established by Mohammad K. boasted imported Swedish looms and outputs to match European production standards. Collectively, he styled these as the NUR foundation (mu'assasat Nur), named after his son, whose broken bicycle had first put the enterprise in motion. At the height of his operations, he employed 900 workers. Several of his senior managers were former teaching colleagues. Other managers, who took the helm in the 2000s, after his fall from grace, suggested that the factories had not been managed well, and that he had struggled to invest productively all the funds that had been deposited with him, leading him simply to pay returns out of surplus deposits.

The state intervened in his operations in 1994, as well as in several other smaller schemes that resembled financial pyramid schemes rather than productive industrial and commercial operations. In June 1994 President Hafez al-Asad signed a law forbidding money gatherers (jami'i al-amwal) to receive deposits from anyone outside their family, and requiring those who had done so to return the funds to depositors within six months. Months earlier, between February and April 1994, state television had aired a serial ("Tarbush Hats") portraying money collectors as unscrupulous actors operating opaque and fraudulent schemes. The television serial prepared the public for the demise of these entrepreneurs and started rumors of the scheme's impending bankruptcy (Boissiere and Anderson 2014, 360). K. insisted that the NUR enterprise was viable, and he was able to return two billion lire of deposits. However, unable to liquidate the rest of the assets in time, he was declared bankrupt and arrested in September 1995. He was subsequently prosecuted for opposing the socialist project and in 1997 was sentenced to fifteen years in prison, achieving early release in 2007.

It is hard to know whether the motives behind the state's interventions were primarily political or economic.[14] One member of Parliament estimated that the money collectors had affected almost 20 percent of Syrian citizens. Another talked of the constituency of those affected as a public. K.'s scheme had attracted sixty-thousand individual depositors, many with other family members depending on them. Some observers viewed this as a latent political base. The regime had sought to prevent the turn to the private sector and economic liberalization from leading to political liberalization. In 1994, when the regime intervened against the schemes, Hafez al-Asad also permitted a select group of entrepreneurs to enter the Syrian parliament. These businessmen remained within patron-client relations with regime personnel (Boissiere and Anderson 2014), which prevented them from making collective political and economic demands. Was K. arrested because he threatened to surpass the bounds of such relationships? Perhaps unsurprisingly, after he had been released from prison, he downplayed his political independence, arguing that he had been undermined because his own patrons fell out of favor in factional in-fighting within the regime.

During the Parliamentary debate that preceded the money gatherers law in June 1994, and in subsequent televised conferences and newspaper articles, politicians and leading commentators argued that unregulated financial schemes were an example of economic backwardness and irrationality, and that in order to develop, the economy required unregulated schemes to be registered and officially regulated as joint stock companies.

In 1995, the state established consultative committees under the governor of Aleppo to decide the future of the money collectors' schemes. A referendum was held to consult depositors about the future of their assets. Of the 58,948 who had invested money with the NUR foundation scheme, 53,807 voted for the return of their deposits; a mere 2,135 voted for the reestablishment of the scheme as a joint-stock company (*al-Tishrin* newspaper, June 30, 1995). The governor's committees resisted the popular desire for the return of deposits and instead proceeded to reestablish the scheme as a joint-stock company.

The decision may have been taken to prevent unemployment or destabilization of market prices by liquidating so many of the NUR foundation's assets at once. Yet the effect was to enable the assets to be redistributed among narrow business networks rather than being returned to the original depositors. The police arrested K. in September 1995. In October, the consultative committees revalued the assets and reduced the value of each coupon by half—a valuation that *al-Tishrin* reported as "doubtful" and "damaging the interests of depositors" (November 1, 1995). In November, the Consultative Committees established a transitional management board to take over the running of the new joint-stock company. Meanwhile, under the share trading scheme established by the Consultative Committees, brokers started buying up the re-issued share certificates on Khandaq Street, the site where Muhammad K. had first established his deposit office. The coupons that he had issued there were now being sold as stock certificates at a tenth of their original value, as brokers reportedly talked down their value.

According to a senior manager of the company, the shares were purchased by "big merchants (tjar kbar) who were not part of the company" for less than 100 lire per share. The same merchants had "an arrangement with the company" to exchange these shares for the company's assets at 500 lire per share. The assets were also undervalued when they were sold; goods worth 800 lire were valued at 500 lire and sold to a merchant for a share coupon, which he had bought at 70 or 90 lire. The manager said, "this is a game (lu'ba): the company is reducing its capital, but it is benefiting the big merchants." A former Economy Ministry official confirmed this arrangement: "Mr H. bought up a lot of shares this way. He paid nominally 28,00,000 lire for a polyester yarn factory. But the factory was worth more. He paid half in cash and half in shares: the shares were worth 500 lire each in the deal, but he had bought them for 100 lire." At the other end of the value chain were small investors who had lost almost everything, seeking to redeem some of their savings and family assets. One who hailed from a poor neighborhood in the east of Aleppo said in 2009, "my grandmother and uncles bought into the scheme. One of my uncles pulled his money out just before the crash. My grandmother lost nearly everything. Many people have died of oppression (al-qahr) and anger."

In the Parliamentary debate in June 1995, the state had been represented as a shepherd of Syria's economic destiny, and the jointstock company as the most rational vehicle for economic development. Yet managers who were aware of the way that the new company's shares were traded, and its assets sold off to a small group of businessmen, regarded the state in this case as a sham. One said that the state was "not a state, but a small group of people, maybe one person or two." The effect of this skewed market in the company's shares and assets was to shrink the constituency of shareholders who had been the economic and potentially political base of the money gatherers. It also radically reshaped the power dynamics within this base, taking value out of the hands of the mass of small coupon-holders and transferring it to a small group of businessmen who had come to an arrangement with the management board of the new company, and who were therefore dependent on regime elites through the governor of Aleppo who had instituted the new board. In a final twist to the tale, Muhammad K. was rumored to have secured his early release from prison in 2007 by promising to manage the company's assets differently. By 2009, he had purchased enough shares in the company to install his son as the chairman of the board and was reported to be controlling the enterprise again from behind the scenes.

Contestations of Urban Notability

This episode in Aleppo's recent history illustrates in concrete terms some of the actual economic forms that emerged in Syria under the banners of economic liberalization (al-infitah) in the 1980s and 1990s and social market economy in the 2000s. Behind the Parliamentary rhetoric of the state as a shepherd of economic development emerged narrow rent-seeking networks in which the state was not a state but a small network of people bringing together senior officials and compliant businessmen. The episode also illustrates one process by which regime elites sought to manage and control the emergence of potentially autonomous social actors who had gathered a significant base among the regime's traditional core of public sector workers. At a moment of social and economic transition in the 1980s, a new cadre of entrepreneurs cultivated a popular base of depositors by providing regular monthly payments at a level that the state's own public sector unions were no longer able to match. But through a series of interventions in the mid-1990s, the regime arrested these entrepreneurs, dismantled their potentially autonomous constituencies, and allowed their assets to be transferred to narrower networks of businessmen. Those with access to enough liquidity acquired assets at artificially low prices. As well as selling off assets in this way, the management of the company also leased out factories at rock-bottom prices, enriching entrepreneurs who took cheap long-term leases but damaging the value of the shares and the equity of the mass of small shareholders.

Mohannad Sanub was one of those who benefited in this way, acquiring a cheap lease on his factory, which had previously been owned by K.'s public of couponholders. In 2001 he took up the lease on one of K.'s textile factories in Ghirba, where he established his madafa and clothed his workers in the colors of the city's football team. As well as benefiting from the redistribution of K.'s assets, Mohannad was able to develop favorable relations with state officials, which afforded him a temporary monopoly in cotton imports. Cotton production had previously been the preserve of the state and protected by import tariffs, but in 2008 the tariffs on Turkish cotton were removed. In 2008 Mohannad received advanced notice of this, giving him an advantage until the policy was publicly announced. This arrangement came at the expense not only of the wider market, but of the state cotton companies in Idlib, Aleppo, and Lattakieh, which were selling the cotton they produced at 160 lire. Mohannad gained access to Turkish cotton at 110 lire a kilo, which he immediately sold at a profit in Aleppo: "everyone wondered how I was getting such cheap cotton—was I stealing it? Then when they found out they rushed to import from Turkey, and the state companies had to lower their price."

Mohannad spent several months in 2009 campaigning for election to the board of Aleppo's Chamber of Industry, seeking to drum up support through the networks in his madafa. But his chances depended on being included on the electoral ticket headed by a family of pedigree. He was unsuccessful in his bid to be included. Although it is difficult to know why he did not succeed, the basis for notability was contested between established families and new entrants to the market. The son of the merchant who headed the electoral ticket which rejected Mohannad deemed sponsorship of the Union Club an extravagant waste of money. His own family had used their wealth to establish a religious charity. His distaste for football sponsorship was rooted not only in religious sensibilities but in a class disposition. Decrying the vast sums of money invested in football sponsorship, he added that "Union Club supporters are the lower classes. I hate it when they win, how they behave—going on the rampage, smashing things in the street." A scion of an old family related by marriage to the House of Umar, he fully expected to be represented on the Board of the Chamber in Industry: "I will be on the Board in the future." Holding a madafa was another claim to notability, but this too was impugned by old families. One Umar merchant who knew that I visited Mohannad's madafa said, "I haven't seen the good of him." He opined that hospitality among merchants used to mark someone's status as a personality, but now it had been debased and had become a purely instrumental act of marketing (di'aya). For his part, Mohannad scorned the abuse of reputation by families of pedigree, commenting that "some old families abuse their reputation to pay late."

We saw in chapter 2 that old urban elites such as the House of Umar contested the legitimacy of state-dependent clans' claims to leadership in Aleppo's Chambers of Commerce and Industry. They did so through exchange ideologies, discourses about trade and about what constituted honorable commerce. They construed their own modes of commerce as authentically urban, and authentic urbanity as the rightful basis for leadership in the city's Chambers. These constructions of urban-rural difference became salient in the context of a divide-and-rule policy by the regime, which divided influence in the chambers between a state-dependent bourgeoisie and an autonomous commercial bourgeoisie. We see something similar in the antipathy among scions of old families toward the modes of notability Mohannad pursued. Criticisms of hospitality as purely instrumental and commercialized, no longer a mark of status, were similar to criticisms of football sponsorship as an irrational use of money associated with lower-class unruliness in the city. Both declared the modes of notability of nouveaux riches newcomers as inauthentic and unfit to qualify someone for urban leadership. These contests for notability were shaped by the ways that the regime instituted state-merchant relations by fostering rival blocs of elites. In part it did so by distributing rent—cheap premises and import monopolies—through patron-client relations. But invited euergetism can also be seen in this light as cultivating a form of urban notability to rival the claims of pedigree.

Most analyses of sociopolitical investments by merchants focus on their support for religious institutions; this chapter, however, has drawn attention to another phenomenon, that of football, sports, and cultural sponsorship. Because the institutions that received this support stood for some aspect of urban identity or heritage, the chapter analyzed this sponsorship as a form of euergetism: donations to the city by wealthy notables. By directing mercantile euergetism toward sports and cultural associations, the regime shaped public discourses of urban identity and attachment, construing the city in civic rather than explicitly religious terms, and promoting an alternative to Islamic discourses of urbanity and civil society.

By permitting and encouraging civic patronage, the regime also positioned leading merchants as a kind of urban notability. Euergetism conferred status as a patron of the city; invited euergetism also signified entry into patron-client relations with political elites. Either could be a stepping-stone to success in managed elections to Aleppo's merchant Chambers, which in turn opened up petitioning channels with elites who had demonstrated their standing with popular constituencies. Notability in this sense was part of the institutionalized modes of governance through which the regime managed merchant elites during periods of economic liberalization. But while in an earlier period, notables had wielded considerable power as local political leaders, the notability conferred by civic patronage and leadership of the chambers was politically attenuated. It did not imply influence over policy-making, but only entry into patron-client networks that enabled protests to be voiced against excesses of state predation. Those who surpassed the bounds of permitted notability, moving beyond celebrity to relations of economic patronage with the public at large, found themselves prosecuted and imprisoned.

Merchant notability was also part of a divide-and-rule policy by the regime. Through a combination of measures—civic patronage, the distribution of rent in patron-client relations, managed elections to the chambers—the regime fostered competition by rival blocs of notables. This rivalry was expressed formally in elections, but also in everyday contestations about the values and meanings of credit, hospitality, and pedigree. These contestations also extended to the realm of civic euergetism. For Mohannad's supporters, the red tablecloth on which he hosted his guests in a public place was a symbol of his popularity, preeminence, and electoral credibility; for his detractors, it was a false sign of notability. Such contestations of urban notability reflected measures put in place by the regime to identify and balance merchant elites in a period of economic liberalization; in other words, to divide and rule. As scholars analyzing the resilience of authoritarian regimes in the face of liberalizing pressures have argued, these were not ad hoc measures, but institutionalized systems of rule that were both relatively durable and responsive to the emergence of new social forces.

7

AFFECTIVE ECONOMIES OF SINCERITY AND ECONOMIC LIBERALIZATION IN ALEPPO

"I never thought I would be cheated (minghishsheh) by the House of Umar!" declares a confident well-dressed woman in her early forties. She is standing in the center of a shop in Aleppo's old city markets, a stone's throw from the city's central Umayyad Mosque. Her vocal outrage is drawing the amused attention of other customers. "Why are you being like this?" (laysh anti haik?), she demands to know of the shopkeeper, a tall man, with a brush mustache, in his late fifties. Sitting at the desk at the back of his shop, the shopkeeper replies as he always does when his customers press him for a discount: "I'd make a loss at that price! We don't charge over the odds here, as God is my witness" (wallahi bakhsar, ma nakhud ziyadeh hon, allahu wakili)! As a regular guest of the shop, I was used to hearing the unflappable responses with which the shopkeeper Fuad met virtually all attempts to bargain down prices. This woman, who was evidently on familiar terms with him, stood over his desk, her foot touching a line between the tips of his toes, and exclaimed to the delighted smiles of the other women in the shop, "you are a cheat!" (inta ghashash). He defended himself robustly against her playful and flirtatious accusations, invoking God's name as he insisted that his margins were modest, and his first price was his last price.

This chapter explores the diverse relations that merchants fashioned between sincerity, Islam, and Aleppine identity. In Aleppo, the business of trade often involved asserting and maintaining relations of mutuality with customers and business partners under the rubric of sincerity (al-sidq). Al-sidq was probably the most frequently invoked moral principle in the markets in Aleppo. However, sincerity did not just entail adhering to the rules of not lying and not overcharging but also implied an affective orientation. In the flow of interaction with customers, invocations of sincerity were more often part of the cordiality and warmth that shopkeepers deployed to conclude a transaction. Sincerity was not just a moral principle but an affect of mutuality and interpersonal affinity. With their retail customers, traders often transacted affects of sincerity by invoking ideas of shared participation in divine provision. When socializing with each other in evening gatherings (sahrat, sg.: sahra), merchants sometimes strengthened social bonds by invoking ideals of emotional sincerity (al-sidq, al-'atifiyyeh) and heartfelt connection, made manifest in serendipitous events, and which they identified as characteristics of Aleppineness.

This is relevant to wider discussions about the relationship between Islam and commerce.[1] Scholars have paid much attention to movements of Islamic economics and Islamic entrepreneurialism, which depend on systematically elaborated knowledge, and which often cultivate a confessionally exclusively sense of the Islamic way of doing commerce. In Aleppo, Islam and commerce intertwined in a third way: what we might call an economic cosmology of grace, or culturally shared ideas about how to access providence or prosperity and make sense of fortune and serendipity. This economic cosmology was not explicitly elaborated by religious experts, and was not confessionally exclusive to Muslims. Moreover, with economic liberalization, circulations of affects of sincerity that had previously been rooted in bourgeois urban gatherings were being rescaled and reconfigured: evening gatherings were being repositioned as nodes in a transregional affective economy. Affect and morality are keys to understanding how changes in global capital flows were being inscribed in Aleppo's merchants.

An Economic Cosmology of Grace

Fuad Umar's shop was simply fitted out. Two large pieces of hardboard, raised a foot off the ground on either side of the shop, served as the main display shelves for different kinds of household items. On the desk at the back of the shop were some of the basic instruments of trade: a calculator, a telephone, a jug of water, a stash of receipts, and some notebooks. Yet interwoven with this rudimentary infrastructure were symbols of transcendence. A copy of the Quran was displayed prominently on the wall above the cash desk—"for blessing" (min shan al-baraka), Fuad said, so that "the hand of God is present" and so that "God gives the increase" (Allah yu'ti al-ziyadeh). Fuad inscribed the basmala, the words "in the name of God the Compassionate the Merciful," in his account book each morning, to invoke the same economy of abundance. A Quranic verse etched onto the glass above the threshold of his shop—"we have granted you a manifest victory" (inna fatahna laka fathan mubinan)—attributed the shop's success to a divine act of opening or giving victory. Fuad also embodied his reliance on a divine provision in his demeanor. He maintained a studied indifference to customers browsing in the shop, responding to inquiries briefly and politely, but otherwise making little or no effort to promote his wares or press his customers toward making a purchase. His studied indifference accorded with the stance that "divine provision comes on its own" (al-rizq byiji li haluh) rather than through his frantic or excessive efforts. In the verbal etiquette of his salesmanship, too, he invoked an economy of divine abundance, saying "God is the provider" (Allah yarzaq), and "may God provide the return for you" (Allah yu'awwid 'alaik), when the customer handed over their cash.

Scholars considering the relation between Islam and commerce have often paid attention to one of two main trends: a modern field of Islamic economics and finance informed by traditions of classical fiqh jurisprudence; and a "market Islam" ethic marrying pious discipline with business acumen, often informed by popular literature on life-coaching and personal development.[2] As Robert Hefner (2023) has observed, both these trends depend on knowledge that is explicit and systematically elaborated by experts. He argues that market ethics in Muslim societies that have been drawn into global capitalist circuits tend not to be ordinary in the sense of tacit and taken-for-granted; instead, they have been developed by specialists into formal ethical systems. But Syria, before the outbreak of the recent conflict, was less drawn into capitalist circuits than the settings considered by Hefner and other anthropologists of Islam.[3] Neither Islamic finance nor market Islam had really taken off, although both were present in an embryonic form. What kind of market ethics developed in such a setting that was relatively less integrated into global capitalist circuits? The first part of this chapter draws attention to traders' notions of sincerity, which they associated with the capacity to depend on and transact divine grace or provision. The economic cosmology of divine provision was largely tacit, embedded in mundane language and etiquette; it was not elaborated by experts into an explicit system. Since it could equally incorporate Jewish and Christian economic actors, I refer to it as an Islamicate (rather than Islamic) cosmology of market exchange.

Grace may seem to be more easily associated with Christianity than Islam, because it is central to Christian theology—a centrality that can lead to a contrast between Christianity as a religion of grace and Islam and Judaism as religions of law and legalism. Yet some scholars (e.g., Ahmed 2015) have recently challenged the traditional tendency in the field of Islamic Studies to treat Islam as primarily a religion of law, and jurisprudence as the preeminent form of Islamic knowledge (see, e.g., Goldziher 1967). Anthropologists, too, observed that notions of grace have been of central importance in Judaism and Islam as well as in Christianity.

As Julian Pitt-Rivers pointed out ([1954] 2011, 441), notions of the same order as grace exist in Judaism, in the concept of loving kindness and divine mercy (hesed), and in Islam, in the concepts of divine mercy (rahma) and divine blessing (baraka). Pitt-Rivers conceived of grace as that which is extra, which goes beyond what is obligatory or owed, as in the mundane example of the gratuity or tip. Grace is counterposed to what is calculable or predictable; it "belongs on the register of the extraordinary (hence its association with the sacred)" (Pitt-Rivers [1954] 2011, 425). In its sense of forgiveness of a debt or a sin, it is "opposed to justice and the law" (Pitt-Rivers [1954] 2011, 437). Like grace, baraka in Islam is associated with divine excess; it cannot be reduced to a calculable or predictable quantity. Having its source in divine transcendence, it surpasses human logic of justice or equivalent exchange. If baraka is opposed to the logic of equivalent exchange, it may be strange to think of it as having a place in commerce. Yet divine grace in this sense was invoked in Aleppo's markets both visually and verbally; as the vignette above illustrates, merchants could advertise their dependence on divine blessing through the mise-en-scène of the shop, and through the etiquette of the sale a seller could invoke divine provision for the buyer. In this cosmology of market exchange, to trade well was to receive grace and then transact it.

One reason that merchants advertised their dependence on divine grace was to assert mutuality with their customers amid suspicions of exploitation. After Bashar al-Asad came to power in 2000 promising economic reform, restrictions were lifted on many imported consumer goods. From the mid-2000s, cheap Chinese commodities and credit had increasingly shaped the consumer goods market in Syria, enabling individuals with no family background in trade to become small importers and wholesalers. As Fuad put it in 2008, "every family is sending a son to China these days." Families such as Fuad's, which had been wholesaling consumer goods for several generations, spoke dismissively of a crowd (zahmeh) of incomers, of rip-off merchants (ghashashin) who overcharged for low quality goods, and of a general decline in trust (ma ba'a fi al-thiqa). These dynamics of economic liberalization could reinforce the perception that Aleppo's souks resembled a bazaar economy in which prices and the quality of goods were uneven, reliable information was scarce, and prices were unfixed (Geertz 1978; Fanselow 1990). Theorists of bazaar economies have argued that where goods are not standardized, and prices cannot easily be compared in relation to quality, relations between buyers and sellers tend to be competitive and characterized by low levels of trust. Brand names and advertising, which might act as efficient channels of information between producers and consumers, are rare; instead, a long chain of middlemen makes the provenance of commodities difficult to determine. In such an environment, buyers typically find it difficult to assess quality, and inferior goods can pose as superior goods. The result is a general "atmosphere of suspicion that everything is adulterated and no trader is honest" (Fanselow 1990, 253). Unless the sellers hope to benefit from repeat custom, they are effectively in competition with the buyer rather than each other; the result is a perception that "honest sellers are driven out of the market, or honesty is driven out of the sellers" (Fanselow 1990, 262).

In a context of emerging competition and the information deficit of a bazaar market, Fuad constantly sought to assure his customers of the integrity of his trading name, and that the relations he sought to establish with them were characterized by mutuality rather than mutual competition. When I asked Fuad why he displayed a copy of the Quran above his cash desk, he said that it was for blessing (min shan al-baraka). Yet Fuad did not actually talk much about the rewards he or his customers could expect from his ritual displays and speech acts in the shop. When I pressed him to explain blessing, he said, "The hand of God is present" and "God gives the increase." But the notion of increase mostly occurred in natural discourse in another way—as that which he did not take from his customers. He often proclaimed to customers milling around the shop: "We don't grasp the increase here" (ma nakhud al-ziyadeh hon). By insisting that his increase in capital came from God, he claimed that it was not taken from customers at their expense. The assertion that his business model was not dependent on profit margins paid for by his customer was encapsulated in a saying he sometimes quoted: "buy at ten and sell at ten, there is blessing in between." The key feature of a bazaar economy is that sellers are not in competition with each other but with the customer; buyers and sellers are locked into a zero-sum competition and form an antagonistic dyad. By construing interactions with customers as a transaction of divine provision (rizq), Fuad sought to locate himself and his customers instead in a triadic economy of abundance in which provision comes from God and circulates between buyers and sellers with the promise of mutual benefit for each. When he said, "we don't grasp the increase here," the implication was, "we rely on God to give it instead."

Merchants could assert relations of mutuality with their customers in various ways. In food shops and those where commodities were weighed out, they could do so by tipping the scales slightly in the customer's favor. In clothes shops, a seller could say to a buyer at the point of purchase, "remember me in its fabric," imbuing the transaction with affective warmth and cordiality. And they could do so in the language and mise-en-scène of the sale, offering the customer a blessing that invoked and enacted divine grace. Pitt-Rivers characterized grace as the counter-principle of calculation, as "opposed to calculation . . . as the free gift is to the contract, . . . as the total commitment is to the limited responsibility, as the notion of community is to that of alterity, . . . as kinship amity is to political alliance, as the open cheque is to the audited account" ([1954] 2011, 437). On the face of it, relations between merchants and their customers fall into the domain of the contract, of precise equivalence, limited responsibility, and calculated alliance, rather than the domain of free gifts, uncounted generosity, unlimited mutuality, and total commitment. Yet, as we saw in chapter 5, one of the skills of commerce was to handle the tension between the logics of connectedness and separation, mutuality, and self-interest; to manage relations of precise obligation and equivalence while also inscribing those relations into the domain of unlimited mutuality. In wholesale trade, this could happen through acts of hospitality and debt forgiveness, construed as a generosity that had a divine source and exceeded the bounds of human accounting. In Fuad's retail shop, brief invocations of divine provision served the same end: performatively embedding relations of equivalence within a domain of excess and grace. The symbolism of divine grace enabled Fuad to adhere to the widely recognized moral aesthetic that, in commerce, relations of equivalence should be inscribed in a domain of mutuality and solidarity.

Heartfelt Exchange: Affect, Mutuality, and the Meanings of Sincerity

For Fuad, not "grasping the increase," but depending on divine provision and transacting grace in his dealings with customers, was a way to enact the virtue of al-sidq. Al-sidq—usually translated as sincerity or honesty—was a resonant moral principle in the markets in Aleppo, particularly among merchant houses, such as the Umars, who were aligned with Sufi traditions. In Sufi vocabulary, al-sidq was one of the states (ahwal) or embodied dispositions—alongside repentance and self-discipline or self-accounting (muhasaba)—which adepts sought to cultivate and demonstrate through proper behavior (adab), thereby creating moral spaces of exchange, and arenas of solidarity and trust (Pinto 2006). In shops influenced by these teachings, al-sidq could be invoked as an Islamic ideal, as in the collocation of sincerity and trustworthiness (al-sidq wa'l-amaneh), exemplary qualities of the Prophet Muhammad, who could be invoked as a model of mercantile virtue. In the prosaic register of postsale reflections, al-sidq could be identified as the essence of Islam, as Fuad explained that "Islam is sincerity and trustworthiness" (al-Islam huwa al-sidq wa'l-amaneh). At one level, al-sidq referred to honesty in describing and selling goods; merchants emphasizing this moral principle often repeated the maxim that "in Islam you are held to account for every word that you say" (bi'l-Islam tithasib 'al kalimeh). Some interpreted al-sidq as requiring merchants to refrain from bargaining (Pinto 2006). For some retailers, it implied a notion of fair price, and a commitment not to charge excessive margins and thereby cheat customers. Fuad and other merchants said that 1,000 percent margins were "immoral profit" (ribh fahish), and that merchants who "sell for 100 lire something worth 10 lire" were "dirty." The rules here, "in Islamic law (fi al-shar')," were nuanced. Fuad's son said that it was "haram in Islam (al-shar') to take a large margin (al-ziyadeh) for basic goods" such as foodstuffs that the poor needed to live on." But where the goods were nonessential and unique in the market, the issue was less clear-cut. Fuad's son hoped to get a monopoly on a line of such goods and charge high margins: "it is not an excellent thing to do, but lawful in Islamic law if the person buys willingly (radyan)."

Despite references to Islamic law, sincerity was not only a moral rule or precept of not overcharging, but also implied an affective stance of cordiality, of selling from the heart (min qalbuh). As the goods were handed over, a merchant might say, "God willing, we are selling sincerely" (inshallah sadiqin ma'k)." Like the phrase sometimes used in clothes and textile shops—"remember me in its fabric"—this gestured toward mutuality and intimacy between merchant and customer. Among those influenced by Sufi teachings, these affective orientations toward the customer could be described using a language of intention. Pinto notes that Sufi adepts who eschewed bargaining explained that "[w]hen you tell the client a price higher than what you would take, this means you have an evil intention in your heart and are also forcing him to do the same by offering a price lower than the one he would pay" (2006, 169). Sincerity or intentionality here was not a matter of speaking deeply felt, self-authored words, as in Protestant conceptions of the virtue (Keane 2007), but rather described an affective stance that refused to confront the customer as an opponent or a victim for the slaughter (al-dhabh).

Sincerity has often been understood as speaking words that are truly one's own, as opposed to speaking words that are superficial, ritualistic, or borrowed from others.[4] In his study of the emergence of the ideal of sincerity in European literature, Lionel Trilling ([1972] 2009) argued that sincerity came to be a concern in public culture in Europe from the 1600s. As seen in Polonius's advice to his son in William Shakespeare's *Hamlet*: "to thine own self be true," this ideal of sincerity expressed a conception of the true self as the inner self, distinct from any social roles a person might play. This ideal of sincerity had emerged out of a largely Protestant history that had discredited ritual language as formulaic and placed a high value on speaking from the heart in public professions of faith and in spontaneous prayer before God. Following Trilling, anthropologists of Christianity have explored the histories and ramifications of such understandings of sincerity. Webb Keane (2002, 2007), notably, identified distinct conceptions of language, materiality, and personhood that were implicit in Protestant concerns to cultivate sincere speech. The early Puritans' preference for plain speech and dress derived from an underlying concern that language and material things could hide or compromise rather than reveal the true self; the person was understood as an interiority that existed behind and prior to its expression in the world through language and materiality. For them, the function of language was to convey that true self as transparently as possible. Dutch Protestant missionaries active in Southeast Asia in the twentieth century also saw ritual speech as ill-suited to the expression of that interior self because, being borrowed from others, it was liable simply to be parroted (Keane 2002, 75). Implicit in this ideal of sincerity was a conception of the person as a self-authoring subject, autonomous of both tradition and social others who might influence or coerce speech.

Sincerity is a concern not only in Protestant traditions. As Niloofar Haeri (2017, 132) argued, Islamic traditions have long emphasized the value of "presence of heart" in prayer, and "intention" as a prerequisite of felicitous worship. Sincerity of the believer in worship is a shared concern across a variety of traditions—including Islam, Judaism, and Protestant and non-Protestant forms of Christianity—where it is "centrally concerned" with the quality of the relationship a believer "constructs with the divine" (124). Concerns about how to achieve sincerity in prayer and anxieties about what kinds of words and things can be allowed to mediate the relationship between the believer and God are found well beyond Protestantism. Mindful of Haeri's intervention, I do not want to fix or essentialize differences between religious traditions in their approaches to sincerity. Instead, I want to ask what differences may be revealed by looking at sincerity in the context of commercial rather than religious interactions—encounters between buyers and sellers rather than believers and God. What might it mean to exchange sincerely or to sell from the heart? And what tacit understandings of exchange, language, and personhood underpinned ideals of sincere exchange in Aleppo's markets?

Affective Economies of Grace and Envy

Merchants in Aleppo spoke of the value of selling "from the heart" (min qalbuh), with "pure intentions" (niyya safiyyeh) and sometimes described this idiomatically as having "good cinnamon" (qirfeh kwayyiseh). To say of a merchant that he had good cinnamon meant that he sold with good grace—willingly and wholeheartedly. Conversely, bad cinnamon meant selling with bad grace—unwillingly and reluctantly, begrudging one's customers what one had sold them. In the discourse of good cinnamon, sincerity or insincerity was not simply a matter of honesty and dishonesty, but of harboring healthy or unhealthy affective stances toward others. Some merchants said that these could manifest as good or bad fortune; a merchant whose cinnamon was good—who sold willingly—would both set the customer at ease (yrayyih al-zabun) and generate prosperity and abundance for them. A person buying from them would find that the goods were blessed (bada'i'a mubarakeh); they would last a long time and, if the purchaser was a trader who wished to sell the goods on, he would find a customer with ease who was willing to pay a good price. Conversely, a merchant forced to sell cheap might sell unwillingly and with resentment, begrudging their buyer the profit they would go on to make. A customer purchasing from such a merchant, whose cinnamon was bad, would struggle to find his own buyers and would likely make a loss. The ethical distinction drawn between willing and unwilling exchange also finds parallels in commercial transactions among the Sumbanese in Indonesia (Keane 2002). Keane reports that in understandings of exchange that dated from before missionization by Dutch Protestants, a valued attitude in exchange was a willingness to transact, which was glossed as sincerity, using the Arabic loan word ikhlas (Keane 2002 87n19).[5]

In this understanding of exchange, the intentions of the seller—their willingness or unwillingness—inhered in the material product, making the transaction felicitous or infelicitous. Materiality here is a medium that harbors the positive potentialities of good will and grace, or the negative potentialities of ill will and the absence of grace. Goods that had been sold with good grace (literally: good intentions) were said to be easy to sell; they were full of grace or blessing (baraka); they flowed easily. Merchants could read negative intentions into goods that proved impossible to sell and were inauspicious. In his madafa, Mohannad once recounted how he had been unable to sell a batch of textiles, which he had paid a certain manufacturer to produce for him; eventually he had had to sell them for less than a quarter of what he had paid for them. Although their quality was good and the manufacturer had excellent machines, Mohannad concluded that "people had said his [the manufacturer's] cinnamon wasn't good." Moreover, the purchaser who finally bought the goods from Mohannad at a steep discount "wasn't even grateful." Such goods, being manifestations of ungrace, were trapped in an affective economy of ill will. Some spoke of hating (kirh) goods that they were unable to sell, feeling resentment whenever they saw the hard-to-shift rolls of fabric still sitting in their showroom.

That goods could bear negative potentialities of ill will or the positive potentialities of grace recalls economic cosmologies observed elsewhere in the region. Julia Elyachar (2005) observed a similar cosmology of market exchange among workshop owners in Cairo in which economic actors sought to protect themselves against envy and cultivate its converse, positive relational value through acts of generosity and favors. In Aleppo, too, cinnamon expressed an economic cosmology of the evil eye and belief in the destructive effects of envy. A merchant with bad cinnamon was said to have an "eye that lingers on what he sells" ('aynuh tghuss 'ala ma yabi'). When the seller's eye—their unhealthy attachment to the object—remained on the commodity, it imbued it with a strongly negative affective charge. Muhyi Umari, a yarn industrialist from a family that had intermarried with the House of Umar said, "If you sell something because you are forced to (ghasman 'annak)—you liquidate assets because you need the cash—or if you sell and afterward see that you missed an opportunity to profit, you sell wishing you hadn't. If what you have sold is a car, maybe someone will crash in it. That is why, when you sell, people should say, from their heart, 'I hope you profit from it.'" This language of grace could propel the object into an economy of grace rather than envy, severing the seller's attachment to the object, and generating positive rather than negative affective charges. Phrases such as "I hope you profit from it," or "may God bring you the reward [for the money you have spent on this]" transacted not just the commodity but something extra: a desire for the customer's benefit; this was what it meant to sell sincerely.

The phrases that formatted the exchange relationship as felicitous should be spoken "from the heart," as Muhyi put it. Yet the mistrust and ambivalence in this notion of sincerity are directed primarily not toward language but toward material exchange. Discussions of sincerity and intention in worship across the religious traditions analyzed by Keane, Haeri, and others, are primarily concerned with the inner self's engagement in, or disengagement from, the words that claim to mediate that inner self. They address the possibility that a person may be speaking without any sense that the words are their own. By contrast, Aleppine merchants' ideals of sincerity-in-exchange—of having good cinnamon or selling from the heart—address a different anxiety, namely that a person may be parting with something to which they remain attached, and envying and resenting their exchange partner as a result. This notion of sincerity-in-exchange implies a different conception of the person from sincerity-in-speech; rather than an interiority that exists prior to materiality, mediation, and language, here the moral dimensions of a person—their good or bad cinnamon—are bound up with their attachments and relations to material things and social persons. The moral dimensions of a person are constituted as those relations are enacted through language; as a person says at the point of exchange, "I hope you profit from it," thus renouncing their own attachments to the transacted commodity.

As Keane (2002, 2007) argued, the ideal of sincerity as self-authored words expressing the "authentic" inner person is tied to a historically contingent ideology of the subject. It emerged from a specific history of modernity in which the self-conscious subject emerged as the site of freedom from social roles, weight of tradition, and coercion of political authority. But among Aleppo's merchants, sincerity meant wishing well and not wishing harm, rather than primarily speaking words that were deeply felt and truly one's own. This ideal of sincere exchange was tied to different ideologies of the subject, and of language and materiality, than those outlined by Keane in his account of Protestant modernity. Here, the subject of sincere commerce was constituted not through freedom from social roles, tradition, and political coercion, but through its dependence on divine grace and capacity to offer it to others. Language was not a veil that was ideally transparent to the true inner self, but a medium for invoking divine provision and instantiating relations of mutuality with others. Materiality was not an encumbrance conceived of as necessarily distinct from the human subject, but a medium in which human intentions and divine abundance could inhere.

More than transparent and self-authored words, then, sincerity implied relations of mutuality and felicitous connection. Merchants spoke of sensing this connection affectively, as interpersonal dynamics of affinity and ease. An industrialist from a Souk Jarba family explained good cinnamon by saying, "there is ease (aryahiyya). Some people, you sit with them, you relax (tartah; literally: "feel at ease"), feel good, they have a pleasant tongue. With others, you enter their factory, and you don't feel at ease somehow—even though they are excellent people (kwayyisin), and the goods are the same, excellent, even cheaper than elsewhere." He sensed sincerity affectively, as a connection in which two people felt at ease and in tune with one another. Some spoke of this affinity between transactors in terms of astrological pairing. Abu Tonji, a yarn importer and wholesaler based in the bazaar, said: "you know about the stars (al-nujum)? In spoken dialect you might talk about "good cinnamon," but scientifically ('ilmiyyan), it is about stars [astrology].... It means two people's stars go together (najmhun 'ala bad). It means your star is matched with his star (najmak 'ala najmuh)."

Many merchants understood the affective dynamics of such interpersonal affinity/sincerity to manifest themselves as serendipity. As I noted above, a seller's good cinnamon made a transaction felicitous, and was apparent in the ease with which the transacted commodity could be sold on. Outside the market, too, it was common to interpret serendipity as evidence of the affective dynamics of sincerity and interpersonal affinity. Fadi, a retail trader whom I visited regularly, called me as I was walking down a busy street in Aleppo. I happened to put my hand into my pocket just at the moment that he called and felt my phone vibrating. I answered and told him that if I had not put my hand on the phone at that instant, I would have missed his call. He replied: "You have a pure intention (niyyatak safiyyeh)! ... this means that there is sincerity. I do not have any agenda (maslaha) with you, and you do not have one with me. It is just pure friendship, for God (al-sadaqa lillah)." Fadi construed sincerity as an affect or atmosphere, interpreting serendipity as evidence of an atmospheric connection or resonance between us.

An Islamicate Cosmology of Grace

Adil Barakat was another merchant who spoke of sincerity as an ethical quality that could be sensed affectively, as an atmosphere between two people. In his early twenties, Adil worked alongside his father in their office in the bazaar, importing and wholesaling yarn. He said, "not everyone knows this term, 'good cinnamon.' Maybe no-one outside our market. But the idea is important: even if people don't know the word, everyone knows about it, they feel it. Some people you feel at ease with (tartah illuh), others you don't. This person is known, his reputation (suma'tuh) is like that." He continued, "Do you think you will be able to explain this cinnamon to your students? It is something real, something you feel. You need to feel it. We feel it. When you are here, you feel it." Adil's mother belonged to a family of elite Islamic religious scholars, and Adil was now active in a regime-approved Islamic youth organization. He keenly articulated its conceptions of value and morality, emphasizing the importance of paying obligatory zakat in full at 2.6 percent per year of investment assets. Yet when it came to discussing "good cinnamon," rather than talking about it as part of a distinctively Islamic approach to business, he emphasized the embodied rather than textual aspects of cinnamon ("you need to feel it") and its distance from formal or systematic knowledge ("not everyone knows this term"). According to Adil, the understanding that sincerity-in-exchange could be sensed affectively was widespread, yet there was no settled cultural agreement on the language in which this understanding could be formally expressed. Abu Tonji's contestation of the proper scientific register for describing this knowledge ("in spoken dialect you might call it 'good cinnamon'") seems to reinforce the point.

Munir, a former business partner of Adil's father, spoke of his familiarity with good cinnamon or sincerity as a form of knowledge that was relatively distant from religious experts and close to practical experience of commerce. A bazaar-based merchant in his fifties, Munir imported yarn from Turkey and manufactured and exported textiles to Europe. Asked about cinnamon, he said, "[a reputation for good] cinnamon comes from good interaction (mu'amaleh kwayyiseh). I give you goods on credit; if you don't sell them, you can give them back to me. It comes from having good ethics (adab), from religion (din), faith. We [merchants] combine work and spirituality: we will benefit you more than a hundred religious scholars!" Munir identified good cinnamon with the virtue, articulated in Islamic scripture, of buying and selling with "tolerance" (al-samh), citing a Prophetic hadith which praises a merchant who is "tolerant (samhan) when he buys, sells and settles debts."[6] Tolerance, or good cinnamon, meant "making the customer comfortable (yrayyih al-zabun), giving him credit, so that he doesn't need to burden himself with bank loans, and not charging him extra for late payments, as the banks do." But Munir also pointed out that Aleppine Jews, too, who had left the city and migrated to New York in the 1990s, recognized the virtue of good cinnamon. He recalled: "in the 1950s, in my father's time, there were a hundred or more Jewish merchants, all in textiles and yarn. We have had a relationship with these Jewish merchants for twenty-five years, until now they are buying from us. They say to us: 'Go buy from such-and-such, because their cinnamon is good.' They have a belief ('aqida) in good cinnamon, even though they are Jewish."

By citing a hadith, Munir related the virtue of good cinnamon to Islam. But he also saw it as entailing a form of knowledge that was acquired through practical experience rather than book learning, and that was mastered by merchants rather than religious scholars. And he highlighted that Jewish merchants also recognized and practiced this knowledge. This suggests that familiarity with this economic cosmology of grace was not limited to Muslims, nor identified with Islam in a confessionally exclusive sense. Indeed, the etiquette of civility—"God is the provider," "may God provide the return for you"—could be spoken to and by Christians as well as Muslims. Such deployments of cordiality and grace were not typically seen as the Islamic way of doing things. We might therefore think of this economic cosmology as Islamicate rather than Islamic.[7] In both these respects—entailing tacit rather than explicit knowledge, and not being exclusive to an Islamic confessional identity—the economic cosmology of grace differs from movements of Islamic economics and Islamic entrepreneurialism, which Hefner (2023) identifies as the main modes by which Islam has been brought to bear on the market in capitalist settings in the modern period.

Sincerity, Emotion, and Easternness

I now turn to a related way in which Aleppo's merchants construed sincerity as an interpersonal, affective connection; namely, through notions of Aleppineness, Easternness, and emotion. They evoked these connections at cultured evening gatherings by commenting on atmospheres of intimacy and serendipitous events.

We have already seen that the city's merchants could construe belief in cinnamon, and sensitivity to affects of sincerity, not only as an Islamic form of knowledge but as an Aleppine mode of commerce. Munir observed that both Muslim and Jewish traders from the city believed in the idea of cinnamon. Some distinguished between a Western cosmology of luck and an (implicitly Eastern) cosmology of grace. Adil's comment, "Do you think you will be able to explain this cinnamon to your students? . . . We feel it. When you are here, you feel it" presented cinnamon as a distinctively local apprehension of the economy, and as something that was culturally alien to Europe—and would therefore need careful explaining to European students. Similarly, after textile merchants in Mohannad's madafa discussed cinnamon, Mohannad's financial partner later added in a gloss for my benefit, "in Europe you call it luck, in Aleppo we don't have 'luck,' we have cinnamon." Like Adil, he presented cinnamon as a fault-line of East-West cultural difference, arguing that European conceptions of economy were disenchanted, whereas Aleppine and Eastern notions of economy had retained their spiritual dimensions.

Similar constructions of sincerity as a marker of East-West cultural difference are found in discourses about music in Aleppo. Jonathan Shannon in his ethnography of tarab music observes that performers and connoisseurs of tarab music in Aleppo construed emotional sincerity as an essential ingredient of a good performance, as a marker of Aleppineness, and as a quality disregarded by and often lacking in Western musical traditions. Tarab is a tradition of Eastern classical music that has been associated with the city of Aleppo from the late Ottoman period; it is an urban phenomenon "native to cities such as Cairo, Beirut and Damascus" (Racy 2003, 15–16), and Aleppo, in particular, has earned the epithet, "the city of tarab" (Shannon 2006). Critical to a good performance are flows of affect referred to as a mood of tarab. This is a kind of intersubjective rapture induced by the music or "the feeling you get when you listen to music and it just makes you want to say Ahh!!" (Shannon 2006, 161). Such a mood only emerges when there is a state of affective connection (tawasul) between the audience and performer. When such conditions obtain, a mood of tarab ripples through the audience: bodies gyrate and sway together, murmurs of appreciation are heard—bodies are united in permeability to this shared affect. Thus, Shannon suggests, "'tarab' comes to gloss the highly complex and intersubjective process of forming this connection—of achieving what Alfred Schutz (1977) called the 'mutual tuning-in relationship'" (Shannon 2006, 170).

According to Arab theorists and connoisseurs, the collective mood of rapture, and a good performance depend on the artist possessing emotional sincerity. Only an artist who displays qualities of emotional sincerity and intuition is able to generate an atmosphere of intimacy and an affective connection with the audience. This capacity for sincerity is seen as a characteristically Eastern, and particularly Aleppine, virtue: as proof of an Eastern spirit (ruh sharqiyya). Shannon wrote: "[e]motionality, as expressed by such qualities as sidq, is for many Aleppines an important if not defining component of their diverse self-conceptions," whereas techno-rationality, identified strongly with the West, was often understood implicitly to be the opposite of Arab emotionality and sentiment (2006, 172, 156, 66, xix). The Syrian music theorist Tawfiq al-Sabbagh argued that whereas European music-making prized technical expertise above all else, Oriental music was to be understood primarily as an "emotive expression" (al-Sabbagh 1950, quoted in Racy 2003, 3). Jihad Ali Racy notes that "totally extraneous to this domain" were "performers and composers of European music" (2003, 15).

Aleppine merchants spoke of emotionality in similar terms as a cultural boundary-marker between East and West. Mohannad's financial partner, Fadi, described emotionality as an aspect of Aleppine spirit. Several months into our acquaintance, as we sat with other merchants, he told me "You've become Aleppine (sirt halabi). You will go back, and you will be different. You will tell different jokes. Your friends will notice a difference. You have more emotionality." Abu Zaki, introduced in the previous chapter, was a well-built man in his late forties with an imposing demeanor, who made a living as an ad hoc importer and exporter and as a broker for Aleppo's textile industrialists. He contrasted the quality of emotionality with the techno-rationality of Western society: "emotions are what make you human. We are not machines. We think you have lost that in the West. There is so much pressure on people, they earn money, they produce more, but they have lost something important. If you are driving somewhere beautiful, in Ireland for example, with trees and nature, what is the first thing that comes to your mind? Don't you think of someone, your sweetheart, a friend, your mother? Don't you want to call them up and say, I am seeing this beautiful thing and thinking of you?" Like the musical theorists and connoisseurs quoted by Shannon, Abu Zaki construed emotional sincerity and sensitivity as a component of an authentically Aleppine modernity, counterposed to European modernity, which was technically powerful but unfeeling and unspiritual.

Sincerity at the Evening Gathering: Affective Economies of Easternness in an Era of Liberalization

For connoisseurs of tarab in Aleppo, a musician's sincerity was an essential ingredient for a good performance; without it, there would be no experience of tarab or rapturous tuning in between the performer and their listeners. Sincerity was, we might say, a critical element in an affective economy, or the circulation of affect, between musicians and their audiences. In twenty-first-century Aleppo, cultured evening gatherings were still understood as occasions to achieve this tuning in: to enact sincerity and an Eastern spirit of sentiment. The evening gathering was a "semi-public affair whose key ingredient is the concept of closeness or intimacy" (Shannon 2006, 140); it was understood to demarcate a zone of distinctively Eastern sociality. Similar observations can be made about the affective dynamics and concepts of selfhood among wholesaler merchants and their brokers in Aleppo. By engaging in intimate sociability during evening gatherings, when they displayed and invoked the affects of emotionality that bound them to each other, some wholesale merchants and their brokers inscribed their relations with each other in a register of mutuality and sincerity. In these circles of Aleppine merchants, just as Shannon observes among Aleppine musicians, emotional sensitivity was a highly valued aspect of the self. It was associated with qualities of sincerity and transparency and could be enacted during evening gatherings of merchants as a sign of the intimacy and closeness that was said to bind these individuals together.

Affects of intimacy and emotion experienced at evening gatherings could be read as indexing the sincerity of other merchants. Abu Zaki had spent an extended period of imprisonment for political activities through the 1980s and early 1990s, after which he had started his career as an accountant, working for a series of small and medium-sized enterprises. As he developed networks within mercantile clienteles, he started to act as an intermediary between industrialists and wholesalers, charging a commission of between 3 percent and 5 percent on deals he brokered. By the late 2000s, he was well-established in these networks and would often spend his mornings driving around the city, between its central districts and its urban periphery, calling on clients. His mobility also extended across Eurasia and beyond. In 2008, he visited China to arrange an order from the wholesale markets of Yiwu and Guangzhou through a Syrian agent, and he spent several months sojourning in Malaysia and southern Russia among members of the Syrian diaspora there, where he also exported some of the goods he had purchased in China. His livelihood depended on his ability to maintain urban, national, and international networks, and to connect these different scales of commerce by, as he put it, making relations (sawi 'alaqat) and maintaining relations within and between them.

As a mobile trader, Abu Zaki could face greater suspicion than sedentary merchants, since the "spatial distance" created by crossing borders allows "contradictory assertions to be made" (Ho 2002, 15, in Marsden 2016, 158). While some mobile brokers used Quranic symbols or ritual practices of prayer to present their moral selves to the merchants with whom they worked, Abu Zaki often displayed his moral self in other ways, in particular by foregrounding his quality of emotionality ('atifiyyeh). This was a multifaceted notion that encompassed sympathy for the suffering of others, emotional sensitivity toward music and poetry, and a capacity for heartfelt, sincere, and intuitive connection with others to whom one was bound in relations of genuine affection and solidarity. Merchants in Aleppo often prided themselves on their emotionality, seeing it as an ideal form of masculine selfhood.

The cultured evening gathering was the site par excellence in which to display this capacity and to experience the intimacy and affective bonds that it mediated. One evening in Aleppo in 2009, Abu Zaki and I attended an evening gathering held in the open courtyard of a renovated traditional-style house in a historic quarter of Aleppo. Our host was a textile industrialist for whom Abu Zaki worked as an ad-hoc broker. During the evening, Abu Zaki recited some verses from classical Arab masters, to which the small gathering listened in rapt attention, murmuring their appreciation "ya salam!" at the end of every line or so, showing that they were moved by the beauty of the poetry. Underlining the intimacy between them, our host told me that sometimes "Abu Zaki and I come here and cry together." Emotional sensitivity was connected to moral qualities of sincerity and transparency (see Shannon 2006). It was seen as typically Aleppine and meant that a person was unable to hide what they were thinking and feeling and would act on it spontaneously.

Evening gatherings could be an occasion to perform this spontaneity and experience the atmospheres and effects of sincerity. One summer evening Mohannad hosted several of his customers and business partners at a restaurant in Aleppo. The venue was an upmarket restaurant where well-heeled diners gathered in pavilions set amid gardens. We all smoked nargileh in the garden before heading into one of the pavilions. The guests included manufacturers like Mohannad, based in the industrial periphery of the city, who exported their textiles to the Gulf and Central Asia; local customers and workshop owners; and agents from further afield—one was visiting from Dubai, and another had recently returned from Britain. After dinner, we sat in the garden, eating from communal plates of fruit and sharing nargileh pipes. The conversation flowed with banter and joking; spirits were high and boisterous. A mood of gaiety rippled on the surface as the participants exchanged quick repartee; Abu Zaki told me afterward that he had sensed a feeling of ease (al-raha) pervading the whole gathering, and that this was a sign of the sincerity of all those gathered: "there was no deceit (ghish), there were no hidden interests." This comment mirrored the way that tarab artists talk about the atmosphere of a musical performance, arguing that a collective sense of rapture depends on an atmosphere that is "authentic—spontaneous, from the heart" (Shannon 2006, 167). For merchants, the evening gathering could be an occasion to enact affects of connection and an intuitive tuning-in with others, processes understood to index an underlying sincerity; such gatherings could be judged by whether or not they produced a tuned-in atmosphere.

Affects of sincerity could be experienced not only through a mood of tuned-in intimacy in face-to-face encounters, but also through long-distance connections mediated by letters and serendipitous phone calls. One evening in 2009, after having returned from several months sojourning in southern Russia with an

Aleppine business partner, Talal, who had settled there, Abu Zaki reflected on the emotional connection that bound him and Talal together. He talked of Talal's emotionality and said, "sometimes I sit reading a letter from Talal and I cry because of the emotionality in the letter." Another evening, when we were driving around the city together, Abu Zaki said, "the person I was sitting drinking coffee with yesterday evening is strong in emotionality, he has a strong personality... we were talking about Talal. I left, got in my car, and just at that moment Talal called and said, 'I was just thinking about you.'" Abu Zaki interpreted this serendipitous phone call, which came at the end of an evening gathering, as evidence of an affective connection between them, and of the sincerity and intuitive sincerity of each party.

There is a tradition, in both Arab musical theory (Racy 2003; Shannon 2006) and in mercantile sociability, of construing the evening gathering as an occasion to evoke and experience affects of sincerity. Yet as Abu Zaki reflected on his relationship with Talal, he also construed an affective economy of sincerity on a much larger scale. Abu Zaki's modest evening gatherings in Aleppo provided occasions for him to experience the affects of emotion and sincerity that bound him to a merchant in the Caucasus. While the cultured evening gathering can be identified as a distinctively urban and Aleppine heritage (Shannon 2006), it can also be seen in the context of Abu Zaki's circuits of mobility as a node in a transregional affective economy. This rescaled affective economy was emerging after the collapse of the Soviet Union, and during a period of economic liberalization, in which Syria's upwardly mobile merchant strata were forging new circuits of mobility within and beyond the Middle East. Abu Zaki was reflecting on his ties to Talal shortly after returning from his sojourn with him in southern Russia. He had stayed in the cities of Sochi and Nalchik, assessing the possibilities of establishing a home in the Caucasus, before deciding to return to Aleppo. Talal was an Aleppine of Circassian heritage who had moved from Syria to Sochi in southern Russia in the 1990s as part of a Circassian national return movement, which saw several thousand Syrian and Jordanian citizens of Circassian background emigrate from the Levant to southern Russia after 1991 after the collapse of the Soviet Union (Shami 1996). In 2009, after returning from the Caucasus, Abu Zaki remained in touch with Talal and continued to arrange the export of Chinese commodities to him.

The Circassian return movement and associated forms of circular mobility such as Abu Zaki's had started to fashion a new geography that overlapped formerly distinct regions of the Middle East and the ex-Soviet world. During the Cold War, dominant political geographies had configured these regions as separate cultural areas, but during the 2000s emerging patterns of mobility and commerce were inscribing them as a single geography. When Abu Zaki, leaving an evening gathering, received a phone call from Talal in Sochi and commented on the serendipity of it, attributing it to Talal's emotional sincerity, he experienced this emerging arena of transregional mobility as a coherent, affectively connected one. On his return to Aleppo, as well as invoking the emotionality that connected him to Talal, he observed that societies in southern Russia and the Arab world both exhibited a kind of intimacy and social solidarity which could not be found in Moscow or Europe: "I like the Caucasus more than Europe and Moscow, because there is more intimacy (hamimiyya): if you have a problem on the street, lots of people will come to help you." By describing the virtues of emotionality and intimacy as Eastern and as shared between the Arab world and the Caucasus, he rationalized the coherence of the affective arena that connected him to Talal.

With the opening to China and the facilitation after 1991 of mobility between Syria and southern Russia, constructs of Easternness and Aleppineness were being articulated in new ways. The affective economy of sincerity that Shannon described within Aleppo's musical gatherings was in some cases being reconfigured on an expansive, transregional scale. Evening gatherings were not only places to reproduce Aleppine tradition and bourgeois status within the city; they were also nodes in affective flows that connected merchants across borders and brought cities that had previously been located in separate culture regions into a common domain of Easternness. By evoking an idea of shared Easternness in these new transregional contexts through references to sincerity and serendipity, merchants could play an active role in restructuring the affective economies in which they operated. In doing so, they brought coherence to transregional commercial circuits which had developed during a period of economic liberalization, especially after the collapse of the Soviet Union in 1991.

Scholars of diaspora, transnationalism, and transregionalism have drawn attention to the role that Islam has played in fashioning expansive geographies and bringing coherence to networks that cross borders, as well as the role played by notions of Muslim modernity in creating transregional zones of connectivity.[8] Scholars have also highlighted the capacity of state-promoted frameworks of transregional mobility, such as the new Silk Road, to produce imaginative geographies that connect Muslim-majority societies to China and have shown how these strategically deploy Muslimness as a transregional identity.[9] Aleppine merchants' affective economies of sincerity and Easternness show that transregional connections could also be fashioned from below. They emerged as merchants drew on—but also restructured and rescaled—imaginative and affective resources rooted in urban locales and traditions.

This chapter explored the ways in which market exchange was moralized in Aleppo through discourses of sincerity. Although many scholars studying the interaction of Islam, commerce, and morality have focused on doctrinally elaborated movements of Islamic economics and pious entrepreneurialism, this chapter looked instead at everyday invocations of sincerity, exploring the meanings of this term in the wider context of economic liberalization. Aleppine merchants could construe sincerity not only as speaking from the heart but selling from the heart: willingly and with good grace (samhan). In shops in the bazaar, they could evoke sincerity through the mundane language of the sale, showing that they depended on and sought to transact divine grace. Conversely, insincerity implied transacting unwillingly or enviously. Grace and ungrace, sincerity and insincerity, were sensed affectively, as atmospheres of ease and mutual affinity, or unease and inauspiciousness. Commerce in Aleppo's bazaar involved transacting not only commodities but positive and negative affects of grace and envy.

The chapter also explored the ways in which market exchange was organized, through discourses of sincerity, into new imaginative and affective geographies in a period of economic liberalization. Though merchants could describe sincerity as an Islamic virtue, they could also construe belief in, and sensitivity to, affects of sincerity as marking out a cultural domain of Aleppineness and Easternness. Such mercantile discourses about commerce mirrored musical connoisseurs' discourses about music, as documented by Racy (2003) and Shannon (2006). Among both musicians and merchants, sincerity could be sensed as an affective "tuning-in," and among both groups it marked a domain of Aleppine cultural authenticity counterposed to European modernity, which was deemed technically advanced but unfeeling. The chapter traced how these ideas of urban heritage gained new significance as circuits of capital and commodities developed between Syria and the Caucasus during the 1990s and especially after 2000. Some Aleppine merchants brought coherence to these emerging circuits by construing them as affective geographies of sincerity, thereby embedding them in an imagined geography of Easternness.

Conclusion
EXCHANGE IDEOLOGIES AND THE FUTURES OF THE SYRIAN NATION

This book analyzed economic liberalization in Syria as a cultural and social process. Its main focus was on the ways in which Aleppo's traders construed, represented, and contested the nature of commerce, and the figure of the merchant, during the first decade of Bashar al-Asad's rule. For merchant elites in the city, this was a period of both change and stasis, as the regime sought to accelerate the liberalization of trade, while also retaining political control. The Alawite-dominated regime kept rival Sunni merchant elites divided through the selective distribution of opportunities for profit, by maintaining rival patron-client networks, and by inviting them to compete for precedence and urban notability in managed elections to merchant chambers. The book focused on pre-Baathist merchant notability, and a newer cadre of Sunni industrialists, both of whom had to contend for influence with a powerful state-dependent contractors' bourgeoisie. It considered two distinctive ways of organizing social membership of the market—patrilineal families and leader-centered gatherings—arguing that both served to incorporate Sunni merchant elites into the regime's patron-client networks. The rivalry between these groups, their forms of social membership of the market, their relations with the state, and the broader process of trade liberalization, shaped the ways in which they understood and represented commerce and what it meant to be a merchant in society. These cultural notions and representations of commerce and merchants were therefore always entangled in processes of state power and social and economic change.

Inspired by work on language ideologies, the book approached commerce, like language, as a form of human exchange that is ideologically construable—capable of being enacted and represented in ways that express social identities, statuses, and memberships. Its central theoretical claim is that ideas about commerce—whether implicit or explicit—mediate social relations; they can express claims of social identity and distinction, reinforce or contest social hierarchies, and draw boundaries of inclusion and exclusion. Questions of what it means to trade in a certain way—what modes of commerce are seen as proper and valuable, or as improper and discredited—are not incidental but central to commerce as a social fact. The meanings of commerce are established—both tacitly in embodied interaction, and explicitly in commentary and metapragmatic discourse—in ways that are shaped by and have deep significance for other social and political processes. Attention to the ways in which commerce and merchants are construed can therefore open up new perspectives on processes of social reproduction, contestation, and change. The book focused on four such processes during a period of politically controlled economic liberalization in Syria under Bashar al-Asad: social and economic rivalries created by the regime's divide-and-rule approach toward merchant elites; the organization of Aleppo's wholesale markets into patriarchal social groups subordinated to the regime's patron-client networks; contestations over what constituted modern forms of commerce after the regime promoted entrepreneurialism as a mode of national development; and the consolidation of transregional trading networks following the collapse of the USSR.

Notions of commerce and of merchants in Syria under Bashar al-Asad were bound up with processes of politically managed economic liberalization that had received renewed impetus since the early 1990s. The early Baathist state had nationalized large swathes of commerce and industry, and much of Aleppo's merchant bourgeoisie had sided against the regime in the late 1970s and early 1980s. However, since the 1990s the regime had increasingly sought to allow space for the private sector to operate and, especially after Bashar al-Asad's accession in 2000, to win over Aleppo's merchant bourgeoisie as a political support base. The overriding logic of its approach to economic liberalization in this period was to attract and mobilize merchant capital while maintaining political control. Some of the ways it did so in Aleppo were by recruiting influential merchants and industrialists into patron-client networks, positioning them as nodes of state-society relations and as a type of urban notability, and balancing rival blocs of merchant elites.

These strategies shaped the ways that economic elites thought about and represented commerce as a social practice. Chapter 2 focused on the tension between state-dependent clans and more autonomous merchant elites, and their contests for notability and influence in the city. The latter asserted their social distinction and urban legitimacy vis-à-vis the former through claims about what constituted Aleppine modes of commerce and exchange. The established families' intertwining exchange ideologies—of commerce, marriage, and language—were ways in which "urban" merchants distinguished themselves from the state and its proxies. They reflected both a history of tension between Aleppo's merchants and the Baathist state in Damascus, and an ongoing a contest for urban notability and leadership between Aleppo's relatively autonomous commercial bourgeoisie and the state-dependent bourgeoisie. This rivalry was expressed formally in elections to Aleppo's Chambers of Commerce and Industry, but it was also expressed in the everyday, through mundane expressions of exchange ideologies which served to create and reinforce distinctions between urban and rural identities. Both electoral contestations and everyday modes of differentiation reflected the regime's divide-and-rule approach to managing merchant elites in Aleppo.

Another feature of economic liberalization in this period was the emergence of merchants as public figures. The regime invited would-be clients to boost their profile by becoming public sponsors of urban institutions. Chapter 6 analyzed how under Bashar al-Asad, leading merchants could position themselves socially as celebrities and civic patrons through acts of euergetism. This revived an older idea of mercantile status—that merchants could be patrons of the city—but also rendered this status into an instrument of political control. The public sponsorship of sports clubs afforded new elites a claim to urban notability, which rivaled that of the old incumbents; it played into the regime's divide-and-rule approach to merchant elites and their incorporation into patron-client networks in the city's merchant chambers. To be identified in this way as a patron of the city was also to be publicly subordinated as a client of the regime. The construal of what it meant to be a leading merchant in this period was connected to the ways in which the regime managed economic elites in a period of politically controlled liberalization. Attention to shifting notions of commerce and of merchants in Syria therefore contributes to analyses of divide-and-rule politics in Syria (Salamandra 2013; Ismail 2019) but focuses on urban and rural identities, and the distinction between pedigree and those of humbler social backgrounds rather than sectarian identities.

Another analytic concern brought into focus in the book was the way that Aleppo's wholesale markets were organized socially. Scholars analyzing how the Syrian regime co-opted elite merchants during periods of economic liberalization have focused on the formation of economic networks and business networks.[1] Although the study of business networks reveals a good ideal about the structure of the state and the interests of crony capitalists, the forms of power, obligation, and status through which the wider merchant bourgeoisie was incorporated into the political economy of the late Baathist state are better revealed by a study of the membership structures of wholesale markets. Chapters 3 and 4 focused on extended patrilineal families, and chapters 5 and 6 on a leader-centered peer network or loyal gathering. These were analyzed as structures of social membership in the markets; structures through which economic actors accessed credit, information, arbitration, and judicial rights. Persons accessed these goods primarily as members of a merchant house (bait) or through their membership of a mercantile gathering (jama'a).

Both these membership structures were shaped by the institutionalized ways in which the regime interacted with merchants. Both became salient in the absence of formal financial and legal structures and institutions that would have enabled economic actors to access credit and rights as individuals. And the regime strengthened them both by empowering patriarchal figures as relays of state-society relations, and by ceding to them the tasks of regulating access to credit and of dispute resolution. In turn, these membership structures inserted merchant elites into the regime's patron-client networks and gave rise to particular notions and ideals of commerce that reinforced the political status quo. Among established merchant families, respectable commerce was figured in the model of the patriarchal family, in the capacity of men to command credit from peers and obedience from sons, and to maintain relations of friendship with contemporaries in the regime. Among leader-centered peer networks of industrialists and brokers who did not hail from established families, commerce was construed as a form of mutuality beyond the family structure. This ideology of mutuality emerged as part of a hospitality economy, in which persons accessed multiple goods—commodities, credit, information, commercial rights—as guests, in exchange for political loyalty to the host, who himself sought preferment from regime elites.

Paying attention to the different ways in which commerce was construed as a social practice also revealed that trade was central to the ways in which political, cultural, and economic elites imagined and contested what it meant to be modern. The notion of merchants as patriarchal authority figures chafed against official discourses of modernity promoted by Bashar al-Asad's government. Official documents championing the social market economy promoted entrepreneurial modernity exemplified by youthful, outward-looking, technocratically skilled, and politically compliant economic subjects who, freed from the heavy hand of tradition, would be able to innovate, express their natural dynamism, and become job creators rather than job seekers. There was little in official discourse to trouble the assumption that such modern entrepreneurs were male. Yet some reformers and would-be social entrepreneurs equated the heavy hand of tradition with patriarchal authority. They espoused the regime's entrepreneurial modernity by figuring certain modes of commerce—trading by sitting in the bazaar and presiding over the labor of sons—as obstacles to national modernity. The heads of patriarchal families, who maintained relations of friendship with political elites, responded by figuring their own modes of commerce in terms of authentic Islamic modernity, as both economically efficient and a bulwark against moral decay in society. On both sides, commerce ideologies were bound up with the contestation of modernity. This contestation reveals a contradiction in the regime's approach to economic liberalization; it championed the entrepreneurial dynamism of individuals, while maintaining patriarchal structures of economic participation in Aleppo.

The final process analyzed in the book in which construals of commerce played a role was the emergence and intensification of transregional trading circuits after the collapse of the USSR in 1991. Chapter 7 argued that Aleppo's merchants could invoke understandings of the economy—as the circulation of divine provision and of affects of sincerity—to negotiate relations of moral identification and solidarity with their customers. In some cases, these relations of identification and solidarity could transcend regional, confessional, and ethnic divides. Ideas of Aleppine and Eastern modes of commerce and interaction could be invoked to establish affinities between Muslim traders in Syria and Jewish traders in New York; and between Arab traders in Aleppo and Circassian traders in the Caucasus. In these cases, commerce ideologies and their accompanying affects of sincerity served to bring coherence to trading geographies that had emerged after the collapse of the USSR.

Cultural economic anthropologists have long explored folk models of the economy, and some of the construals of commerce documented in this book could have been analyzed in some of the terms they have proposed, such as cosmologies of market exchange (Elyachar 2005), cosmoeconomics (Da Col 2012; Gudeman 2012), or economic theologies (Mittermaier 2014, 2019; Henig 2019, 2020). I chose instead to approach these notions as exchange ideologies, in order to emphasize that Aleppine merchants' constructions of exchange, like construals of language, were contestable, bound to specific social and political interests, and construed in interaction. Connotations of exchange, the meanings of particular ways of exchanging, were construed in the minutiae of speech and embodied interaction, in metapragmatic discourse, and in spatial frameworks—whether the mise-en-scène of the shop decorated by Islamic calligraphy, the hospitality room designated as a madafa, or a red tablecloth spread before guests. Gendered social hierarchies too—whether the patriarchal merchant house or the leader-centered gathering—were reproduced and reinforced through the ways in which exchange was construed and represented in interaction. For this reason, exchange ideologies can be seen as a form of micro-politics.[2]

Aleppo in the Syrian Conflict

"O Aleppo, where are you?" chanted a crowd in the Syrian coastal city of Baniyas protesting against the regime of Bashar al-Asad in 2011.[3] The crowd had expected that Aleppo, Syria's commercial and industrial hub, would be one of the cities at the forefront of nationwide protests, especially since many of the city's merchants had supported the previous major challenge to the Asad regime, in 1979–82, funding opposition groups and shutting their shops in solidarity. Yet thirty years after that political challenge to the Asad regime, much of the urban bourgeoisie in Aleppo opted instead to sit on the sidelines. Aleppo was to become perhaps the most heavily contested city in Syria's civil war, yet large swathes of the merchant bourgeoisie remained ambivalent about siding against the regime. One explanation is that as general beneficiaries of economic liberalization, Aleppo's merchants were economically invested in the status quo stability (Hinnebusch and Zintl 2015b). The regime's willingness to use extreme force, its ability to limit defections, the fracturing of the opposition, and a perceived lack of credible alternative, arguably made other calculations too risky (Haddad 2013). Another credible explanation, at least in the early period of the uprising, invokes ideological convergence: the merchants' religious bourgeois ethic of self-reliance and hard work aligned with the regime's post-Baathist neoliberal ideology (Pierret 2015).

Other approaches seek to explain behavior in other terms than interests or explicit ideological commitments. Lisa Wedeen (2019) argued for the significance of ambivalence in keeping many on the sidelines of political protests in Syria, and analyzed the circulations of affect that generated ambivalent attachments to the status quo. Empirically, her analysis focuses on the ambivalent middle—those who did not develop explicit commitments one way or the other. Theoretically, she argues that social actors positioned themselves politically not only on the basis of how they perceived and calculated their interests, nor on the basis of their explicitly avowed ideological preferences, but as a result of affective attachments to fantasies of the good life which the regime had become adept at producing, and which had a partially captivating effect even on those who recognized their incoherence. Wedeen thinks of this effect as the workings of ideology. But it is different from what Paul Friedrich (1989) terms "critical-Marxist" conceptions of ideology. Wedeen's claim is not that social actors misrecognized their interests, but that interests were not the most important factor in explaining motivation and behavior. Equally significant were the forces—the affectively compelling "fantasies," the "epistemic murk"—that generated ambivalence and attachments to the old order, and stopped social actors reaching a point of "creative political judgement" (Wedeen 2019, 4).

This book has not sought to explain merchants' positions in the Syrian conflict, nor to theorize their ambivalence during the crisis. But the processes it analyses may go some way to explaining some Aleppine merchants' initial attachments to the old order in the early stages of the uprising in 2011. The regime's divide-and-rule approach to merchant elites, and their co-option into patron-client networks, meant that they had little interest in forming a common front against the regime, and little opportunity to do so. Moreover, the structures of social membership in the market identified in the book meant that it was not only the notables—the economic elites who participated directly in patron-client relations with the regime—who were invested in the status quo. Below these established elites, aspiring elites were incorporated into the market and civil society through structures that were ultimately subordinated to the regime's patron-client relations with the regime, also giving them a stake in the status quo. Those who had found a place or were promised a future place in the market and in civil society through these structures were also incorporated in that way into the polity.

These structures of social membership afforded elites and aspiring elites not only economic goods but a kind of citizenship: a sense of inclusion in the market, through access to credit and information, and inclusion in civil society, through access to arbitration and petitioning channels. These goods were conferred not through abstract citizenship rights, but through small-scale and local structures—the family and merchant gathering. Through membership in these social formations, individuals were also recognized as moral persons possessing particular obligations and reputations. These membership structures therefore conferred both a kind of inclusion or citizenship in the polity, and a locally meaningful moral identity that mediated that citizenship. By the same token, membership structures were also exclusive and barriers to entry for newcomers. Yet the ability of the regime to co-opt a newcomer such as Mohannad through managed elections and civic sponsorship, and to offer patronage to social formations other than established patrilineal kinship groups, suggests a degree of flexibility in the regime's approach to state-society relations where urban bourgeoisies were concerned, and a capacity to incorporate aspiring economic elites in Aleppo.

The sense of membership in the polity conferred by the social structures of the market was not uniformly distributed, even before 2011. Individuals denied credit, or arbitration rights or favorable outcomes, or some other good, may have thought differently about it from those who found membership worked in their favor more often. Some individuals may have chafed more than others against the constraints imposed on them by membership even before the conflict, for a variety of reasons. And social membership may have meant less and less after the uprising was repressed and the conflict militarized. The Syrian crisis radically shifted the terrain on which individuals apprehended the value and meanings of social membership in the market, and forced many to consider alternatives. One example is Abu Zaki. Before 2011, his unwillingness always to remain silent about his years of political imprisonment in a Syrian jail, and his continuing interest in human rights, had sometimes put him at odds with his friend Mohannad; however, the relationship had remained a close one and he was one of the most loyal members of Mohannad's gathering. The Syrian crisis radically raised the stakes of their different political orientations, making them more rigid. Abu Zaki went into exile where he was freer to speak and publish. Mohannad, facing the looting of his factory, declared himself for the regime's militias. The bonds of loyalty that had underpinned Abu Zaki's membership of Mohannad's gathering were broken.

The crisis led elite merchants to reassess the value of proximity to the regime, and their position within patron-client networks, in different ways. While Mohannad and his financial partner sided with the regime's militias, enjoying their protection, other leading industrialists declared themselves against the regime, fled, and suffered the confiscation and destruction of the assets they left in Syria. Those who remained sometimes reaped the benefits; Mohannad finally succeeded in his ambition to become a board member of Aleppo's Chamber of Industry. Yet below the elite level, the value of social membership of the market, and the sense of inclusion in the polity they conferred, also shifted radically between 2011 and 2012. The militarization of the conflict put the polity in question, destroyed markets, and led to the emergence of a war economy. The role that patrilineal families and loyal gatherings played under the developing conditions of the war economy is a question for further research. What needs did merchants have for credit, arbitration, and petitioning of the regime? What role did the old membership structures play in meeting these needs: how did the structures adapt, rupture or reform? The same questions can be asked of processes of displacement and resettlement.[4] Many merchants left Aleppo for other countries in the region, notably Turkey, Lebanon, Jordan, Egypt, and the United Arab Emirates. What role did older structures of market membership, and the deep connections forged in Aleppo's markets over the years, play in shaping where they went, and whether and how they re-established themselves in commerce?

Connections forged in Aleppo's marketplaces before the conflict facilitated commerce, resettlement, and reemployment after 2011. One example of this is in patterns of migration between Aleppo and the city of Yiwu in China's southeastern Zhejiang Province. Since 2000, Yiwu has become an important wholesale hub supplying markets across the world, including in Syria, with low-grade commodities of everyday use, ranging from toothbrushes and stationery to tools and kitchenware.[5] Syrian merchants began visiting the city and residing there as commercial agents in the late 1990s, with around 50 Syrian trading offices established in the city by 2006, and around 350 by 2011 (Anderson 2020). Merchants from the House of Umar were among those who opened offices in Yiwu in 2007, provisioning importers based in Souk Jarba in Aleppo. When the conflict in Syria was militarized in 2011–12, several hundred Syrian men in their teens and twenties fled the country and the prospect of forced military service, and found refuge and employment in trading offices in Yiwu; in many cases they were relatives of the traders already settled in Yiwu, but in some cases they were also employees of relatives (Anderson 2018a, 2019a).

Ghayth left Aleppo for Yiwu in this way in 2015 at the age of twenty-one. His passage to China was arranged by Mahmoud, a thirty-one-year-old merchant from the House of Umar, who had sold household items in Souk Jarba before his commercial partnership broke up. In 2007, Mahmoud Umar had set out on his own, establishing two shops elsewhere in Aleppo and one in the region of al-Bab in the Euphrates valley. In order to provision these shops, Mahmoud first bought from wholesalers in Souk Jarba, but then started to visit Yiwu, purchasing one or two containers of household items each trip, and storing the goods in his warehouse in the east of Aleppo. By 2014, this area in the east of Aleppo was controlled by opposition fighters. Mahmoud's employee Ghayth, who was unrelated to him, but who credited him with good cinnamon, made several trips crossing enemy lines in order to empty the warehouse for his employer. Then, on one occasion in 2015, on his return to the regime-controlled area in the west of Aleppo, he was arrested and imprisoned by the regime. His release was eventually secured; and Mahmoud Umar arranged for him to travel to Yiwu to work in a trading office there. Before Ghayth left, he made one last trip to the region of al-Bab, controlled by the Islamic State, in order to do a final stock take and close the shop for his employer from the House of Umar. By 2017 Ghayth had established himself as an unofficial export agent in Yiwu, arranging for shipments of goods duty-free through Turkey to areas in northern Syria controlled by Syrian opposition forces. Goods shipped in this way were sold in duty-free hubs in opposition-controlled areas such as Sarmada and Manbij and then sold in Aleppo, smuggled back into Turkey, or transported into northern Iraq. The connection between Mahmoud and Ghayth shows that patrilineal kinship groups, and the bonds of loyalty that grew up in their interstices through employer-employee relationships, operated as structures of social membership not only within Aleppo, but also on a transregional scale.

Another question requiring research is the relationship between displacement, conflict, and urban notability. Several younger men from the House of Umar who could have faced the prospect of military service left Syria, but some older members of the family remained in Aleppo to keep a claim on their property and to maintain a presence in the city. How did displacement and the conflict change merchants' perceptions of the city, of the status of urban notability, and the ways in which they sought to claim it? By 2020, a senior member of the Umar house had been appointed to the board of the Chamber of Industry, and members of Fuad Umar's family were starting to rebuild some of their shattered shops in Souk Jarba. Those merchant elites who remained in Aleppo undoubtedly saw opportunities for economic and political influence by maintaining and extending their presence in the markets and chambers. But given the changing political landscape, and the increasing influence of rurally based clans who have been active as militias, what ideas of urbanity, civic leadership, and patronage of the city are different social actors deploying in and through their reconstruction efforts and representation in the chambers?

Exchange Ideologies in the Diaspora

This, in turn, raises the question of exchange ideologies and construals of commerce. The book has argued that structures of social membership in the market and ideologies of commerce and exchange are two sides of the same coin. What new understandings of commerce and of merchants have arisen under conditions of war and displacement, and how are they related to changing structures of market membership and notability? Within Syria, the war economy saw the emergence of new sources of revenue and new forms of predation. During the turn to reconstruction, the regime is seeking new sources of revenue, and clan militias and families of pedigree continue to vie for influence. What notions of prestigious and illegitimate modes of commerce are at play, and how are they connected to construals of language, marriage, and exchange with the regime? Beyond Syria: what role do notions of Aleppine modes of commerce play in underpinning trading networks in the diaspora, and in connecting Syria to the diaspora?

Although much of this research remains to be done, I conclude the book with some initial observations about exchange ideologies that have emerged in the Syrian merchant diaspora. As the conflict in Syria was militarized, battle lines rigidified particularly along divisions of religion, ethnicity, and sect. Aleppine merchants displaced to the city of Yiwu observed from afar. But by reflecting on commerce and its relation to society and the Syrian polity, they also engaged in debates about the preconflict and postconflict nation. The following observations are drawn from interviews with merchants conducted in 2016. They show how Syrian and other Arab merchants construed commerce in ways that contested an emerging culture of sectarianism in the region, and as a means of fashioning an alternative national imaginary.

They presented a commercial ethic of interaction as an alternative to forms of religiosity and morality that emphasized identity and difference. Several remembered a time before 2011 when this commercial ethic of interaction had been the prevailing form of (implicit) religiosity and had marginalized more explicit and identity-focused modes of religiosity. To make the point, they recounted cases where people discovered that they had been ignorant of another person's true confessional identity. These were, in part, nostalgic reflections on a moral culture that had been lost, and which wistfully recalled a time before the rise of sectarianism when confessional differences had been unmarked. But in recalling and celebrating an implicit mercantile ethic of interaction, they were also engaging in an active process of heritage-making, constructing a shared idea of Syrianness and Muslimness at a time when these notions were contested and in flux.

These accounts contribute to a recent body of scholarship which considers how heritage can be both affected and generated by war and conflict and can "participate in the recovery and remaking of communities" (Sørensen and Viejo-Rose 2015, 1). This scholarship has been particularly valuable in highlighting how, as well as destroying heritage or precipitating attempts to mitigate destruction, conflict can generate new sites of heritage and add symbolic meanings to existing sites (Sørensen and Viejo-Rose 2015, 8). It is well-recognized that the heritage that is affected and remade through conflict comprises both tangible and intangible forms. But the data I present here suggest that as well as knowledge, skills, and abilities, the valued stock of intangible heritage can comprise forms of ignorance and indifference as well as positive bodies of knowledge. As Roy Dilley (2010, 177) argues, "moral value is placed upon knowledge and ignorance in various ways."[6] In some social and political contexts, ignorance can be considered a virtue. In recalling a world in which ignorance of confessional identity did not matter, because it did not alter the ways in which a person was actually known, these merchants placed a form of not-knowing at the heart of their conceptions of valued Syrian heritage.

Abu Samad was an Aleppine industrialist who had established a series of manufacturing enterprises in Aleppo in the 1980s, producing shoes and cardboard boxes for the domestic market, and underwear for department stores across Europe. He had taken advantage of the increased economic opening under Bashar al-Asad to import cars and tractors from Korea, and had also established an exhibition center next to his car dealership in the north of Aleppo. In the civil conflict that broke out in 2011, this area became a battleground between competing factions; many of his premises were badly damaged, and cars and heavy machinery were looted. He was able to move one of his factories to the regime-controlled city of Lattakia; but having to contend with a pervasive lack of stability, and an erratic electricity supply, he decided to leave the country, moving his wife and four sons to Dubai, and then moving again with two of his sons to China, where he settled in the city of Yiwu, a city of two million people and the site of the largest wholesale market of small commodities in the world. Here he established a design and manufacturing business, producing gift boxes and Arabic language textbooks for wholesale customers in the Emirates, Kuwait, and Saudi Arabia.

I met and interviewed Abu Samad in Yiwu in 2016. As I sat across from him in a booth in the city's wholesale Futian market, Abu Samad began to reflect on the conflict and on what had been lost. He showed me a series of photographs on his mobile phone—the roundabout in the center of the city, which he had paid to have built and donated to the Baath Party; pictures of his car dealership and exhibition center in the north of the city, in various stages of construction. He showed me a picture of his pride and joy—a country house he had built outside of the city, with a well-manicured garden. He remembered how he used to cultivate this with his own hands, every morning, rising at dawn before taking a coffee with his wife a couple of hours later, and then heading into the office for a long day of work. Then Abu Samad flicked forward to images of his business premises after they had been torn up and plundered by looters. He remembered the life he had left behind through images of construction, cultivation, and family intimacy; juxtaposing them with images of destruction and chaos of the kind that now accompany any news story of Aleppo. Against this backdrop of crisis, the images through which he recalled his past life spoke most of all of ordinariness: a man tending his garden, the forecourt of a car dealership, a roundabout in the middle of town. They spoke of his success and civic standing, of course, but also recalled the everyday, the mundane, and unremarkable: a time when life had been full of unmarked routines—a morning coffee between husband and wife, a drive into the office.

Many of the Syrian businessmen I met in Yiwu referred to the situation in their country as "the crisis" (al-azmeh), a term that suggests a departure from normality and the hope of a return to it. It implies a series of binaries: disruption and routine; exceptional and ordinary; marked and unmarked. I had expected Abu Samad to reflect on the assets he had forfeited or been forced to leave behind, and on the prospects for recovering them after the conflict. But the montage of images instead suggested a longing for the everyday, for a time when daily life could be taken for granted, assumed, and left unremarked upon. He expressed his nostalgia for the unmarked in another way. He had recently received a phone call from another Syrian manufacturer, a prominent industrialist who had sat on the board of the city's Chamber of Industry. This man had called Abu Samad to tell him of the death of a mutual friend. Everyone had known the deceased to be a Christian, whose family origins were in a town in Syria known for its famous monastery. When his family had buried him, people were shocked that he had been interred according to Muslim rites. The man, it turned out, had been Muslim all along, but no one had known. Everyone had simply assumed that, coming from a monastery town, he was a Christian. "We had been living and interacting with him all the time, and never known," Abu Samad said. "People never used to talk about these things."

The point for Abu Samad was that while confessional identity might matter at the end of life, prior to that point, this individual was fully known through the way in which he conducted himself in social exchange and commercial interaction. This conception of what it took to know someone was, he suggested, another aspect of life that had simply been taken-for-granted in Syria before the conflict. The way to know someone was through their implicit ethic of interaction rather than through any explicit identity markers. This ethos was expressed through the formulation that "religion is about interaction" (al-din muʻamaleh). In Islamic jurisprudence, the category of social interaction (muʻamaleh) is often distinguished from the category of ritual obligations and worship (al-ʻibadeh). To say "religion is about the ethics of interaction" is to say that religion is not primarily about the devotional practices which distinguish different ritual identities. Abu Samad offered this conception of true religion as a criticism of the emphasis on sectarian identity and difference that many in Yiwu saw as undermining national unity across the Arab world. He saw a mode of religiosity that emphasized identity and difference as a foreign import. He saw the current emphasis on the Sunni-Shia distinction, in particular, as something puzzling, asking me where it had come from, since it was not indigenous to the region. This kind of analysis of the rise of sectarianism should not be stigmatized as a "conspiracy theory" (see Pipes 1999), but seen as a rhetorical strategy that seeks to challenge the hegemony of identity-focused modes of religion, and to undermine their legitimacy by classifying them as non-indigenous impositions which had little to do with authentically Syrian ways of living religion in everyday life.

The rise of sectarianizing forces and other modes of religiosity that emphasized rigid constructions of identity in the late twentieth and early twenty-first centuries has not been limited to Syria nor to Arab or Muslim settings. And among the Arabic-speaking merchants whom I interviewed in Yiwu, expressions of nostalgia for an age of innocence, when confessional differences were said to be unmarked or unremarked upon in daily life, were current beyond the Syrian diaspora. Yahya was an Algerian businessman in his early thirties, who managed an export office in the city in which he was also a junior partner to two older businessmen based in Algeria. When I met him in the summer of 2016, he was trying to source forty pre-fabricated homes required by a petrochemical company for their workers who were drilling in the Algerian desert. Toward the end of the evening spent in his apartment in the center of Yiwu, he offered a similar narrative to Abu Samad's. He recalled a popular merchant who had traded for years in Algeria; he had lived among the community, doing business and dealing or interacting (al-taʻamul) with others in a respectable way. When he died, his will was opened, revealing instructions that he should be buried according to Jewish rites. This occasioned some surprise: no one had known what his confessional identity was and had simply assumed that he was Muslim.

Yahya's point was not that the man had felt it prudent to conceal his Jewish identity in a Muslim-majority society, nor was he implying surprise that a Jewish merchant should have interacted in a respectable way. Like Abu Samad's nearly identical narrative, the point was that during their lifetime, the deceased had been known fully through the ways in which he had conducted himself in commercial interaction. Whether or not his and Abu Samad's narratives offered a historically accurate general account of the degree of knowledge and perception of confessional identities in these societies was beside the point: the message of the parable, which Yahya made explicit, was the normative one that "religion is interaction." The core of religion, Yahya implied, was decency and sincerity of conduct not unique to any particular confessional tradition rather than the devotional practices which marked particular ritual identities. Neither Abu Samad nor Yahya were advocating an explicit framework of tolerance or pluralism that would celebrate diversity or mediate between competing religious identities. Rather they were idealizing an implicit practical habitus or way of dwelling in the world, in which religious identity and difference were left diffuse rather than systematically elaborated.[7] After 2011, when Syrian traders found themselves contending with an intensely sectarianized environment, and mobile merchants often found themselves contending with suspicion arising from global discourses in which Syria was associated with Islamism and sectarianism, they have emphasized their understanding of sincere interaction as the essence of proper moral personhood, true religion, and prewar Syrian culture. By sustaining and evoking these memories, merchants were mobilizing intangible heritage to contest sectarianized notions of culture and polity that, having been marginal, they now saw as becoming mainstream.

These narratives illustrate the central argument of the book, that the ways in which commerce is construed and represented are often part of wider political processes and contestations, and can be a lens on those processes. Before 2011, Aleppine merchants construed and represented their modes of exchange in ways that were shaped by the regime's attempt to retain political control while fostering a degree of economic liberalization. Merchants' exchange ideologies shed light on the regime's divide-and-rule approach to economic elites and the contests for notability that it generated; its patron-client relations and state patriarchy; and its partly contradictory promotion of entrepreneurial modernity. Exchange ideologies of Aleppine commerce reveal how merchants reimagined boundaries of moral community in adaptive ways that took advantage of new opportunities for transregional mobility after the collapse of the USSR. These final reflections from the diaspora show that after 2011, exchange ideologies became a medium for contesting the nature of the Syrian polity. Most anthropology of trade focuses on economic practices and on the forms of ethnic or religious identity that bind trading networks together. This book focused instead on the socially and politically pertinent ways in which commerce was imagined and represented. Studying commerce in this wider sense can provide insights not just into economic strategy but into wider Syrian worlds.

Notes

ACKNOWLEDGMENTS

1. In accordance with anthropological conventions, pseudonyms have been used throughout the book.

INTRODUCTION

1. For studies of language ideologies and identity in the Arab world, see Suleiman 2011, 2013, 2019; Hachimi 2013; Lian 2020.

2. See Hatem 2000, in Joseph 2005, 158; Al-Mughni and Tetreault 2000; Jad, Johnson, and Giacaman 2000; Lazreg 2000; Swirski 2000, in Joseph 2005, 158.

3. Women from lower socioeconomic positions did sometimes provide menial labor in spaces of male sociability.

4. In family homes, gender segregation was observed when men were present from outside the family.

5. Rabo (2005) reports that the role of female capital in Aleppo's markets was limited.

6. As Woolard observes (1998, 6), ideology in this sense is similar to Bourdieu's conception of doxa—practical knowledge that "rarely rises to discursive consciousness"—and the concept of habitus, the embodied structures that generate it.

7. For further critiques of the reification of language, see Briggs 1998; Kulick 1992; Lucy 1993; Mannheim 1986; Rumsey 1990; all cited in Woolard 1998.

8. See Kienle 1994, Haddad 2020.

9. See Kienle 1994; Perthes 1997; Haddad 2012, 2020.

10. On the relationship between the state and patriarchal forms in the Middle East, see Charrad 2000; Hatem 1986; Joseph 1996b; Altorki 2000; Amawi 2000; Hoodfar 2000; Lazreg 2000; Giacaman, Jad, and Johnson 2000.

11. On this topic, see Salamandra and Stenberg 2015; Sottimano and Selvik 2008.

12. On the ways in which entrepreneurialism has been used to figure modernity, see Sloane 1998; Osella and Osella 2009; Hoesterey 2015.

13. Deeb 2011; Shannon 2006; Peterson 2011; Kassab 2010.

14. I conducted research into trans-Asian commerce in Yiwu in southeastern China between 2016 and 2019 as part of a project led by Professor Magnus Marsden and funded by the European Research Council.

15. See Salamandra 2004.

16. See Salamandra 2004; Ismail 2018.

17. See, for example, Viejo-Rose 2013; Sorensen and Viejo-Rose 2015.

1. ALEPPO IN SPACE AND TIME

1. In 2008, Muslim merchants in Aleppo's markets tended to speak fondly of their interactions with Aleppine Jewish traders and, in some cases, retained economic partnerships with them.

2. The term akabir implied both respectable behaviour and elevated status.

3. This section draws on Abboud 2018.

4. Daher (2019, 6) reports that Iraq "became Syria's largest single export destination with sales of $2.3bn in 2010 out of a total of $12.3bn."

5. See Aita 2004, Hourani 2004, Habeeb 2002, Abboud 2010.

6. Daher (2019, 6) reports that "Trade liberalisation led to a significant increase in imports of foreign products—a surge of 62 percent between 2005 and 2010—rather than exports of Syrian products, which grew by only 34 percent in the same period."

7. Under Bashar al-Asad, selected businessmen (similarly to religious leaders) gained prominence as the heads of charities dispensing social welfare. This continued a trend started in the 1990s in which the state licensed some charities as part of the shift to private enterprise, after most had been repressed during the 1980s (Abboud 2018).

2. EXCHANGE IDEOLOGIES OF URBAN-RURAL DIFFERENCE

1. On nostalgia for an older, more moral era—but coded as tribal rather than urban, see Rabo 1986 and Chatty 1986.

2. See, e.g., Malinowski 2013 and Mauss 2002.

3. Mansur Hussain, Al-'asha'ir fi Halab wa'l-thawra [Clans in Aleppo and the Revolution]. Al-Jisr newspaper, July 13, 2019, online.

4. Asasneh clan, Facebook profile, https://www.facebook.com/profile.php?id=100069106311982.

5. Mansur Hussain, Al-'asha'ir fi Halab wa'l-thawra [Clans in Aleppo and the Revolution].

6. Mansur Hussain, Al-'asha'ir fi Halab wa'l-thawra [Clans in Aleppo and the Revolution].

7. Mansur Hussain, Al-'asha'ir fi Halab wa'l-thawra [Clans in Aleppo and the Revolution].

8. Scholars observed that far from being a purely technical commercial mechanism, modern accounting is "irredeemably social" (Miller 1994, 4; McPhail, Gorringe and Gray, 2004) because it is a way of making moral claims by seeking to persuade audiences that particular business transactions and persons are morally legitimate (Strathern 2000).

9. Commercial accounting has functioned as a technology of the self, enabling a person to trace and work on their moral development, across a range of historical and cultural settings. For early modern European merchants, account books were a means of acquiring a "prudent disciplined mind" (Espeland and Carruthers 1991; see also Jacobs and Walker 2004 for a contemporary example). In eighteenth-century Europe, clean and neat account books were valued as embodiments of a clean and neat conscience (Yamey 1981). In nineteenth-century Britain, evangelicalism promoted an "ordered existence of assiduousness and moral rectitude" exemplified in careful financial accounting, as well as time-keeping and getting up early (Davidoff and Hall 2018). Even in secular contexts where the religious significance of accounting has been forgotten, such as middle-class mid-nineteenth-century Germany, careful book-keeping retained an air of virtue. It was a way of acquiring and demonstrating mercantile honor; to learn accounting was to acquire not just a technical skill but an attitude toward life—a middle-class ethos of orderliness and rationality (Maltby 1997).

10. The focus here is on the relationship between entrustment (rather than commerce in general) and ordered sociality. Nevertheless, this echoes constructs about the relationship between commerce and civility observed in other settings. Adam Smith saw commerce as capable of refining morals and manners (Anderson and Marsden 2023); in early modern Europe, commerce was increasingly approved by intellectual elites on the basis that it encouraged people to focus on their interests and thereby tame their more harmful passions (Hirschman 1997). Susan Bayly noted that commerce has been viewed in moral and religious traditions in Asia as a "pre-requisite of ordered sociality" (2007, 159; see also Marsden 2016, 8).

3. MERCHANT PATRIARCHY AND THE STATE

1. See Sharabi 1988, Moghadam 2004.
2. See Pateman (1988) for an argument about the history of this shift in Europe.
3. Kandiyoti (1988) connects classic patriarchy (patrilineal, patrilocal, extended tribal kinship group) to agrarian production.
4. Keddie (1990) and Eickelman (1989) connect patriarchy in the region to tribal and clan structures; Fernea (2003) argues that while patriarchy tends to decline with urbanization, it is at home in the clan of merchant capitalist kinship.
5. Hajj is an honorific title referring to a man who has undertaken the pilgrimage to Mecca, taken as a sign of respectability and seniority.
6. Merchants would sometimes refuse to take responsibility for the debts of their close relatives, including their sons; this tended to be accepted but would also rebound on their family reputation and their ability to introduce others to the market.
7. See Charrad 2000; Hatem 1986; Joseph 1996b; Altorki 2000; Amawi 2000; Hoodfar 2000; Lazreg 2000.
8. See Singerman 1995; Ismail 2006.
9. On economies of favor, see Humphrey 2016; Makovicky and Henig 2016; Henig 2016
10. On the relationship between short- and long-term spheres of exchange, see Parry and Bloch (1989).
11. See Haddad (2020). On the influence in Aleppo's Chamber of Commerce of the regime's affiliated "clans" and their clients, see Ismail (2018).
12. See Joseph (2005).
13. For a fine-grained study of reputation among Aleppo's traders, see Rabo (2005).
14. As Joseph notes, connective selfhood has been studied in other cultural contexts and theorized by feminists (Keller 1982; Chodorow 1978).

4. ECONOMIC PATRIARCHY AND CONTESTED MODERNITIES

1. On connective selfhood, see Joseph (1994).
2. The chapter explores the relationship between patriarchal structures in the economy and modes of apprehending the future; it does not argue that all those presented in the chapter were critiquing or seeking to change systems of economic patriarchy. While Saad was engaged in such a critique, Hamdi and arguably the participants in the stock market speculated with a view to taking their place as economic patriarchs in the future. And while Saad envisioned training young women alongside young men, aged rather than gendered domination was the focus of his critique of the politics of the father. I am grateful to Alice Wilson for raising this point.
3. See Deeb 2006; Shannon 2006; Winegar 2006; Kassab 2010; Peterson 2011.
4. Compare Abu-Lughod's (1986) argument about the relationship between licensed transgression and patriarchal social organization among the Awlad Ali in Egypt.
5. This section reproduces some ethnography and analysis from my PhD dissertation, "Threads of Virtue: The Ethical Lives of Syrian Textile Traders," University of Edinburgh, 2011.
6. The market had attracted investment from merchants and wealthy families across the city, peaking in 1993 before the collapse of one of the largest yarn manufacturers.
7. See also Anderson (2013).
8. See *Syria Today* magazine, the first English-language current affairs journal in Syria, whose founder worked for a government-approved NGO under the patronage of Asma al-Asad (Tabler 2011).
9. The English-language counterpart to the Arabic journal *al-Iqtisad wa'l-Naql*.
10. Fitra: the inborn disposition, which in Islamic thought connects humans to God.

5. THE HOSPITALITY ECONOMY

1. See Meneley 2016; Dazi-Heni 1994; Slyomovics 1998; Salamandra 2004; Jamous 1992; Bourdieu 1980; Shyrock 2004, 2008, 2012, 2019; Dresch 1998; Marsden 2012, 2016; Antoun 2000. Here I include Central Asia within the broader Middle East (see Green 2014). See Shryock 2004; Walton 2000; Lashley and Morrison 2000; Selywn 2000.

2. On this question, see Haddad 2013; Donati 2020; Perthes 1995, Kienle 1994.

3. See Khalaf (2020) for this argument.

4. Khalaf 2020; Schneider and Schneider 2008; Chu 2002, quoted in Marsden 2016; Lashley 2000; Ritzer 2004, 2007; Warde and Martens 2000.

5. Dresch 1998; Lindholm 1982; Humphrey 2012; Candea and Da Col 2012.

6. Meneley 1996; Jamous 1992,168, 170; Bourdieu 1980.

7. See Ben Jelloun 1999; Derrida 1999; Derrida and Dufourmantelle 2000, quoted in Shryock 2008.

8. See "Politics and Friendship: A Discussion with Jacques Derrida", Centre for Modern French Thought, University of Sussex, December 1, 1997, http://hydra.humanities.uci.edu/derrida/pol+fr.html.

9. See also Gregory 2012.

10. Compare Borneman's (2007) findings of a culture of male-male intimacy in Aleppo's bazaar, although his focus is on homosexuality rather than the valorization of homosociality.

11. Desai and Killick 2010; Mains 2013; Bell and Coleman 2020.

12. Compare Allerton 2012.

13. See Roitman 2005.

14. See Guindi 2012, Eickelman 1989.

15. al-Hasbani 1992; Antoun 1972, 2000; Shyrock 2004; Dazi-Heni 1994.

16. On this question, see Heydemann 2007; Heydemann and Leenders 2013; Pierret and Selvik 2009; Hinnebusch 2012.

17. See, for example, Hinnebusch and Zintl 2015a; Pierret 2015; Haddad 2013; Donati 2020; Perthes 1995; Kienle 1993.

18. See Antoun 2000; Shryock 2004.

19. For similar arguments, see Qleibo 1992; al-Hasbani 1992; Slyomovics 1998; Baylouny 2010.

20. See also Shyrock 2019.

6. CIVIC PATRONAGE

1. See also Rifai 2020.

2. This focus on the proximity of merchants to religious scholars has been observed elsewhere in the Middle East. Gilles Kepel (2002) argues that in Egypt, Palestine, and North Africa, an important component of the Islamist movement was the pious bourgeoisie—merchant lineages from the bazaar who had lost out in the process of decolonization. And in Iran, where ulema were long an autonomous social force, a "mosque-bazaar alliance" was the incubator for revolts against the state from the end of the nineteenth century through to the advent of the Islamic republic (Ashraf 1988), when the Islamic regime weakened its autonomy (Keshavarzian 2007).

3. For studies of recombinant authoritarianism, see Heydemann 2013; Heydemann and Leenders 2013; Donati 2020; Brownlee 2002 and 2007; Lust-Okar 2005; Posusny and Angrist 2005; Pratt 2007; Schlumberger 2007.

4. Osella and Osella 2009; Pierret 2013; Haynes 1987; De Neve 2000; Laidlaw 1995; Mines 1994; Mosse 2003; Price 1996.

5. Gygax 2021, Gygax and Zuiderhoek 2021.

6. For similar arguments, see Encarnación 2003; Jamal 2009; Cavatorta 2012.
7. On authoritarian iterations of civil society in Syria, see Terc 2015; Wedeen 2019.
8. See Amara 2011; Tuastad 2014.
9. See Pierret and Selvik 2009 for a notable example.
10. See Zubaida 1992; Roussillon 1990; al-Sayyid 1993; Clark 2004.
11. Mahmood 2005. Hirschkind 2006.
12. See Anderson 2018b.
13. The account in this chapter of K.'s career and the state intervention that followed is an adaptation of sections of Boissiere and Anderson (2014).
14. The Syrian Money Collectors law closely mirrored Egyptian legislation that had addressed the emergence of a parallel Islamic banking system that had drained state coffers (Sadowski 1991).

7. AFFECTIVE ECONOMIES OF SINCERITY AND ECONOMIC LIBERALIZATION IN ALEPPO

1. See Kuran 1997, 2004; Warde 2000; Henry and Wilson 2004; Haenni 2005; El-Gamal 2006; Hefner 2006; Tripp 2006; Osella and Osella 2009; Rudnyckyj 2010; Njoto-Feillard 2012; Atia 2013; Hoesterey 2015; Tobin 2016; Sloane-White 2017.
2. See Hefner 2023 for this categorization. On Islamic economics and finance, see Kuran 1997, 2004; Warde 2000; Henry and Wilson 2004; El-Gamal 2006; Hefner 2006; Tripp 2006; Tobin 2016. For works on market Islam and comparable phenomena, see Haenni 2005; Hoesterey 2015; Osella and Osella 2009; Rudnyckyj 2010; Njoto-Feillard 2012; Atia 2013; Sloane-White 2017.
3. Tobin 2016; Osella and Osella 2009; Sloane-White 2017; Njoto-Feillard 2012.
4. See Keane 2007; Haeri 2017.
5. Willingness has been reported as a salient ethical attitude in ritual as well as commercial transactions in other contexts. Many in the Sakalava polity in Northwest Madagascar had adopted Islam in the eighteenth century after contact with Arab traders, and some adopted Catholicism in the nineteenth century after contact with European traders and colonial armies, while in both cases also retaining traditional religious practices. Lambek (2008) noted among Sakalava ethnic groups in the late twentieth century, a sacrificial animal that shrieked on the way to the slaughter was said to be unwilling to give its life, and was spared on the grounds that it would be infelicitous to slaughter it. Lambek writes that "it is evidently not giving itself willingly and signals that neither is its owner offering it willingly" (2008, 149).
6. Bukhari collection, hadith number 2076. Bukhari, M, and Ali, M. 1956. *English Translation of Sahih Al-Bukhari*. Lahore: Ahmadiyya Anjuman Ishaat-i-Islam.
7. The term Islamicate was coined by Marshall Hodgson (1974, 56–60). Gagan Sood (2001, 117) observes that while Islamic is usually associated with the religious traditions of Muslims, Islamicate is a more capacious term that refers to "social and cultural complexes ... under Islamic dominion" and which, in particular, acknowledges "the meaningful involvement in the life of the region's polities of non-Muslim individuals, corporations and groups."
8. See Ho 2004, 2006; Jaffrelot and Louër 2017; Ghazal 2014; Kane 2015; Stephan-Emmrich 2018; Osella and Osella 2007, 2009.
9. Marsden 2021; Anderson 2020; Erie 2016.

CONCLUSION

1. Haddad 2013; Donati 2020.
2. On the concept of micro-politics, see Hann 1994; Osella and Osella 1998.

3. See Wedeen 2019.

4. See Chang (2018) for an analysis of the reconfiguration of Syrian merchant networks in the diaspora after 2011.

5. On the development of the city of Yiwu as a transnational trading hub, see Pliez 2012; Marsden 2015, 2016, 2017; Belguidoum and Pliez 2016.

6. See also Dilley and Kirsch 2015.

7. On the contrast between diffuse and systematized forms of religion, see Marsden and Retsikas 2012.

References

Abboud, S. 2010. "Syrian Trade Policy." St Andrews Papers of Contemporary Syria. *Syria Studies* 2, no. 2: 3–32.
———. 2015. Locating the "Social" in the Social Market Economy. In *Syria from Reform to Revolt: Political Economy and International Relations*, ed. R. Hinnebusch and T. Zintl, 45–65. Syracuse, NY: Syracuse University Press.
———. 2018. *Syria: Hot Spots in Global Politics*. Chichester: John Wiley & Sons.
Abu-Lughod, L. 1986. *Veiled Sentiments: Honor and Poetry in a Bedouin Society*. Berkeley: University of California Press.
———, ed. 1998. *Remaking Women: Feminism and Modernity in the Middle East*. Princeton: Princeton University Press.
Ahmed, S. 2015. *What Is Islam?* Princeton: Princeton University Press.
Aita, S. 2004. *Al-qita' al-sina'i fi ittifaqiyyat al-sharaka al-suriyya al-urubiyya*. [The Industrial Sector in the Syrian-European Association Agreement.] Damascus: Syrian Economic Society.
Akin, D. 1999. "Cash and Shell Money in Kwaio, Solomon Islands." In *Money and Modernity: State and Local currencies in Melanesia*, ed. D. Akin and J. Robbins, 103–30. Pittsburgh: University of Pittsburgh Press.
Alexander, J., and P. Alexander. 1991. "What's a Fair Price? Price-Setting and Trading Partnerships in Javanese Markets." *Man*, New series 26, no. 3: 493–512.
Allerton, C. 2012. "Making Guests, Making 'Liveliness': The Transformative Substances and Sounds of Manggarai Hospitality." *Journal of the Royal Anthropological Institute* 18: S49–S62.
Al-Mughni, H., and M. A. Tetreault. 2000. "Citizenship, Gender and the Politics of Quasi States." In *Gender and citizenship in the Middle East*, ed. S. Joseph, 237–60 Syracuse: Syracuse University Press.
Al-Sabbagh, T. 1950. *Al-dali al-musiqi al-'amm fi atrab al-angham* [The general music manual of the most pleasing modes]. Syria: Matba'at al-Ihsan li-Maytam al-Rum al-Kathulik.
Al-Sayyid, M. K. 1993. A Civil Society in Egypt? *Middle East Journal* 47, no. 2: 228–42.
Altorki, S. 2000. "Citizenship in Saudi Arabia." In *Gender and Citizenship in the Middle East*, ed. S. Joseph (ed), 215–36. Syracuse: Syracuse University Press.
Amara, M. 2011. *Sport, Politics and Society in the Arab World*. New York: Springer.
Amawi, A. 2000. Gender and Citizenship in Jordan. In *Gender and Citizenship in the Middle East*, ed. S. Joseph, 158–84. Syracuse: Syracuse University Press.
Anderson, P. 2013. "The Politics of Scorn in Syria and the Agency of Narrated Involvement." *Journal of the Royal Anthropological Institute* 19, no. 3: 463–81.
———. 2018a. "Aleppo in Asia: Mercantile Networks between Syria, China and post-Soviet Eurasia since 1970." *History and Anthropology* (Suppl.): S67–S83.
———. 2018b. "'An Abundance of Meaning': Ramadan as an Enchantment of Society and Economy in Syria." *HAU: Journal of Ethnographic Theory* 8, no. 3: 610–24.
———. 2019a. "Beyond Syria's War Economy: Trade, Migration and State Formation across Eurasia." *Journal of Eurasian Studies* 10, no. 1: 75–84.
———. 2019b. "Games of Civility: Ordinary Ethics in Aleppo's Bazaar." *Ethnos* 84, no. 3: 380–97.

———. 2020. "Not a Silk Road: Trading Networks between China and the Middle East as a Dynamic Interaction of Competing Eurasian Geographies." *Global Networks* 20, no. 4: 708–24.

Anderson, P., and M. Marsden 2023. "The Ethics of Trade and Commerce." In *The Cambridge Companion to the Anthropology of Ethics*, ed. J. Laidlaw. Cambridge: Cambridge University Press.

Antoun, R.T. 1972. *Arab Village: A Social Structural Study of a Transjordanian Peasant Community*. Bloomington: Indiana University Press.

———. 2000. "Civil Society, Tribal Process, and Change in Jordan: An Anthropological View." *International Journal of Middle East Studies* 32, no. 4: 441–63.

Arslanian, F. 2009. "Growth in Transition and Syria's Economic Performance." In *Syria's Economy and the Transition Paradigm*, ed. S. Abboud and F. Arslanian, 33–74. St Andrews: St Andrews Papers on Contemporary Syria.

Ashraf, A. 1988. "Bazaar-Mosque Alliance: The Social Basis of Revolts and Revolutions." *International Journal of Politics, Culture, and Society* 1, no. 4: 538–67.

Atia, M. 2013. *Building a House in Heaven: Pious Neoliberalism and Islamic Charity in Egypt*. Minneapolis: University of Minnesota Press.

Balanche, F. 2014. "Alep et ses territoires: Une métropole syrienne dans la mondialisation" [Aleppo and its territories: a Syrian metropolis in the context of globalization]. In *Alep et ses territoires: Fabrique et politique d'une ville 1868–2011* [Aleppo and its territories: the making and politics of a city, 1868–2011], ed. J-C. David and T. Boissiere, 39–66. Beyrouth-Damas: Presses de l'Ifpo.

Barker, J., E. Harms, and J. A. Lindquist, eds. 2013. *Figures of Southeast Asian Modernity*. Honolulu: University of Hawaii Press.

Baylouny, A. M. 2010. *Privatizing Welfare in the Middle East: Kin Mutual Aid Associations in Jordan and Lebanon*. Bloomington: Indiana University Press.

Bayly, C. A. 1988. *Rulers, Townsmen and Bazaars: North Indian Society in the Age of British Expansion, 1770–1870*. Cambridge: Cambridge University Press.

Bayly, S. 2007. *Asian Voices in a Postcolonial Age: Vietnam, India and Beyond*. Cambridge: Cambridge University Press.

Belguidoum, A., and O. Pliez. 2016. "Yiwu: The Creation of a Global Market Town in China." *Articulo—Journal of Urban Research* 12, online journal, doi: 10.4000/articulo.2863.

Bell, S., and S. Coleman, eds. 2020. *The Anthropology of Friendship*. Abingdon-on-Thames: Routledge.

Ben Jelloun, T. 1999. *French Hospitality: Racism and North African Immigrants*. New York: Columbia University Press.

Blaydes, L. 2010. *Elections and Distributive Politics in Mubarak's Egypt*. Cambridge: Cambridge University Press.

Boissière, T. 2005. "Précarité économique, instabilité de l'emploi et pratiques sociales en Syrie." *Revue des Mondes Musulmans et de la Méditerranée* 105–6: 109–31.

Boissiere, T., and P. Anderson. 2014. "L'argent et les affaires a Alep: Succes et faillite d'un 'ramasseur d'argent' dans les annees 1980–2009" [Money and commerce in Aleppo: the rise and fall of a 'money gatherer' 1980–2009]. In *Alep et ses territoires: fabrique et politique d'une ville 1868–2011* [Aleppo and its territories: the making and politics of a city, 1868–2011], ed. J-C. David and T. Boissiere, 351–68. Beyrouth-Damas: Presses de l'Ifpo.

Borneman, J. 2007. *Syrian Episodes*. Princeton: Princeton University Press.

Bourdieu, P. 1977. *Outline of a Theory of Practice*. Cambridge: Cambridge University Press.

———. 1979. *Algeria 1960*. Trans. Richard Nice. Cambridge: Cambridge University Press.

---. 1980. *Le sens pratique* [The logic of practice]. Paris: éditions de Minuit.
---. 1987. *Distinction: A Social Critique of the Judgement of Taste*. Cambridge, MA: Harvard University Press.
Bourdieu, P., A. Darbel, J. P. Rivet, and C. Seibel. 1963. *Travail et travailleurs en Algérie* [Work and workers in Algeria]. Paris: Mouton.
Briggs, C. 1998. "Constructing Dominant Ideologies of Language in Warao Men's Gossip." In *Language Ideologies: Practice and Theory*, ed. B. Schieffelin, K. Woolard and P. Kroskrity, 229–55. Oxford: Oxford University Press.
Brison, K. 1999. "Money and the Morality of Exchange among the Kwanga, East Sepik province, Papua New Guinea." In *Money and Modernity: State and Local Currencies in Melanesia*, ed. D. Akin and J. Robbins, 151–63. Pittsburgh: University of Pittsburgh Press.
Brownlee, J. M. 2002. "Low Tide after the Third Wave: Exploring Politics under Authoritarianism." *Comparative Politics* 34 no. 4: 477–98.
---. 2007. *Authoritarianism in an Age of Democratization*. Cambridge: Cambridge University Press.
Bukhari, M., and M. Ali. 1956. *English Translation of Sahih Al-Bukhari*. Lahore: Ahmadiyya Anjuman Ishaat-i-Islam.
Caldwell, J. C., 1978. A theory of fertility: from high plateau to destabilization. *Population and development review* 4, no. 4: 553–77.
Candea, M. 2012. "Derrida en Corse? Hospitality as Scale-Free Abstraction." *Journal of the Royal Anthropological Institute* 18: S34–S48.
Candea, M., and G. Da Col. 2012. "The Return to Hospitality." *Journal of the Royal Anthropological Institute* 18: S1–S19.
Carey, M. 2017. *Mistrust: An Ethnographic Theory*. Chicago: Hau Books.
Carruthers, B. G., and W. N. Espeland. 1991. "Accounting for Rationality: Double-Entry Bookkeeping and the Rhetoric of Economic Rationality." *American Journal of Sociology* 97, no. 1: 31–69.
Carsten, J., ed. 2000. *Cultures of Relatedness: New Approaches to the Study of Kinship*. Cambridge: Cambridge University Press.
Cavatorta, F., ed. 2012. *Civil Society Activism under Authoritarian Rule: A Comparative Perspective*. London: Routledge.
Chang, C. A. 2018. "Transformation of the Syrian Business Community after the 2011 Uprising: The Formation of a War-Induced Business Diaspora and the Reorganisation of their Networks." PhD diss., University of Edinburgh.
Charrad, M. 2000. "Becoming a Citizen." In *Gender and Citizenship in the Middle East*, ed. S. Joseph, 70–87. Syracuse: Syracuse University Press.
Chatty, D. 1986. *From Camel to Truck: The Bedouin in the Modern World*. New York: Vantage Press.
---. 2010. "The Bedouin in Contemporary Syria: The Persistence of Tribal Authority and Control." *Middle East Journal* 64, no. 1: 29–49.
Chodorow, N. 1978. *The Reproduction of Mothering*. Berkeley: University of California Press.
Chu, Y. K. 2002. *The Triads as Business*. Routledge.
Clark, J. A. 2004. *Islam, Charity, and Activism: Middle-Class Networks and Social Welfare in Egypt, Jordan, and Yemen*. Bloomington: Indiana University Press.
Cooke, M. 2007. *Dissident Syria: Making Oppositional Arts Official*. Durham, NC: Duke University Press.
Da Col, G. 2012. "The Poisoner and the Parasite: Cosmoeconomics, Fear, and Hospitality among Dechen Tibetans." *Journal of the Royal Anthropological Institute* 18, no. 1: S175–S195.

Daher, J. 2019. *Syria's Manufacturing Sector: The Model of Economic Recovery in Question*. Florence: European University Institute.

———. 2020. *The Syrian Chambers of Commerce in 2020: The Rise of a New Business Elite*. Florence: European University Institute.

Davidoff, L., and C. Hall. 2018. *Family Fortunes: Men and Women of the English Middle Class, 1780–1850*. Abingdon-on-Thames: Routledge.

Dazi-Heni, F. 1994. "Hospitalité et politique: La diwâniyya au Koweit" [Hospitality and politics: the diwaniya in Kuwait]. *Maghreb-Machrek* 143, no. 1: 109–23.

De Neve, G. 2000. "Patronage and 'Community': The Role of a Tamil 'Village' Festival in the Integration of a Town." *Journal of the Royal Anthropological Institute* 6, no. 3: 501–19.

Deeb, L. 2011. *An Enchanted Modern*. Princeton: Princeton University Press.

Deeb, L., and J. Winegar. 2012. "Anthropologies of Arab-Majority Societies." *Annual Review of Anthropology* 41: 537–58.

Derrida, J. 1999. *Adieu to Emmanuel Levinas*. Stanford, CA: Stanford University Press.

Derrida, J., and G. Bennington. 1997. *Politics and Friendship: A Discussion with Jacques Derrida*. Centre for Modern French Thought, University of Sussex. http://hydra.humanities.uci.edu/derrida/pol+fr.html.

Derrida, J., and A. Dufourmantelle. 2000. *Of Hospitality*. Stanford, CA: Stanford University Press.

Desai, A., and E. Killick, eds. 2010. *The Ways of Friendship: Anthropological Perspectives*. New York: Berghahn Books.

Dilley, R. 2010. "Reflections on Knowledge Practices and the Problem of Ignorance." *Journal of the Royal Anthropological Institute* 16: S176–S192.

Dilley, R., and T. G. Kirsch, eds. 2015. *Regimes of Ignorance: Anthropological Perspectives on the Production and Reproduction of Non-Knowledge*. New York: Berghahn Books.

Donati, C. 2020. "The Economics of Authoritarian Upgrading in Syria: Liberalization and the Reconfiguration of Economic Networks." In *Middle East Authoritarianisms*, 35–60. Stanford, CA: Stanford University Press.

Dresch, P. 1998. "Mutual Deception: Totality, Exchange, and Islam in the Middle East." In *Marcel Mauss: A Centenary Tribute*, ed. W. James and N. Allen, 111–33. New York: Berghahn Books.

Dukhan, H. 2014. "Tribes and Tribalism in the Syrian Uprising." *Syria Studies* 6, no. 2: 1–28.

Eagleton, T. 2014. *Ideology*. Abingdon-on-Thames: Routledge.

Eickelman, D. F. 1989. *The Middle East: An Anthropological Approach*. Upper Saddle River, NJ: Prentice Hall.

Eisenstein, Z. R. 2020. *The Color of Gender*. Berkeley: University of California Press.

El-Barghuthi, O. T., 1924. Rules of Hospitality. *Journal of the Palestine Oriental Society* 4, no. 4: 175–203.

El-Gamal, M. A. 2006. *Islamic finance: Law, Economics, and Practice*. Cambridge: Cambridge University Press.

Elsheshtawy, Y. 2006. "From Dubai to Cairo: Competing Global Cities, Models, and Shifting Centers of Influence." In *Cairo Cosmopolitan: Politics, Culture, and Urban Space in the Globalized Middle East*, ed. D. Singerman and P. Amar, 235–50. Cairo: American University in Cairo Press.

Elyachar, J. 2005. *Markets of dispossession*. Durham, NC: Duke University Press.

———. 2010. "Phatic Labor, Infrastructure, and the Question of Empowerment in Cairo." *American Ethnologist* 37, no. 3: 452–64.

Emirbayer, M., and J. Goodwin. 1994. "Network Analysis, Culture, and Problem of Agency." *American Journal of Sociology* 99: 1411–54.

Encarnación, O. G. 2003. "Civil Society Reconsidered." In *The Myth of Civil Society: Social Capital and Democratic Consolidation in Spain and Brazil*, ed. O. Encarnación, 163–76. New York: Springer.

Erie, M. S. 2016. *China and Islam: The Prophet, the Party, and Law.* Cambridge: Cambridge University Press.

Fabos, A. H. 2008. *"Brothers" or Others?: Propriety and Gender for Muslim Arab Sudanese in Egypt.* Vol. 22. New York: Berghahn Books.

Fadlalla, A. 2007. *Embodying Honor: Fertility, Foreignness, and Regeneration in Eastern Sudan.* Madison: University of Wisconsin Press.

Fanselow, F. 1990. "The Bazaar Economy or How Bizarre Is the Bazaar Really?" *Man*, New series 25, no. 2: 250–65.

Friedrich, P. 1989. "Language, Ideology, and Political Economy." *American Anthropologist* 91, no. 2: 295–312.

Gal, S., and J. T. Irvine. 1995. "The Boundaries of Languages and Disciplines: How Ideologies Construct Difference." *Social Research* 62, no. 4: 967–1001.

Geertz, C. 1978. "The Bazaar Economy: Information and Searching in Peasant Marketing." *American Economic Review* 68: 28–32.

Gelvin, J. L. 2006. "The 'Politics of Notables' Forty Years After." *Review of Middle East Studies* 40, no. 1: 19–30.

Ghazal, A. N. 2014. "Transcending Area Studies: Piecing Together the Cross-Regional Networks of Ibadi Islam." *Comparative Studies of South Asia, Africa and the Middle East* 34, no. 3: 582–89.

Gilsenan, M. 1996. *Lords of the Lebanese Marches: Violence and Narrative in an Arab Society.* Berkeley: University of California Press.

Glick Schiller, N., and A. Çağlar. 2016. "Displacement, Emplacement and Migrant Newcomers: Rethinking Urban Sociabilities within Multiscalar Power." *Identities* 23, no. 1: 17–34.

Goitein, S. D. 1999. *A Mediterranean Society: The Jewish Communities of the Arab World as Portrayed in the Documents of the Cairo Geniza, Vol. 1: Economic Foundations.* Berkeley: University of California Press.

Goldziher, I. 1967. *Muslim Studies*, Vol. 1. Albany: SUNY Press.

Goodman, J. E. 2005. *Berber Culture on the World Stage: From Village to Video.* Bloomington: Indiana University Press.

Green, N. 2014. "Rethinking the 'Middle East' after the Oceanic Turn." *Comparative Studies of South Asia, Africa and the Middle East* 34, no. 3: 556–64.

Gregory, C. A. 2012. "On Money Debt and Morality: Some Reflections on the Contribution of Economic Anthropology." *Social Anthropology* 20, no. 4: 380–96.

Gudeman, S. 1986. *Economics as Culture: Models and Metaphors of Livelihood.* London: Routledge.

———. 2012. "Vital Energy: The Current of Relations." *Social Analysis* 56, no. 1: 57–73.

Guindi, F. E. 2012. "Milk and Blood: Kinship among Muslim Arabs in Qatar." *Anthropos* 107, no. 2: 545–55.

Gygax, M. D. 2021." Classical Athens and the Invention of Civic Euergetism." In *Benefactors and the Polis: The Public Gift in the Greek Cities from the Homeric World to Late Antiquity*, ed. M. D. Gygax and A. Zuiderhoek, 69–95. Cambridge: Cambridge University Press.

Gygax, M. D., and A. Zuiderhoek, eds. 2021. *Benefactors and the Polis: The Public Gift in the Greek Cities from the Homeric World to Late Antiquity.* Cambridge: Cambridge University Press.

Habeeb, H. H. 2002. *The Euro-Mediterranean Partnership Pros and Cons: An Arab View.* Irvine, CA: Universal Publishers.

Hachimi, A. 2012. The urban and the urbane: Identities, language ideologies, and Arabic dialects in Morocco. *Language in Society* 41, no. 3: 321–41.
———. 2013. "The Maghreb-Mashreq Language Ideology and the Politics of Identity in a Globalized Arab World." *Journal of Sociolinguistics* 17, no. 3: 269–96.
Haddad, B. 2012. "Syria's State Bourgeoisie: An Organic Backbone for the Regime." *Middle East Critique* 21, no. 3: 231–57.
———. 2020. *Business Networks in Syria*. Stanford, CA: Stanford University Press.
Haenni, P. 2005. *L'islam de marché* [Market Islam]. Paris: Le Seuil.
Haeri, N. 2017. "Unbundling Sincerity: Language, Mediation, and Interiority in Comparative Perspective." *HAU: Journal of Ethnographic Theory* 7, no. 1: 123–38.
Hatem, M. 1986. "The Enduring Alliance of Nationalism and Patriarchy in Muslim Personal Status Laws: The Case of Modern Egypt." *Feminist Issues* 6, no. 1: 19–43.
———. 2000. "The Pitfalls of the Nationalist Discourses on Citizenship in Egypt." In *Gender and Citizenship in the Middle East*, ed. S. Joseph, 33–57. Syracuse: Syracuse University Press.
Haynes, D. E. 1987. "From Tribute to Philanthropy: The Politics of Gift Giving in a Western Indian City." *Journal of Asian Studies* 46, no. 2: 339–60.
Heal, F. 1990. *Hospitality in Early Modern England*. Oxford: Oxford University Press.
Hefner, R. W. 2006. "Islamic Economics and Global Capitalism." *Society* 44, no. 1: 16–22.
Hefner, R. 2023. "Modern Capitalism and Ethical Plurality." In *The Cambridge Companion to the Anthropology of Ethics*, ed. J. Laidlaw. Cambridge: Cambridge University Press.
Henig, D. 2016. "A Good Deed Is Not a Crime." In *Economies of Favour after Socialism*, ed. D. Henig and N. Mackovicky, 181–202. Oxford: Oxford University Press.
———. 2019. "Economic Theologies of Abundance: Halal Exchange and the Limits of Neoliberal Effects in Post-War Bosnia–Herzegovina." *Ethnos* 84, no. 2: 223–40.
———. 2020. *Remaking Muslim Lives: Everyday Islam in Postwar Bosnia and Herzegovina*. Urbana: University of Illinois Press.
Henry, C. M., and R. Wilson, eds. 2004. *The Politics of Islamic Finance*. Edinburgh: Edinburgh University Press.
Herzfeld, M. 1987. "'As in Your Own House': Hospitality, Ethnography, and the Stereotype of Mediterranean Society." In *Honor and Shame and the Unity of the Mediterranean*, ed. D. Gilmore, 85–89. Washington, DC: American Anthropological Association.
———. 2012. "Afterword: Reciprocating the Hospitality of These Pages." *Journal of the Royal Anthropological Institute* 18: S210–S217.
Heydemann, S. 2007. *Upgrading Authoritarianism in the Arab World*. Washington, DC: Saban Center for Middle East Policy at the Brookings Institution.
———. 2013. "Tracking the 'Arab Spring': Syria and the Future of Authoritarianism." *Journal of Democracy* 24, no. 4: 59–73.
Heydemann, S., and R. Leenders, eds. 2013. *Middle East Authoritarianisms: Governance, Contestation, and Regime Resilience in Syria and Iran*. Stanford, CA: Stanford University Press.
Hill, J. H., and B. Mannheim. 1992. "Language and World View." *Annual Review of Anthropology* 21, no. 1: 381–404.
Hinnebusch, R. 1993. "State and Civil Society in Syria." *Middle East Journal* 47, no. 2: 243–57.
———. 2004. *Syria: Revolution from Above*. Abingdon-on-Thames: Routledge.
———. 2008. Modern Syrian Politics. *History Compass* 6, no. 1: 263–85.
———. 2012. "Syria: From 'Authoritarian Upgrading' to Revolution?" *International Affairs* 88, no. 1: 95–113.
———. 2015. "President and Party in Post-Baathist Syria: From the Struggle for 'Reform' to Regime Deconstruction." In *Syria from Reform to Revolt: Political Economy and*

International Relations, ed. R. Hinnebusch and T. Zintl, 21–44. Syracuse: Syracuse University Press.
Hinnebusch, R., and T. Zintl. 2015a. "Introduction." In *Syria from Reform to Revolt: Political Economy and International Relations*, ed. R. Hinnebusch and T. Zintl, 1–17. Syracuse: Syracuse University Press.
———. 2015b. "The Syrian Uprising and Bashar al-Asad's First Decade in Power." In *Syria from Reform to Revolt: Political Economy and International Relations*, ed. R. Hinnebusch and T. Zintl, 285–310. Syracuse: Syracuse University Press.
Hirschkind, C. 2006. *The Ethical Soundscape: Cassette Sermons and Islamic Counterpublics*. New York: Columbia University Press.
Hirschman, A. 1997. *The Passion and the Interests: Political Arguments for Capitalism Before its Triumph*. Princeton: Princeton University Press.
Hivernel, J. 2000. "Bâb al-Nayrab, un faubourg d'Alep, hors la ville et dans la cité" [Bab al-Nayrab, a suburb of Aleppo, within and beyond the city]. *Études rurales* 215–37.
Ho, E., 2002. "Before parochialization: diasporic Arabs cast in creole waters." In *Transcending Borders: Arabs, Politics, Trade and Islam in southeast Asia*, ed. H. De Jonge and N. Kaptein, 11–35. Leiden: Brill.
———. 2004. "Empire through Diasporic Eyes: A View from the Other Boat." *Comparative Studies in Society and History* 46, no. 2: 210–46.
———. 2006. *The graves of Tarim*. Berkeley: University of California Press.
Hodgson, M. G. 1974. *The Venture of Islam, Vol. 2*. Chicago: University of Chicago Press.
Hoesterey, J. 2015. *Rebranding Islam: Piety, Prosperity and a Self-Help Guru*. Stanford, CA: Stanford University Press.
Hoffman, K. E. 2008. *We Share Walls: Language, Land, and Gender in Berber Morocco*. Chichester: John Wiley & Sons.
Hoodfar, H. 2000. "Iranian Women at the Intersection of Citizenship and the Family Code: The Perils of Islamic Criteria." In *Gender and Citizenship in the Middle East*, ed. S. Joseph, 287–313. Syracuse: Syracuse University Press.
Hourani, A. 1968. "Ottoman Reform and the Politics of Notables." In *Beginnings of Modernization in the Middle East: The Nineteenth Century*, ed. W. Polk, R. Chambers and R. Chambers, 41–68. Chicago: Chicago University Press.
———. 2004. *The Effects of Interest Rate Change in the Context of Economic Reform*. [In Arabic.] Damascus: Syrian Economic Society.
Humphrey, C. 2012. "Hospitality and Tone: Holding Patterns for Strangeness in Rural Mongolia." *Journal of the Royal Anthropological Institute* 18: S63–S75.
———. 2016. "A New Look at Favours." In *DEconomies of Favour after Socialism*, ed. Henig and M. Makovicky, 50–72. Oxford: Oxford University Press.
Ilahiane, H. 2004. *Ethnicities, Community Making, and Agrarian Change: The Political Ecology of a Moroccan Oasis*. Lanham, Maryland: University Press of America.
Inhorn, M. C. 1996. *Infertility and Patriarchy: The Cultural Politics of Gender and Family Life in Egypt*. Philadelphia: University of Pennsylvania Press.
Irvine, J., and S. Gal. 2000. "Language Ideology and Linguistic Differentiation." In *Regimes of Language*, ed. P. Kroskrity, 35–84. Santa Fe, NM: School of American Research.
Ismail, S. 2006. *Political Life in Cairo's New Quarters: Encountering The Everyday State*. Minneapolis: University of Minnesota Press.
———. 2013. "Piety, Profit and the Market in Cairo: A Political Economy of Islamisation." *Contemporary Islam* 7, no. 1: 107–28.
———. 2018. *The Rule of Violence: Subjectivity, Memory and Government in Syria*. Cambridge: Cambridge University Press.
Jacobs, K., and S. P. Walker. 2004. "Accounting and Accountability in the Iona Community." *Accounting, Auditing & Accountability Journal* 17, no. 3: 361–81.

REFERENCES

Jad, I., P. Johnson, and R. Giacaman. 2000. "Transit Citizens: Gender and Citizenship under the Palestinian Authority." In *Gender and Citizenship in the Middle East*, ed. S. Joseph, 137–557. Syracuse: Syracuse University Press.

Jaffrelot, C., and L. Louër, eds. 2017. *Pan-Islamic Connections: Transnational Networks Between South Asia and the Gulf*. Oxford: Oxford University Press.

Jamal, A. A. 2009. *Barriers to Democracy*. Princeton: Princeton University Press.

Jamous, R. 1992. "From the Death of Men to the Peace of God: Violence and Peace-Making in the Rif." In *Honor and Grace in Anthropology*, ed. J. Peristiany and J. Pitt-Rivers, 167–92. Cambridge: Cambridge University Press.

Jones, K. B. 1993. *Compassionate Authority: Democracy and the Representation of Women*. Abingdon-on-Thames: Routledge.

Joseph, S. 1993. "Connectivity and Patriarchy among Urban Working-Class Arab Families in Lebanon." *Ethos* 21, no. 4: 452–84.

———. 1994. "Brother/Sister Relationships: Connectivity, Love, and Power in the Reproduction of Patriarchy in Lebanon." *American Ethnologist* 21, no. 1: 50–73.

———. 1996a. "Gender and Citizenship in Middle Eastern States." *Middle East Report* 198 (Jan to Mar): 4–10.

———. 1996b. "Patriarchy and Development in the Arab World." *Gender & Development* 4, no. 2: 14–19.

———, ed. 1999. *Intimate Selving in Arab Families: Gender, Self, and Identity*. Syracuse: Syracuse University Press.

———. 2005. "The Kin Contract and Citizenship in the Middle East." In *Women and Citizenship*, ed. M. Friedman, 149–69. New York: Oxford University Press.

Kandiyoti, D. 1988. "Bargaining with Patriarchy." *Gender & Society* 2, no. 3: 274–90.

———. 2008. "Islam and Patriarchy: A Comparative Perspective." In *Women in Middle Eastern History: Shifting Boundaries in Sex and Gender*, ed. N. Keddie and B. Baron, 23–42. New Haven: Yale University Press.

Kane, E. 2015. *Russian Hajj: Empire and the Pilgrimage to Mecca*. Ithaca: Cornell University Press.

Kassab, E. S. 2010. *Contemporary Arab thought: Cultural Critique in Comparative Perspective*. New York: Columbia University Press.

Keane, W. 2002. "Sincerity, "Modernity," and the Protestants." *Cultural Anthropology* 17, no. 1: 65–92.

———. 2007. *Christian Moderns: Freedom and Fetish in the Mission Encounter*. Berkeley: University of California Press.

Keddie, N. R. 1990. "The Past and Present of Women in the Muslim World." *Journal of World History* 1, no. 1: 77–108.

Keller, E. 1982. "Science and Gender." *Signs* 7: 589–602.

Kepel, G. 2002. *Jihad: The Trail of Political Islam*. Cambridge: Harvard University Press.

Keshavarzian, A. 2007. *Bazaar and State in Iran: The Politics of the Tehran Marketplace*. Cambridge: Cambridge University Press.

Khalaf, S. N. 2020. *Social Change in Syria: Family, Village and Political Party*. Abingdon-on-Thames: Routledge.

Khoury, P. S. 1983. *Urban Notables and Arab Nationalism: The Politics of Damascus, 1860–1920*. Cambridge: Cambridge University Press.

———. 1990. "The Urban Notables Paradigm Revisited." *Revue des mondes musulmans et de la Méditerranée* 55, no. 1: 215–30.

Kienle, E. 1994. "Introduction." In *Contemporary Syria: Liberalization between Cold War and Cold Peace*, ed. E. Kleine, 1–13. London: British Academic Press.

Kubala, P. 2007. "Review of 'Among the Jasmine Trees: Music and Modernity in Contemporary Syria' by Jonathan Shannon." *Arab Studies Journal* 15, no. 1: 125–28.

Kulick, D. 1992. "Anger, Gender, Language Shift and the Politics of Revelation in a Papua New Guinean Village." *Pragmatics* 2, no. 3: 281–96.
Kuppinger, P. 1998. "The Giza Pyramids: Accommodating Tourism, Leisure and Consumption." *City & Society* 10, no.1: 105–19.
———. 2006. "Pyramids and Alleys: Global Dynamics and Local Strategies in Giza." In *Cairo Cosmopolitan: Politics, Culture, and Urban Space in the Globalized Middle East*, ed. D. Singerman and P. Amar 313–44. Cairo: American University in Cairo Press.
Kuran, T. 1997. "The Genesis of Islamic Economics: A Chapter in the Politics of Muslim Identity." *Social Research* 62, no. 2: 301–38.
———. 2004. *Islam and Mammon: The Economic Predicaments of Islamism*. Princeton: Princeton University Press.
Laidlaw, J. 1995. *Riches and Renunciation: Religion, Economy and Society among the Jains*. Oxford: Clarendon Press.
Lambek, M. 2008. "Value and Virtue." *Anthropological Theory* 8, no. 2: 133–57.
Lapidus, I. M. 1967. *Muslim Cities in the Later Middle Ages*. Cambridge: Harvard University Press.
Lashley, C. 2000. "Towards a Theoretical Understanding." In *In Search of Hospitality: Theoretical Perspectives and Debates*, ed. C. Lashley and A. Morrison, 1–17. Abingdon-on-Thames: Routledge.
Lashley, C., and A. Morrison. 2000. *In Search of Hospitality: Theoretical Perspectives and Debates*. Abingdon-on-Thames: Routledge.
Lazreg, M. 2000. "Citizenship and Gender in Algeria." In *Gender and Citizenship in the Middle East*, ed. S. Joseph, 58–69. Syracuse: Syracuse University Press.
Lian, C. 2020. *Language, Ideology and Sociopolitical Change in the Arabic-Speaking World: A Study of the Discourse of Arabic Language Academies*. Edinburgh: Edinburgh University Press.
Light, I., and G. Karageorgis. 1994. "The Ethnic Economy." In *The Handbook of Economic Sociology*, ed. N. Smelser and R. Swedberg, 647–71. Princeton: Princeton University Press.
Lindholm, C. 1982. *Generosity and Jealousy: The Swat Pukhtun of Northern Pakistan*. New York: Columbia University Press.
Lucy, J. A. 1993. "Reflexive Language and the Human Disciplines." In *Reflexive Language: Reported Speech and Metapragmatics*, ed. J. Lucy, 9–32. Cambridge: Cambridge University Press.
Lust-Okar, E. 2006. "Elections under Authoritarianism: Preliminary Lessons from Jordan." *Democratization* 13, no. 3: 456–71.
Mahmood, S. 2005. *Politics of Piety: The Islamic Revival and the Feminist Subject*. Berkeley: University of California Press.
Mains, D. 2013. "Friends and Money: Balancing Affection and Reciprocity among Young Men in Urban Ethiopia." *American Ethnologist* 40, no. 2: 335–46.
Makovicky, N., and D. Henig. 2016. "Introduction—Re-Imagining Economies (after socialism): Ethics, Favours and Moral Sentiments." In *Economies of Favour after Socialism*, ed D. Henig and M. Makovicky, 1–20. Oxford: Oxford University Press.
Malinowski, B. 2013. *Argonauts of the Western Pacific: An Account of Native Enterprise and Adventure in the Archipelagoes of Melanesian New Guinea [1922/1994]*. Abingdon-on-Thames: Routledge.
Maltby, J. 1997. "Accounting and the Soul of the Middle Class: Gustav Freytag's Soll und Haben." *Accounting, Organizations and Society* 22, no. 1: 69–87.
Mann, P. S. 1994. *Micro-Politics: Agency in a Postfeminist Era*. Minneapolis: University of Minnesota Press.

Mannheim, B. 1986. "Popular Song and Popular Grammar, Poetry and Metalanguage." *Word* 37, no. 1-2: 45-75.
Marsden, M. 2012. "Fatal Embrace: Trading in Hospitality on the Frontiers of South and Central Asia." *Journal of the Royal Anthropological Institute* 18: S117-S130.
———. 2015. "From Kabul to Kiev: Afghan Trading Networks across the Former Soviet Union." *Modern Asian Studies* 49, no. 4: 1010-48.
———. 2016. *Trading Worlds: Afghan Merchants across Modern Frontiers*. Oxford: Oxford University Press.
———. 2017. "Actually Existing Silk Roads." *Journal of Eurasian Studies* 8, no. 1: 22-30.
———. 2021. *Beyond the Silk Roads*. Cambridge: Cambridge University Press.
Marsden, M., and K. Retsikas, eds. 2012. *Articulating Islam: Anthropological Approaches to Muslim Worlds*. Berlin: Springer Science & Business Media.
Mauss, M. 2002. *The Gift: The Form and Reason for Exchange in Archaic Societies*. Abingdon-on-Thames: Routledge.
McPhail, K., T. Gorringe, and R. Gray. 2004. "Accounting and Theology, an Introduction." *Accounting, Auditing & Accountability Journal* 17, no. 3: 320-26.
Meier, P. 2014. "Le conte de deux villes: Alep du point de vue des marchands du souk" [A tale of two cities: Aleppo from the perspective of souk traders]. In *Alep et ses territoires: fabrique et politique d'une ville 1868-2011* [Aleppo and its territories: the making and politics of a city, 1868-2011], ed. J-C. David and T. Boissiere, 319-32. Beyrouth-Damas: Presses de l'Ifpo.
Meininghaus, E. 2016. *Creating Consent in Ba'thist Syria: Women and Welfare in a Totalitarian State*. London: Bloomsbury.
Meneley, A. 2016. *Tournaments of Value: Sociability and Hierarchy in a Yemeni Town*. Toronto: University of Toronto Press.
Meriwether, M. L. 1999. *The Kin Who Count: Family and Society in Ottoman Aleppo, 1770-1840*. Austin: University of Texas Press.
Miller, P. 1994. "Accounting as Social and Institutional Practice: An Introduction." In *Accounting as Social and Institutional Practice*, ed. Anthony G. Hopwood and Peter Miller, 1-39. Cambridge: Cambridge University Pres.
Mines, M. 1994. *Public Faces, Private Lives: Community and Individuality in South India*. Berkeley: University of California Press.
Mittermaier, A. 2014. "Beyond Compassion: Islamic Voluntarism in Egypt." *American Ethnologist* 41, no. 3: 518-31.
———. 2019. *Giving to God: Islamic Charity in Revolutionary Times*. Berkeley: University of California Press.
Moghadam, V. M. 2004. "Patriarchy in Transition: Women and the Changing Family in the Middle East." *Journal of Comparative Family Studies* 35, no. 2: 137-62.
Momdjian, M. 2017. "The Levantine Merchant Consuls of Aleppo; The Commercial Elites 1750-1850." PhD diss., UCLA.
Monroe, K. V. 2016. "Exploring Nature, Making the Nation: The Spatial Politics of Ecotourism in Lebanon." *PoLAR: Political and Legal Anthropology Review* 39, no. 1: 64-78.
Mosse, D. 2003. *The Rule of Water: Statecraft, Ecology and Collective Action in South India*. Oxford: Oxford University Press.
Munn, N. D. 1992. *The Fame of Gawa: A Symbolic Study of Value Transformation in a Massim (Papua New Guinea) Society*. Durham, NC: Duke University Press.
Nagy, S. 1998. "'This Time I Think I'll Try a Filipina': Global and Local Influences on Relations between Foreign Household Workers and Their Employers in Doha, Qatar." *City & Society* 10, no. 1: 83-103.
Njoto-Feillard, G. 2012. *L'Islam et la réinvention du capitalisme en Indonésie* [Islam and the reinvention of capitalism in Indonesia]. Paris: Editions Karthala.

Osella, C., and F. Osella. 1998. "Friendship and Flirting: Micro-Politics in Kerala, South India." *Journal of the Royal Anthropological Institute* 4, no. 2: 189–206.
———. 2007. "'I am Gulf': The Production of Cosmopolitanism in Kozhikode, Kerala, India." In *Struggling with history: Islam and cosmopolitanism in the Western Indian Ocean*, ed. E. Simpson and K. Kress, 323–56. London: Hurst.
———. 2009. "Muslim Entrepreneurs in Public Life between India and the Gulf: Making Good and Doing Good." *Journal of the Royal Anthropological Institute* 15: S202–S221.
Parry, J., and M. Bloch. 1989. "Introduction." In *Money and the Morality of Exchange*, ed. J. Parry and M. Bloch, 1–32. Cambridge: Cambridge University Press.
Pateman, C. 1988. *The Sexual Contract*. Palo Alto, CA: Stanford University Press.
Peebles, G. 2010. "The Anthropology of Credit and Debt." *Annual Review of Anthropology* 39: 225–40.
Peirce, C. S. 1960. *Collected Papers of Charles Sanders Peirce*. Volumes I–VIII, ed. C. Hartshorne, P. Weiss, and A. W. Burks. Cambridge, MA: Belknap Press of Harvard University Press.
Perthes, V. 1992. "The Syrian Private Industrial and Commercial Sectors and the State." *International Journal of Middle East Studies* 24, no. 2: 207–30.
———. 1997. *The Political Economy of Syria under Asad*. London: I.B. Tauris.
———. 2004. *Syria under Bashar al-Asad: Modernisation and the Limits of change*. International Institute for Strategic Studies Adelphi Paper 366. Oxford: Oxford University Press.
Peterson, M. A. 2011. *Connected in Cairo: Growing Up Cosmopolitan in the Modern Middle East*. Bloomington: Indiana University Press.
Phillips, A. 1993. *Democracy and Difference*. University Park: Pennsylvania State Press.
Pierret, T. 2013. *Religion and State in Syria: The Sunni Ulama from Coup to Revolution*. Cambridge: Cambridge University Press.
———. 2015. "Merchant Background, Bourgeois Ethics." In *Syria from Reform to Revolt: Vol. 2, Culture, Religion, and Society*, ed. C Salamandra and L. Stenberg, 130–46. Syracuse, NY: Syracuse University Press.
Pierret, T., and K. Selvik. 2009. "Limits of 'Authoritarian Upgrading' in Syria: Private Welfare, Islamic Charities, and the Rise of the Zayd Movement." *International Journal of Middle East Studies* 41, no. 4: 595–614.
Pinto, P. 2006. "Sufism, Moral Performance and the Public Sphere in Syria." *Revue des Mondes Musulmans et de la Méditerranée* 115–16: 155–71.
———. 2007. "Pilgrimage, Commodities, and Religious Objectification: The Making of Transnational Shiism between Iran and Syria." *Comparative Studies of South Asia, Africa and the Middle East* 27, no. 1: 109–25.
———. 2009. "Creativity and Stability in the Making of Sufi Tradition: The Tariqa Qadiriyya in Aleppo, Syria." In *Sufism Today: Heritage and Tradition in the Global Community*, ed. C. Raudvere, 117–35. London: I.B. Tauris.
———. 2011. "'Oh Syria, God Protects You': Islam as Cultural Idiom under Bashar al-Asad." *Middle East Critique* 20, no. 2: 189–205.
———. 2017. "Mystical Metaphors: Ritual, Symbols and Self in Syrian Sufism." *Culture and Religion* 18, no. 2: 90–109.
Pitt-Rivers, J. [1954] 2011. "The Place of Grace in Anthropology." *HAU: Journal of Ethnographic Theory* 1, no. 1: 423–50.
———. 1963. "The Stranger, the Guest and the Hostile Host: Introduction to the Laws of Hospitality." In *Contributions to Mediterranean Sociology: Mediterranean Rural Communities and Social Change: Acts of the Mediterranean Sociological Conference*, ed. J. Peristiany, 14–30. Paris: Mouton & Co.

Pliez, O. 2012. "Following the New Silk Road between Yiwu and Cairo." In *Globalisation from Below: the World's Other Economy*, ed. G. Mathews, G. Lins Ribeiro, and C. Alba Vega, 19–35. London: Routledge.
Posusney, M., and M. Angrist. 2005. *Authoritarianism in the Middle East: Regimes and Resistance*. Boulder, CO: Lynne Rienner.
Powell, W. M., and L. Smith-Doerr. 1994. "Networks and Economic Life." In *The Handbook of Economic Sociology*, ed. N. Smelser and R. Swedberg, 368–401. Princeton: Princeton University Press.
Pratt, N. C. 2007. *Democracy and Authoritarianism in the Arab World*. Boulder, CO: Lynne Rienner.
Price, P. G. 1996. *Kingship and Political Practice in Colonial India*. Cambridge: Cambridge University Press.
Qleibo, A. H. 1992. *Before the Mountains Disappear: An Ethnographic Chronicle of the Modern Palestinians*. Cairo: Kloreus Books.
Rabo, A. 1986. "Change on the Euphrates: Villagers, Townsmen and Employees in Northeast Syria." PhD diss., Stockholm University.
———. 2005. *A Shop of One's Own: Independence and Reputation among Traders in Aleppo*. London: I.B. Tauris.
Racy, A. J. 2003. *Making Music in the Arab World: The Culture and Artistry of Tarab*. Cambridge: Cambridge University Press.
Rae, J. 1999. "Tribe and State: Management of Syrian Steppe." PhD diss., University of Oxford.
Rifai, L. 2020. *The Sunni Religious Establishment of Damascus: When Unification Creates Division*. Washington, DC: Carnegie Endowment for International Peace.
Ritzer, G. 2004. "The Inhospitable Hospitality Industry." *Hospitality Review* 6, no. 3: 40–46.
———. 2007. "Inhospitable Hospitality?" In *Hospitality: A Social Lens*, ed. C. Lashley, P. Lynch, and A. Morrison, 143–54. Amsterdam: Elsevier.
Robbins, J. 2001. "Ritual Communication and Linguistic Ideology: A Reading and Partial Reformulation of Rappaports Theory of Ritual." *Current Anthropology* no. 5: 591–614.
Roitman, J. 2005. *Fiscal Disobedience: An Anthropology of Economic Regulation in Central Africa*. Princeton: Princeton University Press.
Rosa, J., and C. Burdick. 2017. "Language Ideologies." In *The Oxford Handbook of Language and Society*, ed. O. Garcia, N. Flores and M. Spotti, 103–24. Oxford: Oxford University Press.
Roussillon, A. 1990. "Entre al-Jihad et al-Rayyan: Phénomenologie de l'islamisme égyptien" [Between al-Jihad and al-Rayyan: phenomenology of Egyptian Islamism]. *Maghreb Machrek: monde arabe* 127: 17–50.
Rudnyckyj, D. 2010. *Spiritual Economies: Islam, Globalisation, and the Afterlife of Development*. Ithaca: Cornell University Press.
Rumsey, A. 1990. "Wording, Meaning, and Linguistic Ideology." *American Anthropologist* 92, no. 2: 346–61.
Sadowski, Y. M. 1991. *Political Vegetables? Businessmen and Bureaucrats in the Development of Egyptian Agriculture*. Washington, DC: Brookings Institution Press.
Said, S. 2010. "The Effect of Trade Liberalization on Syrian Industry: The Case of Textile and Olive Oil Industry." St Andrews Papers of Contemporary Syria. *Syria Studies* 2, no. 2: 33–65.
Salamandra, C. 2004. *A New Old Damascus: Authenticity and Distinction in Urban Syria*. Bloomington: Indiana University Press.

———. 2013. "Sectarianism in Syria: Anthropological Reflections." *Middle East Critique* 22, no. 3: 303–6.
Salamandra, C., and L. Stenberg, eds. 2015. *Syria from Reform to Revolt: Vol. 2, Culture, Religion, and Society*. Syracuse: Syracuse University Press.
Salemink, O. 2016. "Described, Inscribed, Written Off: Heritagisation as (Dis)connection. In *Connected and Disconnected in Viet Nam: Remaking Social Relations in a Post-Socialist Nation*, ed. P. Taylor, 311–46. Canberra: ANU Press.
———. 2021. "Introduction: Heritagizing Asian Cities: Space, Memory, and Vernacular Heritage Practices." *International Journal of Heritage Studies* 27, no. 8: 769–76.
Schielke, S. 2015. *Egypt in the Future Tense: Hope, Frustration, and Ambivalence before and after 2011*. Bloomington: Indiana University Press.
Schilcher, L.S. 1985. *Families in Politics: Damascene Factions and Estates of the 18th and 19th Centuries*. Stuttgart: Franz Steiner Verlag.
Schlumberger, O., ed. 2007. *Debating Arab Authoritarianism: Dynamics and Durability in Nondemocratic Regimes*. Stanford, CA: Stanford University Press.
Schmitt, C. [1922] 2005. *Political Theology: Four Chapters on the Concept of Sovereignty*. Chicago: University of Chicago Press.
Schneider, J., and P. Schneider. 2008. "The Anthropology of Crime and Criminalization." *Annual Review of Anthropology* 37: 351–73.
Schutz, A. 1977. "Making Music Together: A Study in Social Relationship." In *Symbolic Anthropology*, ed. J. Dolgin, 106–19. New York: Columbia University Press.
Scott, J. C. 1990. *Hidden Transcripts: Domination and the Arts of Resistance*. New Haven: Yale University Press.
Seif, R. 1998. "Private Sector Development—Scenarios for the Future." In *Scenarios for Syria: Socio-Economic and Political*, ed. V. Perthes, 59–70. Baden-Baden: Nomos Verlagsgesellschaft.
Selvik, K. 2008. "It's the Mentality, Stupid: Syria's Turn to the Private Sector." *St Andrews Papers on Modern Syrian Studies* 1, no. 1: 33–54.
Selwyn, T. 2000. "An Anthropology of Hospitality." In *In Search of Hospitality: Theoretical Perspectives and Debates*, ed. C. Lashley and A. Morrison, 18–37. Abingdon-on-Thames: Routledge.
Shami, S. K. 2000. "Prehistories of Globalization: Circassian Identity in Motion." *Public Culture* 12, no. 1: 177–204.
Shannon, J. H. 2003a. "Emotion, Performance, and Temporality in Arab Music: Reflections on Tarab." *Cultural Anthropology* 18, no. 1: 72–98.
———. 2003b. "Sultans of Spin: Syrian Sacred Music on the World Stage." *American Anthropologist* 105, no. 2: 266–77.
———. 2006. *Among the Jasmine Trees: Music and Modernity in Contemporary Syria*. Middletown, CT: Wesleyan University Press.
Sharabi, H. 1988. *Neopatriarchy: A Theory of Distorted Change in Arab Society*. New York: Oxford University Press.
Shryock, A. 2004. "The New Jordanian Hospitality: House, Host, and Guest in the Culture of Public Display." *Comparative Studies in Society and History* 46, no. 1: 35–62.
———. 2008. "Thinking about Hospitality, with Derrida, Kant, and the Balga Bedouin." *Anthropos* 103, no. 2: 405–21.
———. 2012. "Breaking Hospitality Apart: Bad Hosts, Bad Guests, and the Problem of Sovereignty." *Journal of the Royal Anthropological Institute* 18: S20–S33.
———. 2019. "Keeping to Oneself: Hospitality and the Magical Hoard in the Balga of Jordan." *History and Anthropology* 30, no. 5: 546–62.

Silverstein, M. 2003. "Indexical Order and the Dialectics of Sociolinguistic Life." *Language & Communication* 23, no. 3–4: 193–229.

Silverstein, P. 2011. "Masquerade Politics: Race, Islam and the Scale of Amazigh Activism in Southeastern Morocco." *Nations and Nationalism* 17, no. 1: 65–84.

Singerman, D. 1995. *Avenues of Participation: Family, Politics, and Networks in Urban Quarters of Cairo*. Princeton: Princeton University Press.

Sloane, P. 1998. *Islam, Modernity and Entrepreneurship among the Malays*. New York: Springer.

Sloane-White, P. 2017. *Corporate Islam: Sharia and the Modern Workplace*. Cambridge: Cambridge University Press.

Slyomovics, S. 1998. *The Object of Memory: Arab and Jew Narrate the Palestinian Village*. Philadelphia: University of Pennsylvania Press.

Smith, E. 2009. "In His Heart and Soul He's Egyptian, the Nile Flows through His Veins: Bakkar as Egyptian and African." *Critical Interventions* 3, no. 1: 123–39.

Sood, G. D. 2011. "Circulation and Exchange in Islamicate Eurasia: A Regional Approach to the Early Modern World." *Past & Present* 212, no. 1: 113–62.

Sørensen, M. L. S., and D. Viejo-Rose, eds. 2015. *War and Cultural Heritage*. Cambridge: Cambridge University Press.

Sottimano, A., and K. Selvik. 2008. "Changing Regime Discourse and Reform in Syria." *Syria Studies* 1, no. 1: 1–55.

Steinberg, J. 1987. "The Historian and the Questione Della Lingua." In *The Social History of Language*, ed. J. Steinberg, P. Burke, and R Porter, 198–209. Cambridge: Cambridge University Press.

———. 2015. "Muslim Organizations in Bashar's Syria: The Transformation of the Shaykh Ahmad Kuftaro Foundation." In *Syria from Reform to Revolt*, ed. C. Salamandra and L. Stenberg. Vol. 2: *Culture, Religion, and Society*, 147–68. Syracuse University Press.

Stephan-Emmrich, M. 2017. "Playing Cosmopolitan: Muslim Self-Fashioning, Migration, and (Be-)longing in the Tajik Dubai Business Sector." *Central Asian Affairs* 4, no. 3: 270–91.

Strathern, M. 2000. "New Accountabilities." In *Audit Cultures: Anthropological Studies in Accountability, Ethics and the Academy*, ed. M. Strathern, 1–18. London: Routledge.

Suleiman, Y. 2011. *Arabic, Self and Identity: A Study in Conflict and Displacement*. Oxford: Oxford University Press.

———. 2013. *Arabic in the Fray*. Edinburgh: Edinburgh University Press.

———. 2019. *Arabic Language and National Identity: A Study in Ideology*. Edinburgh: Edinburgh University Press.

Swirski, B. 2000. "The Citizenship of Jewish and Palestinian Arab Women in Israel." In *Gender and Citizenship in the Middle East*, ed. S. Joseph, 314–44. Syracuse University Press.

Tabler, A. 2011. *In the Lion's Den: An Eyewitness Account of Washington's Battle with Syria*. Chicago Review Press.

Terc, M. 2015. "'To Promote Volunteerism among School Children': Volunteer Campaigns and Social Stratification in Contemporary Syria." In *Syria from Reform to Revolt: Political Economy and International Relations*, ed. R. Hinnebusch and T. Zintl, 133–53. Syracuse: Syracuse University Press.

Thompson, J. 1984. *Studies in the Theory of Ideology*. Berkeley: University of California Press.

Tobin, S. A. 2016. *Everyday Piety: Islam and Economy in Jordan*. Ithaca: Cornell University Press.

———. 2020. "Self-Making in Exile: Moral Emplacement by Syrian Refugee Women in Jordan." *Journal of Religious Ethics* 48, no. 4: 664–87.

Toynbee, A. 1961. *Between Oxus and Jumna*. Oxford: Oxford University Press.

Tracy, J. 2009. "Syria's Arab Traders as Seen by Andrea Berengo, 1555–1556." *Oriens* 37: 163–76.
Trilling, L. [1972] 2009. *Sincerity and Authenticity*. Cambridge: Harvard University Press.
Tripp, C. 2006. *Islam and the Moral Economy: The Challenge of Capitalism*. Cambridge: Cambridge University Press.
Tuastad, D. 2014. "From Football Riot to Revolution. The Political Role of Football in the Arab World." *Soccer & Society* 15, no. 3: 376–88.
Tucker, J. E. 1993. "The Arab Family in History. 'Otherness' and the Study of the Family." In *Arab Women: Old Boundaries, New Frontiers*, ed. J. E. Tucker, 195–207. Bloomington: Indiana University Press.
Veyne, P. [1976] 1990. *Bread and Circuses: Historical Sociology and Political Pluralism*. Trans. B. Pearce. London: Allen Lane.
Viejo-Rose, D. 2013. "Reconstructing Heritage in the Aftermath of Civil War: Revisioning the Nation and the Implications of International Involvement." *Journal of Intervention and Statebuilding* 7, no. 2: 125–48.
Walby, S. 1989. "Theorising Patriarchy." *Sociology* 23, no. 2: 213–34.
Walton, J. 2000. "The Hospitality Trades: A Social History". In *In Search of Hospitality: Theoretical Perspectives and Debates*, C. Lashley and A. Morrison, 56–76. Abingdon-on-Thames: Routledge.
Warde, I. 2000. *Islamic Finance in the Global Economy*. Edinburgh University Press.
Warde, A., and L. Martens. 2000. *Eating Out: Social Differentiation, Consumption, and Pleasure*. Cambridge: Cambridge University Press.
Weber, M. [1947] 2009. *The Theory of Social and Economic Organization*. Simon and Schuster.
Wedeen, L. 2019. *Authoritarian Apprehensions*. University of Chicago Press.
Weiner, A. 1992. *Inalienable Possessions*. Berkeley: University of California Press.
Weiner, S. 2016. "Rethinking Patriarchy and Kinship in the Arab Gulf States." *Women and Gender in Middle East Politics*. George Washington University: The Project on Middle East Political Science, Studies 19: 13–16.
Weulersse, J. 1946. *Paysans de Syrie et du Proche-Orient* [Peasants of Syria and the Near East]. Paris: Gallimard.
Williams, C. 2006. "Reconstructing Islamic Cairo." In *Cairo Cosmopolitan: Politics, Culture, and Urban Space in the Globalized Middle East*, ed. D. Singerman and P. Amar, 269–94. Cairo: American University in Cairo Press.
Winegar, J. 2006. *Creative Reckonings: The Politics of Art and Culture in Contemporary Egypt*. Stanford, CA: Stanford University Press.
Woolard, K. A. 1998. "Introduction: Language Ideology as a Field of Inquiry." In *Language Ideologies: Practice and Theory*, ed. B. Schieffelin, K. Woolard and P. Kroskrity, 1–50. Oxford: Oxford University Press.
———. 2008. "Why Dat Now?: Linguistic-Anthropological Contributions to the Explanation of Sociolinguistic Icons and Change." *Journal of Sociolinguistics* 12, no. 4: 432–52.
Wynn, L. L. 2007. *Pyramids and Nightclubs: A Travel Ethnography of Arab and Western Imaginations of Egypt, from King Tut and a Colony of Atlantis to Rumors of Sex Orgies, Urban Legends about a Marauding Prince, and Blonde Belly Dancers*. Austin: University of Texas Press.
Yamey, B. S. 1981. "Some Reflections on the Writing of a General History of Accounting." *Accounting and Business Research* 11, no. 4: 127–35.
Zaloom, C. 2006. *Out of the Pits: Traders and Technology from Chicago to London*. Chicago: University of Chicago Press.
Zubaida, S. 1992. "Islam, the State and Democracy: Contrasting Conceptions of Society in Egypt." *Middle East Report* 179: 2–10.

Index

accountability: and credit networks, 51; as marker of mercantile personhood, 2, 9, 42–43, 53–57, 78–79; and mistrust, 45–46, 47–48
accounting: and family relations, 79, 91–92; in the hospitality economy, 101–2; in ideologies of commerce and language, 9–10; in ideologies of urban-rural difference, 49–50, 51, 52–57, 176nn8–9; Islam and self-accounting ethos, 53–56, 91, 145–46; moral, 49–50, 91–92; reputational, 36
affect in commercial relations, 21–22, 140–41, 145–50, 152–55, 156–57, 165. *See also* emotion/emotionality; sincerity
affection (mahabbeh), 65–66, 102–3, 108, 110–11, 155
Alawite minority and regime, 8–9, 27–29, 43–44, 159–60. *See also* state, Baathist
Aleppo: under Bashar al-Asad, 31–35; civic patronage in ideological constructions of, 124–28; history of state-merchant relations in, 27–31; subordination of hinterland of, 25; in the Syrian conflict, 164–69; urban geography of, 24–25; "Capital of Islamic Culture" festival, 127–28
ambivalence: Aleppine, in the Syrian conflict, 164–66; about civic patronage, 127–28, 129; in the hospitality economy, 96–97, 99–107, 108–10, 117
arbitration. *See* dispute resolution
Archeological Society, Aleppo, 128
al-Asad, Asma, 87–88
al-Asad, Bashar: Aleppo under, 31–35; civic patronage encouraged by, 124–25; and contested modernities, 77–78, 87–90, 93–94, 97–98; economic liberalization under, 12–17, 35–39; ulema-merchant nexus under, 119–20. *See also* liberalization, economic (infitah)
al-Asad, Hafez, 15–16, 28–31, 37, 43–44, 130, 134
Asia and Aleppo, 31, 34–35
authenticity, claims of: in bourgeois rivalries, 92; cultural, in Aleppo, 24, 159; and economic liberalization, 36, 38; of economic patriarchal forms, 89–94; in ideologies of urban-rural difference, 43, 44–45, 51, 56–57;

in modernity, 16, 89–94, 163–64; and notability, 36, 129, 138; urban, 9–10, 14–15, 20, 38, 44, 51, 56–57, 138. *See also* sincerity
authoritarianism: and economic liberalization, 12, 13, 17, 35–36, 67–68, 96–97; and the hospitality economy, 96–97, 113, 114, 116–18; and notability, 131, 139; recombinant, civic patronage in, 120; in state-merchant relations, 28–29; upgrading of, 12–13, 114–18
authority, patriarchal: and contested modernity, 76–77, 79–80, 83, 85, 89–90, 93–94; in dispute resolution, 6–7, 59–60, 61–62, 163; in exchange ideologies, 1–2, 8–9, 10–11, 163–64; and filial submission, 76–77, 79; in the hospitality economy, 98–99, 106–7, 110–11, 112–13, 114–15; kin contract in, 60, 62–64, 69–70; legitimation of, 4, 6, 60–75, 92–93; in market membership, 4–7, 62–64, 69–70; and predation, 59–60; self-regulation and reputation in, 61–62, 68–75; in social order, 70; and state-merchant relations, 5–6, 59–70, 74–75
autonomy, vis-à-vis the state: of Aleppo, 6–7; of clans, 37–38; and economic liberalization, 13, 14–15, 37–38; in ideologies of urban-rural difference, 40–41, 54–55; of merchant bourgeoisies, 28–30, 37–38; of merchant notables, 129, 130–31, 136–37, 138; and patriarchal authority, 60, 73–74; of ulema in Iran, 178n2
Awqaf, Ministry of, 90

Baathist coup of 1963, 27–28
Baathist ideology, 16–17, 89–90, 164–65
banking sector, 34, 101
bargaining, 1–3, 6, 140–41, 145–46
Battle of Aleppo (2012–2016), 23–24
bazaars: in Aleppine history and geography, 24–25, 26; bargaining in, 143–44; bazaar-based merchants, 16–17, 51, 55–56, 151–52, 158–59; economic patriarchy and contested modernities in, 79–84, 89–90, 92–93, 94; economies of, 143–44; exchange ideologies in, 2–3

197

betting, 79–84
bourgeoisie, independent merchant: in Aleppine history and geography, 30–31, 34, 36, 39; in contesting urban leadership and legitimacy, 48–49; in economic liberalization, 13–15; and ideologies of urban-rural difference, 8–9, 40–41, 43–49, 161–62; in managed elections, 67–68; as notables, 36–37, 39, 138
bourgeoisie, state-dependent: in Aleppine history and geography, 28–29, 34; civic patronage by, 138; in economic liberalization, 13–15; and ideologies of urban-rural difference, 8–9, 40–41, 43–50, 56, 161–62; in managed elections, 67–68
bribery, 63–64, 66–67, 90–91, 114. *See also* corruption, constructs of
brokers: display of affective sincerity by, 154–56; in the hospitality economy, 98–99, 101–3, 105–6, 116, 117–18; in ideologies of urban-rural difference, 51; in state-merchant relations, 65–66, 72–73, 74–75; and urban notability, 133, 135
bureaucratic state/bureaucratic practices: and economic liberalization, 14, 36; in economic patriarchy and contested modernities, 84–85, 86–87, 92; and the hospitality economy, 113; in the revival of notability, 129–36; in sustaining patriarchal hierarchies, 62–63, 69, 75. *See also* state, Baathist

calculation, 100–101, 103–6, 144–45, 164–65
celebrity, merchant. *See* notables/notability
charisma, 7–8, 109–10
China, 22, 23, 32, 33–34, 143–44, 158, 167–68, 170–73
cinnamon, good/bad, 147–54. *See also* sincerity
citizenship, 4–5, 60, 62–64, 166–67
civic domain, 35–36, 39, 55, 67–68, 120, 122–26, 127–29, 138–39, 162. *See also* euergetism; football; heritage
civility, 9–10, 25, 42–43, 47–48, 59–60, 116–17, 152
civil society, 87–88, 113–18, 119–20, 123–28, 138, 165–66
civil war, Syrian, 23–24, 45–46, 164–69, 170
clans, rural, 9–10, 37–38, 42, 43, 44–49, 53–55, 56, 61
class, socioeconomic. *See also* bourgeoisie, independent merchant; bourgeoisie, state-dependent; status, socioeconomic
clientelism. *See* patron-client/patronage networks
Commerce, Chamber of, 48–49, 62, 67–68, 130–32, 138, 161–62
commerce ideology, defined, 2–3
Commercial Arbitration, Law of, 110–11, 114–15
commodities, 80, 115–16, 117–18, 143–44, 148–49, 150, 158–59
compliance, political, 30–31, 38–39, 44–45, 87–89, 123–24, 131, 136–37
confessional identity, 44, 141, 152, 169–70, 172–73. *See also* religion/religiosity
connectivity, patriarchal, 4–5, 71–75, 79–80, 82–83, 86–87, 92
contestation: of ideologies, 7, 50–51, 160–62, 169–70, 173–74; of post-Baathist modernities, 15–17; of urban leadership and legitimacy, 48–49, 50–51, 55–57, 161–62; of urban notability, 14–15, 26–27, 136–39, 161–62. *See also* modernity
contractors, state, 9, 13, 28–29, 37, 45–46, 160. *See also* bourgeoisie, state-dependent
control, political, 96–97, 114, 117–18, 160, 161–62, 173–74. *See also* divide-and-rule strategies
co-optation of merchants by the state: civic patronage in, 124–25; and contested modernities, 93; in economic liberalization, 13–15, 35, 37, 162–63; in state-merchant relations, 30–31, 67–68; in the Syrian conflict, 165–66. *See also* patron-client/patronage networks
corruption, constructs of, 16, 37–38, 63–64, 66–67, 90–91, 114–15, 133
cosmologies, economic, 141–45, 147–50, 151–53, 164. *See also* grace, economic cosmologies of
courts, state. *See* juridical institutions
credit/debt: clans excluded from networks of, 37–38; and connective personhood, 71–72; in economic patriarchy, 79; forgiveness of, 144–45, 151–52; in the hospitality economy, 21, 96–100, 101–9, 117; in ideologies of commerce and language, 8, 9–10; in ideologies of urban-rural difference, 47, 51, 52, 53–55; in market membership, 5–7; and patriarchal authority, 59–60, 61–62, 65–66, 69–70; of pre-Baathist notables, 36; subordination in relations of, 105–7; Syrian, in Aleppine textile trade, 31, 39
"critical-Marxist" ideology, 165
cronyism/crony capitalism, 12, 14, 28–29, 37–38, 44–45, 93–94, 162–63. *See also* patron-client/patronage networks

INDEX   199

culture: of Aleppo, 24, 159; business, modernization of, 86; economic liberalization as process of, 20, 35–39, 86–87, 160; old urban, 91–92. *See also* Easternness, constructs of

Derrida, Jacques, 100–101
development, economic and industrial, 29, 31–32, 33–35, 38–39, 89, 92–93, 133, 136–37. *See also* liberalization, economic (infitah)
diaspora, 21–22, 26, 33, 143–44, 155, 158, 167–68, 169–74
discipline: authoritarian, 117; in commercial accounting, 9–10, 52–55; in father-son relations, 10, 19, 89, 91; in the hospitality economy, 106–7, 116–17; in merchant patriarchy, 62, 68–69, 74–75
displacement, 126–27, 167, 168–69
dispute resolution: by Aleppine merchants, 36, 37–38; and economic liberalization, 35–36; in the hospitality economy, 96, 110–16, 117–18; in ideologies of urban-rural difference, 9, 42; patriarchal authority in, 6–7, 59–60, 61–62, 163; in reproduction of patriarchal authority, 59–60, 61–62, 68–70, 75
divide-and-rule strategies: bourgeois rivalries in, 8–9, 14–15, 37–38, 40–41, 161–62; civic patronage in, 125–26, 138, 139, 162; in economic liberalization, 13–15, 160–62; elections in, 13–15, 67–68, 161–62; ideologies of urban-rural difference in, 40–41, 56–57; madafa dispute resolution in, 113–14; rural clans in, 37–38; in the Syrian conflict, 165–66. *See also* control, political

Easternness, constructs of, 92, 152–58, 159, 164
economics, Islamic, 141, 142–43, 152, 158–59
education, 77, 84–87
Egypt, 126, 131
elections: civic patronage in, 67–68, 121–22, 123, 124, 130–31; in divide-and-rule strategies, 13–15, 67–68, 161–62; and economic liberalization, 13–15; in the hospitality economy, 21, 96–97, 110, 116; in ideologies of urban-rural difference, 48, 57; managed, 67–68, 114–15, 124, 139, 160, 166; notability in, 35–36, 39, 137–39; in state-merchant relations, 30–31
Elyachar, Julia, 148–49
emotion/emotionality, 21–22, 92, 140–41, 152–58. *See also* sincerity
entrepreneurs/entrepreneurship: in affective economies of sincerity, 141, 152, 158–59; under Bashar al-Assad, 33–35; and economic patriarchy, 77–78, 84–87; in exchange ideologies and Syria's future, 160–61, 163–64, 173–74; as figures of modernity, 15–17, 34–35, 77–78, 87–90, 92–94, 163–64; hospitality in, 95–97; in notability, 7–8, 39, 132–34, 136–37; in state-merchant relations, 29–31
envy, affective economies of, 147–50, 158–59. *See also* cosmologies, economic; sincerity
ethics: in affective economies of sincerity, 142, 147–48, 151–52, 179n5; of interaction, 169–70, 172; in Islamic conceptions of commerce, 3; neoliberal, 89, 164–65; and technocratic modernity, 88–89. *See also* morality/moral culture
ethnography. *See* fieldwork
euergetism, 121–24, 125, 127–28, 129, 131–32, 138–39, 162. *See also* patronage, civic
Eurasia, 23–24
Euro-Mediterranean Partnership, 32–33

father-authority. *See* authority, patriarchal
father-son relations, 1–2, 71–75, 76, 77, 79–80, 82, 87, 89, 91. *See also* genealogies; generations
favor, economies of, 63–67
fieldwork, 17–20, 53, 119
football: clubs, 121–22, 123, 125, 133–34; sponsorship of, as civic patronage, 119, 120, 121–23, 125, 127–28, 129–30, 137–38; sponsorship of, in contests of notability, 35, 39, 129–30, 137–38, 162; sponsorship of, in state-merchant relations, 26–27, 30–31, 67–68
foreign exchange crisis, 1980s, 133
formality/informality: in affective economies of sincerity, 142, 151; in arbitration, 68–69, 110–11, 112–13; in economic patriarchy, 76–77; in the hospitality economy, 99–101, 103–6, 110–11, 112–13, 114; in ideologies of urban-rural difference, 45–46; of market membership, 4, 5–7, 163; of speech, in ideologies of language, 8; in state-merchant relations, 31, 61, 64–66, 68–69
Forward Magazine, 88–89
Fouad, Fouad Mohamed, 24
free trade agreements, 7–8, 12–13, 16, 32, 33, 86–87
French Mandate (1920–1946), 24, 27, 43–44, 130
friendship, 63–67, 103–7, 108, 110–11, 163–64

INDEX

gatherings (jama'a): in affective economies of sincerity, 141, 154–58; as base for notability, 7–8; defined, 8, 14; in the hospitality economy, 21, 97–98, 105–6, 110–11, 115–17; as structure of market membership, 4, 5–6, 162–63; in the Syrian conflict, 166–67. *See also* hospitality/hospitality economy

genealogies, 61, 71–72, 130

generations, 71–73, 74–75, 85–86, 93–94, 96, 97–98

geographies, imagined, 157–59

gifts/gift giving, 100–101, 104–5, 108, 117, 122–23, 124–25, 126–27

grace, economic cosmologies of, 141–45, 147–50, 151–53. *See also* sincerity

Great Britain, 18–19

Greater Arab Free Trade Area, 32

guarantors, 62–63, 69–71, 72–73

guest-host relations, 96–101, 102, 107–13, 116–17. *See also* hospitality/hospitality economy

Hariri affair, 18
Hassun, Ahmad, 124–25
Haykal, Abussalam, 88–89
heritage, 91–94, 120, 122, 127–28, 169–71
hierarchies: in economic patriarchy, 78–79, 83–84; in the hospitality economy, 8, 113–14, 116–17; in ideologies of urban-rural difference, 55–56; in market membership, 4–7; of notability, 26–27, 36, 37–38, 132; in state-merchant relations, 62–64, 67, 69, 75
honesty, 2, 90–91, 143–44, 145–46, 147–48
hospitality/hospitality economy: ambivalence in, 96–97, 99–107, 108–10, 117; bribes in metaphors of, 66–67; credit and debt in, 21, 96–97, 98–100, 101–9, 117; elections in, 21, 96–97, 110, 116; guest-host relations in, 96–101, 102, 107–13, 116–17; in ideologies of commerce and language, 8; madafas in, 107–18; in market access, 21, 95–97, 116–17; mutuality and kinship in, 21, 99–100, 101–13, 117–18, 163; power relations in, 21, 99–100, 106–7, 116–18. *See also* gatherings (jama'a); madafas (places of hospitality)

houses, merchant (buyut, sg. bait), 4, 7–8, 9, 14, 59, 61, 162–63

identity: Aleppine, 6–7, 24, 120, 140–41, 152–54; civic frameworks of, 120, 121–22, 125–27; confessional, 44, 141, 152, 169–70, 172–73; in exchange ideologies of difference, 41–42, 55–56; in ideologies of urban-rural difference, 56–57; Islamic, 140–41, 152, 158, 169–70; Jewish, 26; language and commerce ideologies in constituting, 2, 4, 10–11, 20, 42–43, 46–48; rural and urban, in Aleppo, 43–49

indexicality, 10–12, 42

Industry, Chamber of, 48–49, 67–68, 116, 130–32, 137–38, 161–62, 167, 168–69

industry in Aleppo, 25, 27–28, 29–31, 33–34

Institut Français d'Etudes du Proche Orient, 18

interaction, commercial ethic of, 169–70

intimacy, 64, 65–66, 67, 99–105, 110–11, 146, 152–58. *See also* mutuality/mutual identification

Islam: and affective economies of sincerity, 21–22, 140–43, 145–46, 158–59; civility in, 9–10, 47–48, 59–60; and constructs of authentic modernity, 89, 90–91, 163–64; Day of Accounting in, 54; Islamic civil society, 124–28; Islamic economics, 141, 142–43, 152, 158–59; morality of trade in, 1–2, 145–46; post-9/11 securitization of, 18–19; prayer and accounting in, 52; prohibition of betting in, 80–84; and ulema-bazaar nexus, 119–22, 178n2. *See also* Sufism/Sufi piety movements

Islamicate mode of exchange, 151–52

Islamist rebellion (1979–1982), 29

the Jazira, 24–25
Jews/Judaism, 26, 142–43, 151–53, 172–73
Joseph, Suad, 4, 62, 74, 79
juridical institutions, 5–7, 14, 61–63, 69–70, 75, 110–15

Keane, Webb, 146–47
kinship/kinship groups: and displacement in the Syrian conflict, 167–68; in the hospitality economy, 99–100, 102–3, 104–5, 107–13, 116–17; patriarchal kin contract, 4–5, 60, 61–64, 68–70, 71–75; in state-merchant relations, 60, 64–66. *See also* patrilineality

language ideology, 2–4, 6, 8–12, 20, 41–42, 47–48, 50–51, 160, 175n1

leadership: civic patronage in claiming, 119–20, 121, 127, 128, 129–31, 138–39; ideologies of urban-rural difference in contesting, 48–49, 51, 56–57; political, 63, 121, 127, 129–31, 138–39; religious, 90–91, 119–20, 121; social, 128, 129–30; urban, 9, 48–49, 51, 56–57, 138–39, 161–62

INDEX   201

leisure, 53, 64, 104, 131. *See also* sahra (evening gathering)
liberalization, economic (infitah): affective economies of sincerity in, 141, 143–44, 154–59; in Aleppo, under Bashar al-Asad, 31–35; and authoritarianism, 12, 13, 17, 35–36, 67–68, 96–97; and civic patronage, 120, 123, 162; and contested modernity, 15–17, 89–90, 93–94; co-optation of merchants in, 13–15, 35, 37, 162–63; as cultural process, 20, 35–39, 86–87, 160; divide-and-rule strategies in, 13–15, 160–62; economic and business networks in, 162–63; exchange ideologies in, 12–17; hospitality economy in, 114, 116–18; industrial renaissance, 7–8, 31–32, 33–34; merchants as public figures in, 35–39; and notability, 14–15, 21, 35–39, 130, 132–37, 161, 162; political control in, 114, 117–18, 160, 161–62, 173–74; state-merchant relations in, 14–15, 29–31; and the Syrian conflict, 164–65
luck. *See* serendipity

madafas (places of hospitality), 95–97, 98–100, 101–18, 119, 137–38, 148, 152–53. *See also* hospitality/hospitality economy
market membership, social structures of: and Aleppo's position in the Syrian conflict, 166–67; in economic liberalization, 14; in the hospitality economy, 21, 95–97, 116–17; and incorporation into the polity, 165–67; patriarchy in, 4–7, 8, 62–64, 69–70, 71, 73–74, 162–63, 169; role of gatherings in, 4, 5–6, 162–63
marriage, 36, 46–48, 70
masculinity, 1–2, 14, 155–56
material practices, 9–10, 49–50, 52–56. *See also* accounting
mawani relations, 65–66, 102–5, 108, 110–11. *See also* mutuality/mutual identification
militarization of the Syrian conflict, 166–68, 169
militias, 37, 45–46, 49, 166–67, 168–69
mobility: and diasporic geographies, 21–22; transregional, 155, 157–58, 173–74
modernity: constructs of "authentic," 89–94, 154, 159, 163–64; and economic patriarchy, 21, 76–87, 89–94, 163–64; entrepreneurial, 15–17, 34–35, 77–78, 87–90, 92–94, 163–64, 173–74; Islamic, 89, 90–91, 158, 159, 163–64; post-Baathist, 15–17, 87–94; Protestant, 146–50; technocratic, 77–89, 92–94, 163–64
money collectors/gatherers, 29–30, 134–36
monopolies, 34, 43, 44–45, 137–38, 145–46

morality/moral culture: civic patronage as, 121–22, 126; in commercial accounting, 52–55, 176n8; and commercial ethics of interaction, 101–3, 105, 107, 169–70; of exchange in Islam, 1, 54, 78, 145–46, 148–49, 151–52, 158–59; in ideologies of urban-rural difference, 9, 40, 42–43; in merchant patriarchy, 62–63, 64–65, 73, 74–75; and modes of commerce, 1–3, 10, 20. *See also* affection (mahabbeh); betting; credit/debt; ethics; friendship; intimacy; kinship; mutuality/mutual identification; sincerity
music, 92, 153–55, 156, 157, 158, 159
mutuality/mutual identification: in affective economies of sincerity, 140–41, 143–50, 153, 154–55, 158–59, 164; in the hospitality economy, 21, 99–100, 101–13, 117–18, 163; ideologies of, 8; in state-merchant relations, 65–66, 67. *See also* intimacy

nahda (Arab cultural and scientific renaissance), 7–8, 23–24, 31–32
neoliberalism, 13, 32–33, 93–94, 165
nostalgia, 27, 35–36, 37, 89–90, 169–70, 172–73
notables/notability: in Aleppo's social order, 26–27; celebrity as a claim to, 21, 68, 119, 123–24, 132, 139; and civic patronage, 21, 34–36, 119–20, 121–24, 128, 129–39; contestation of, 7–8, 14–15, 26–27, 136–39, 162–63; and economic liberalization, 14–15, 21, 35–39, 130, 132–37, 161, 162; pedigree as claim to, 130, 137–38; as public figures, 35–39; regime subordination of, 120, 131–32, 162; in state-merchant relations, 14–15, 27–28; status competition among, 120, 122–23, 130–31, 139; and the Syrian conflict in Aleppo, 168–69. *See also* status, socioeconomic
NUR foundation, 133–36

obedience, 1–2, 6, 10–11, 87–88
obligations: in euergetism, 122–23; in the hospitality economy, 21, 98–99, 102, 104–6, 110, 116, 117; in state-merchant relations, 65–66
Ottoman Empire era in Aleppo, 22–24, 25–26, 27, 129–30

patrilineality: in the hospitality economy, 113; in market membership, 4, 5–6, 20, 160; in patriarchy, 61–62; and reputation, 68–69, 74–75; in state-merchant relations, 59–60, 166. *See also* kinship/kinship groups

202 INDEX

patronage, civic: economic liberalization in creating, 120, 123, 162; and football sponsorship, 119–24; in ideological constructions of Aleppo, 124–28; in notability, 21, 34–36, 119–20, 121–24, 128, 129–39; in the rise of Sunni industrialists, 39; and the state, 67–68, 120, 124–25, 129–39

patron-client/patronage networks: civic patronage in, 162; in economic liberalization and political control, 13–15, 120, 160, 161; hospitality in, 96–97; in the madafa economy, 116–18; and market membership, 163; and notability, 129–30, 131, 134, 138–39; in state-merchant relations, 28–29, 64–65; and the Syrian conflict, 165–66, 167. *See also* cronyism/crony capitalism

pedigree, families of: attitudes toward the state of, 36–37, 90–91; in rivalries with new industrialists, 7–8, 137–38; in rivalries with state-dependent "clans," 36–37, 43, 56–57, 169. *See also* authenticity, claims of

periphery of Aleppo, 24–25, 33–35

personality, 7, 64–65, 66, 109–10, 156–57. *See also* charisma; notables/notability

personhood, 46–48, 53–54, 71–75, 77, 79, 146–47, 173. *See also* accountability; connectivity, patriarchal; reputation

petitioning channels: in access to public goods, 166; and economic liberalization, 14–15; and notability, 36–37, 129, 131–32, 138–39; in state-merchant relations, 5–6, 61–62, 67–68, 75

philanthropy. *See* euergetism

piety, 36, 71–72, 84, 124–25, 126. *See also* Sufism/Sufi piety movements

places of hospitality. *See* madafas (places of hospitality)

political economy, 14, 15–16, 21, 28–30, 44–45, 96–97, 116–17, 162–63

predation, 59–60, 131–32, 138–39

preeminence/preeminent personality, 26–27, 35–36, 39, 41, 109–10, 130–31, 139–40

prestige: claims to urban, 127, 128; clans excluded from networks of, 37–38; commerce as tradition of urban, 41–42, 43, 53–54; in the madafa economy, 117; of notables, 39; traditions of urban, 79, 91–92; urban, in late Ottoman period, 27

privilege, networks of, 29, 30–31, 38–39, 114

profit: and economic liberalization, 137, 160; in the hospitality economy, 97, 99; in Islam, 1, 54, 144, 145–46, 147–49; and notability, 39, 133, 137; profit-sharing, 133; in speculation, 78–79

provision, divine, 140–43, 144–45, 149–50. *See also* cosmologies, economic

publics, 21, 30, 35, 121–23, 130, 134, 137, 139

public sector, 28–30, 31–32, 34, 44–45, 132–33, 136–37

quality standards, 32–33

Rappaport, Roy, 11–12

reciprocity, 76–77, 98–99, 117–18

recursivity, fractal, 42

reform, economic, 12, 27–28, 31–32, 87–89, 92, 143–44

religion/religiosity: commercial ethic of interaction in, 169–70, 172–73; in economic cosmologies of grace, 141–43, 179n5; and economic patriarchy, 77; religious patriarchy, 90–91; sincerity of worship in, 146–50; in state-merchant relations, 27. *See also* confessional identity; Islam

rent seeking, 136–37

reputation: in Aleppo's social order, 26–27; civic patronage in, 133–34, 137–38; in economic patriarchy, 79, 83; in the hospitality economy, 96, 105–6, 110–11; in ideologies of urban-rural difference, 48–49, 54–56; patriarchal constructs of, 3, 5–7; of pre-Baathist notables, 36; in regulation of the market, 5–6, 58, 61–63, 68–75; tolerance/grace in, 105, 151–52; varying with exchange ideologies, 7–8, 9–10

respect/respectability: and accounting practices, 51; in Aleppo's social order, 26–27, 36; in dispute resolution, 37; in economic patriarchy, 71–72, 73, 75–79; for male elders, in constructs of "authentic" modernity, 89, 93–94; patriarchal constructs of, 2–3, 5–6, 163; in state-merchant relations, 64–65

responsibility, 60, 62–63, 71, 72–74, 79, 87, 89

Robbins, Joel, 11–12

rural-tribal organizations. *See* clans, rural

sahra (evening gathering), 141, 154–59. *See also* leisure

Salamandra, Christa, 44, 92

scholars, religious, 27, 90–91, 119–20, 127, 129–30, 151–52, 178n2

sectarianism, 43–44, 125–26, 127–28, 162, 169–74

secularism, 27–28, 119–20, 173–74

securitization, post-9/11, 18–19
security state, 28–29, 37–38, 43, 45–46, 59–60, 66, 84–85, 86–87
selfhood, 77, 146–47, 154–55
serendipity, 150, 152–53. *See also* sincerity
Shabiha, 44–46
shaykhs, 90–91, 119–20, 121
Silk Route, 23–24
sincerity: affective economies of, 156–59; affects of, 140–41, 150-157164; in constructs of Aleppineness/Easternness, 152–54; in Islam, 140–43, 145–47, 151–52; manifest in serendipity, 150; as opposite of envy and reluctance, 147–49; varying with ideologies of language and selfhood, 146–47, 149–50; as virtue in commercial exchange, 140–41, 145–52. *See also* grace, economic cosmologies of; liberalization, economic (infitah)
social market economy, 12, 31–32, 136–37, 163
social order: concepts of, 26–27, 36, 42, 47–48, 55, 56–57; notables in, 26–27, 36; preeminence in, 26–27; reproduction and legitimation of, 59–60, 65–66, 68–75
sociolinguistics, 10–12, 41–42. *See also* language ideology
speech, ritual, 144, 146–47, 149–53, 155, 179n5
sports. *See* football
state, Baathist: economic liberalization by, 12–17, 31–35, 161; in the history of state-merchant relations in Aleppo, 27–31; in ideologies of urban-rural difference, 40–41, 43–44, 55, 56; notability under, 14–15, 35–39, 129–36, 138–39, 161–62; and patriarchal structures of market membership, 6–7, 62, 162–63; use of civic patronage by, 124–25, 129–39. *See also* Alawite minority and regime
state bourgeoisies. *See* bourgeoisie, state-dependent
state-merchant relations: civic patronage in, 67–68, 120, 124–25, 129–39; clientelism in, 28–29; in economic liberalization, 14–15, 29–31; formality in, 31, 61, 64–66, 68–69; friendship in, 63–67, 163–64; in the history of Aleppo, 27–31; in the hospitality economy, 96–97; in ideologies of commerce and language, 8–9; influence in, 59–60, 61–62, 63–65, 67–68, 75; notables/notability in, 14–15, 27–28, 37–38; patriarchy in, 5–6, 21, 59–70, 74–75

state-society relations: civic patronage in, 124–28; economic liberalization in, 14–15, 35–39, 161, 163; in the madafa economy, 113–18; male elders as relays of, 67–68; notability in, 129–36; in the Syrian conflict, 166
status, socioeconomic: in Aleppine history, 27–29, 31, 35, 39; civic patronage in, 121, 122–24, 125–26, 127–28, 129–32, 137–39, 162; and economic liberalization, 14–15; in the hospitality economy, 109–10, 113–15, 116, 117–18; and rivalries, 8–9, 129–31. *See also* notables/notability
stock market (bursa). *See* betting
Sufism/Sufi piety movements, 2, 91, 124–25, 127, 128, 129–30, 145–46
Sunni Muslims, 9, 26–29, 44–45, 120–21
Syrian Young Entrepreneurs' Association, 88–89

tarab (genre of music/atmosphere of rapture), 153–56, 159
techno-rationality, Western, 153–54
tolerance, as ethic of commerce, 151–52, 173
training, vocational, 84–87
transcendence, 100–101, 141–43
transregionalism, 16, 31, 32–35, 141, 157–58, 161, 164, 167–68, 173
trust/trustworthiness: in heartfelt exchange, 145–46; in the hospitality economy, 101–2, 113–14, 117–18; in ideologies of urban-rural difference, 42–43, 55, 176n10; patriarchal constructs of, 6–7, 86. *See also* accountability; mawani relations; mutuality/mutual identification; sincerity

Umayyad Mosque, 24–25
urbanity: in Aleppo, 25; authentic, constructs of, 9–10, 14–15, 20, 37–38, 44, 51, 56–57, 138; and civic patronage, 120, 127–28, 138; commerce in, 20, 56–57; in divide-and-rule strategies, 14–15; in ideologies of urban-rural difference, 9–10, 44, 51, 55, 56–57
urban-rural difference: accountability in ideologies of, 9, 42–43, 45–46, 47–48, 51, 53–57; accounting and material practices in, 49–57, 176nn8–9; constructs of authenticity in, 43, 44–45, 51, 56–57; in economies of favor, 66; state-affiliation in, 37–38

vouching, institution of, 62–63, 68–70, 71, 74–75

INDEX

waqf (religious endowments), 27, 90–92, 127
Wedeen, Lisa, 88, 165
wholesale merchants/market, 3, 64–66, 69, 79–84, 155, 162–63
willingness, 21–22, 147–49, 179n5. *See also* sincerity

Woolard, Kathryn, 10, 11, 50–51, 56
workforce, modernization of, 84–87
worship, 147, 149, 172. *See also* religion/religiosity

yarn market speculation, 79–84
Yiwu, China, 167–69, 170–73